OXFORD TELEVISION STUDIES

General Editors **Charlotte Brunsdon**
John Caughie

Inventing Television Culture

Inventing Television Culture
Men, Women, and the Box

Janet Thumim

OXFORD

UNIVERSITY PRESS

Great Clarendon Street, Oxford OX2 6DP

Oxford University Press is a department of the University of Oxford.
It furthers the University's objective of excellence in research, scholarship,
and education by publishing worldwide in

Oxford New York

Auckland Cape Town Dar es Salaam Hong Kong Karachi
Kuala Lumpur Madrid Melbourne Mexico City Nairobi
New Delhi Shanghai Taipei Toronto

With offices in

Argentina Austria Brazil Chile Czech Republic France Greece
Guatemala Hungary Italy Japan South Korea Poland Portugal
Singapore Switzerland Thailand Turkey Ukraine Vietnam

Published in the United States
by Oxford University Press Inc., New York

© Janet Thumim 2004

British Library Cataloguing in Publication Data
Data available

Library of Congress Cataloging in Publication Data
Data available

ISBN 0–19–874223–1

1 2 3 4 5 6 7 8 9 10

Typeset by Graphicraft Limited, Hong Kong
Printed in Great Britain
on acid-free paper by
Biddles Ltd, King's Lynn, Norfolk

Oxford Television Studies

General Editors
Charlotte Brunsdon and **John Caughie**

OXFORD TELEVISION STUDIES offers international authors—both established and emerging—an opportunity to reflect on particular problems of history, theory, and criticism which are specific to television and which are central to its critical understanding. The perspective of the series will be international, while respecting the peculiarities of the national; it will be historical, without proposing simple histories; and it will be grounded in the analysis of programmes and genres. The series is intended to be foundational without being introductory or routine, facilitating clearly focused critical reflection and engaging a range of debates, topics, and approaches which will offer a basis for the development of television studies.

For my son Joshua, my daughters Nancy
and Ella, and the rest of the
twenty-first-century audience

Acknowledgements

T<small>HIS</small> book aims to offer a practical feminist approach to cultural history—in particular to the formation of television culture in the UK. The questions explored here have exercised me for many years, and I am indebted to numerous people for their participation in discussions which have stimulated the refinement of my ideas. Amongst these I should like to record particular thanks to Pat Holland, Sylvia Harvey, and Gillian Swanson for illuminating conversations at crucial stages of the work; to my Bristol colleagues Sarah Street and Baz Kershaw for their helpful support; and to successive groups of students following the MA in Television Studies at the University of Bristol. I want also to acknowledge the benefit of the broad and speculative consideration of television culture which I have enjoyed with my Ph.D. students, especially Paul Ryan, Christine Truran, and Helen Piper. Similarly I have valued opportunities to present ongoing work, particularly at the Console-ing Passions and Screen conferences. Despite all this support there have still been times when I despaired of ever finishing the project, and I am both proud and grateful to acknowledge the rigorous and scholarly encouragement of my daughter, Nancy Thumim. She has read and reread drafts, helped me to tease out the complexities of sometimes unmanageably disparate materials, and generally both assisted in, and insisted upon, the completion of the work.

Thanks are due to the series editors, Charlotte Brunsdon and John Caughie, both for their invitation to contribute to this innovative series and for their substantive and enabling comments on the initial proposal—I'm sorry it took me so long. Andrew Lockett, then at Oxford University Press, was most helpful and engaged with the initial stages of the project, as was Elizabeth Prochaska with its completion: thanks to both of them. I am grateful to Jackie Kavanagh and Jeff Walden of the BBC's written archives at Caversham, to Andrew Whitehouse at BBC viewings, and to Miranda Scrase at the ITC library's archive for their informed assistance with my queries. Peter Salmon was instrumental in allowing me into the Granada Archive, where Adrian Figgess and Peter Heinze offered invaluable and enthusiastic help: warm thanks to them and to Granada for permitting access to their rich materials. I gratefully acknowledge the University of Bristol's support in the form of research leave, particularly for the one-year fellowship which has enabled completion of the book, and the Faculty of Arts Research and Conference funds which have provided generous assistance with a succession of archive visits and conference attendances.

During the long gestation of this book archival research has been transformed by digital technology. I hope that this contribution to our understanding of the early development of television culture in the UK will prove useful in informing the next generation of scholars' use of these archives.

Contents

Abbreviations

AHRB	Arts and Humanities Research Board
A-R	Associated Rediffusion
ATV	Associated Television
BAFTA	British Academy of Film and Television Arts
BBC	British Broadcasting Corporation
EOC	Equal Opportunities Commission
GATS	General Agreement on Trades and Services
IBA	Independent Broadcasting Authority
ITA	Independent Television Association
ITC	Independent Television Commission
ITN	Independent Television News
ITV	Independent Television
MOI	Ministry of Information
NFTVA	National Film and Television Archive
NVLA	National Viewers and Listeners Association
OB	Outside Broadcasting
PMG	Postmaster General
VR	Viewer Research
TAM	Total Audience Measurement
WAC	BBC Written Archives at Caversham
WPU	Women's Programme Unit
WTO	World Trade Organization

Note

Dates in brackets after television programmes refer to dates of transmission.

Introduction: Early Television Culture in the UK

Television and Culture

At the start of the twenty-first century there is little argument over the proposition that broadcast television's output has consequences for the cultural identity of its audiences. It is this proposition, precisely, which informs the current negotiations over GATS in which the pressing need for an 'Instrument for Cultural Diversity' is recognized as an essential safeguard against the possibility—or likelihood—of the WTO's global market stifling regional creativity. As Elizabeth MacDonald of the Canadian Film and Television Production Agency put it, 'Our challenge is to preserve our identity when our children watch exclusively US programmes. . . . We have come to the conclusion that a country that loses its voice and ability to communicate with itself may cease to exist.'[1] The global trade in audio-visual material is a relatively new phenomenon—certainly in its current volume—though the anxieties to which it gives rise are not so new. This book aims to explore some of the cultural anxieties provoked by early television, considering the extent to which we can understand it not only to *reflect* cultural change in the mid-twentieth century, but also to *produce* it. The anxiety generated by the potential of WTO and GATS for the future viability of local, regional, and, indeed, national identity, is directly analogous to that experienced in the later 1950s/1960s over the consequences of mass access to broadcast television for British national culture and identity.

Television history is tricky to research because of its volume, ubiquity, and ephemerality; this is further complicated in the early period because so little broadcast material has been preserved. Television was valued for its immediacy and much material was transmitted live in a once-only performance. Material shot on film was expensive, as was also the practice of 'telerecording' on tape: when this became available in the latter fifties its use was strictly

---

1 Elizabeth MacDonald, Canadian Film and Television Production Agency, speaking in the plenary session 'Culture and Commerce: International Trade and National Culture' at the AHRB Centre for British Film and Television Studies 'Trading Culture: a conference exploring the "indigenous" and the "exportable" in film and television culture' at Sheffield Hallam University, July 2002.

rationed. Hence all that remains of programming from the period, apart from scripts and production notes, is some of the material shot on film, the occasional telecine of a whole programme, and from the end of the 1950s some telerecording of material then regarded as significant enough to warrant such expense—though this remained the exception rather than the rule well into the 1960s. Decisions as to what to preserve were taken according to the currently perceived value of the material—that is to say its inherent interest, its likely use as material for future repeats, or its potential export value. There does remain, however, a vast quantity of written ephemera. But in deploying such material the researcher must remain aware of questions concerning the legitimacy of twenty-first-century concepts in evaluating mid-twentieth-century material. John Ellis's ideas of 'witnessing' and 'working through',[2] for example, were developed through his consideration of television in the 1990s yet seem useful in understanding some dynamics of the institution as it was in the 1960s. Ephemeral materials such as newspaper reviews, management and production memoranda, schedules, and publicity were not intended to bear the weight of historical scrutiny. However, such documents do allow insight into contemporary preoccupations, into organizational and management practices, even into nuances of 'tone of voice' and interpersonal dynamics, and so appear to reveal much about the assumptions of their time. What we glean from all this, with the benefit of hindsight—of knowing, as our historical subjects could not, what happened next—is some understanding of the micro-dynamics of social and historical processes. Central to our understanding, too, must be the recognition that the pace of change is uneven and that contradictory imperatives may be at work. While we may wish to celebrate the lively national attention to gender politics characteristic of the later 1960s, and to trace some of its starting points in the culture of the 1950s, we must also acknowledge how very slow change can be. The recent publication of an EOC survey, for example, showed that only 10% of senior posts in the UK are held by women, despite a workforce comprising 45% women, confirming that the issue of gender equality in the workforce still remains a live one in the early years of the twenty-first century.[3] Bearing such caveats in mind, this book explores the period 1955–65—the start of a plural broadcasting environment in the UK—considering how the developing institution conceived the forms and practices which, from the mid-1960s to the mid-1990s, constituted the television institution at the centre of democratic and cultural life in Britain. Within this broad exploration we shall pay particular attention to the ways in which women and the

---

2 Ellis (2000).

3 *Guardian*, 5 Jan. 2004, p. 6.

feminine were defined—knowing, as we do, that such definitions became contentious ones for the women's liberation movement of the later 1960s and 1970s.

The formative decade 1955–65 was characterized by speculative experiments with both programme forms and audience address, and by a self-conscious attention to the reception of each new intervention. Both broadcasters and their audiences were alert to the uncharted territory which the plural broadcasting environment heralded. Some of the resultant forms were quickly established, becoming central to all subsequent programming and scheduling practices, while some had all but disappeared by the mid-1960s. In the early 1950s the BBC drew heavily on its experience of radio broadcasting but from 1955 attention was firmly on the output of 'the competitor' and its successes and failures. While the national audience for broadcast television was still under construction, as it were, television's special address to women was highly significant since their engagement was thought to be crucial to the establishment of the viewing 'habit' at the centre of domestic life in the UK. Both the BBC and ITV broadcast programmes directly and specifically addressed to women and scheduled in the daytime. But once television *was* established, this experimental address to a section of the audience, expressed in scheduling as much as in content, was abandoned: after 1964 there was no such differentiation.

The Magazine Format

The magazine format, widely deployed across a variety of programme genres, derived from models in the print media already successfully transferred to radio. This programme form was, and still remains, one of the most successful for broadcast television. It provides a familiar and predictable structure within which a succession of novelties may be offered to an audience likely to be interested in some, if not all, of the items. Because a variety of discrete items may be presented, it allows for heterogeneity within its audiences and because the items are necessarily short it can be relatively cheap to produce. Studio presentations may be alternated with pre-recorded film or videotaped inserts and last-minute adjustments to the programme's contents or running time are not difficult to achieve. The magazine, therefore, is 'safe' relative to other programme forms and no doubt for this reason it was, and is, ubiquitous. This is the form now taken by the news, by many current affairs programmes, and by countless programmes appealing to special interest groups of one kind or another—sports programmes, gardening, cooking, motoring, children's and youth programmes. Even though the special interest group in general may be solicited in the name or kind of magazine, the format still allows producers to acknowledge, and cater for, a variety of particular concerns within it. Though deriving from the print media and refined in radio broadcasting, arguably it finds its fullest development in broadcast television. Indeed it might be broadly understood to describe the endless and continuous succession of items constituting television's output as a whole: the magazine, we might say, is the paradigm for television itself. Television depends on attracting and securing a mass audience—the institutional apparatus is unthinkable otherwise. Even so-called minority programming must number its viewers in tens of thousands, hence the imperative to develop programme forms which could fulfil the public service remit (to which the ITA as well as the BBC was obligated, though in rather different terms) without alienating too much of the potential audience for too long. In the daytime and early evening schedules programmes which allowed for short bursts of viewer attention, rather than those requiring sustained concentration over a longer period, were found to fulfil the requirement to attract an audience—hence the variety show and magazine formats were particularly favoured.

But while the fiscal and organizational advantages of the magazine form may have secured its dominance during the tumultuous decade from 1955, it also privileged habits in both producers and viewers which, in the longer term, were perhaps not so advantageous. On the one hand it encouraged the succinct, which all too easily became the superficial, and on the other hand in assuming a short attention span in the potential audience it probably inhibited an in-depth approach to material, colluding, effectively, in producing the habit of fragmented attention, unfinished speech, the 'weaving of voices' to which Raymond Williams has alluded.[4] Magazine programmes were, by and large, concerned with essentially factual material though, depending on the intended audience, this was often enlivened by 'entertainment'. Cecil McGivern, the BBC's Controller of Programmes, Television in the mid-1950s, urged this strategy on the producers of the afternoon magazine *About the Home*:

> I feel there is a tendency to give too many facts, and to make your audience punch drunk. I suggest there should be a reduction in the number of facts given and a deliberate insertion of resting spots. This can be anything, but you might get away from words, and some music on gramophone records or a piece of celluloid would be invaluable.[5]

---

4 Williams (1989: 12).

5 Memo from Cecil McGivern, Controller of Programmes BBC Television, to the Editor, Women's Programmes, 21 Jan. 1955. WAC file no. T32/1/6.

Magazine programmes were frequently scheduled at times when the audience was presumed to be inattentive, such as in the early evening. However, this programming strategy was at the same time deployed to attract attention and thus to secure the audience for the more prestigious peak viewing time, hence the novelty of items and the speed of their succession. These features of the form, combined with its ubiquitous presence, must have played a part in the mounting unease with which contemporary commentators regarded television's place in national culture. Certainly it is rare, in perusing the national press reviews of the period, to find reference to any but the most celebrated magazine programmes such as the BBC's *Panorama* and *Tonight* or ITV's *This Week*. The magazine programme, it seems, was understood as part of television's basic diet, along with Light Entertainment's variety shows and popular drama series, and as such was largely ignored by critics whose writing focused instead on 'quality' drama or factual programmes and on high-profile 'show business' performers.

| Generic Invention | In seeking to fulfil their acknowledged responsibility to audiences, broadcasters drew heavily on precedents established in other communicative forms. Indeed since television was initially understood primarily in terms of the technological achievement it represented it was, at first, used simply to *purvey* material conceived in the first instance as, for example, a concert, or a play, or a 'topical' talk. It is significant to note also that the British Broadcasting Company—the predecessor of the Corporation—was established in 1922 at the instigation of a consortium of radio receiver manufacturers in order that the purchasers of sets might have something to receive. Radio was certainly the dominant source for both programme form and programme content, not to mention its model for television's institutional management pattern which, inevitably, informed production decisions. But, in its attempt to distinguish itself from radio broadcasting, television naturally emphasized those aspects of its operation which depended on vision; hence as the service developed it is possible to discern additional sources to those available in radio's examples. And, as the audience expanded and broadcasters became more experienced, increasing attention was paid to audience research reports and to more public discussion of the pros and cons of television. Talks, discussions, and, to a certain extent, documentaries also derived from press models developed for radio: here special interest publications, such as those concerned with science, nature, or 'hobbies' like gardening, offered precedents for address and content, not to mention rich sources of specialist guest personnel. Documentaries, |

while also familiar from radio talks, had a wider background. Here the British documentary movement in film in the 1930s, instigated by John Grierson, and the wartime MOI films (which drew on personnel trained by Grierson and his associates), had already laid the basis for a form which, arguably, was to find on television its most successful outlet. By the end of the 1950s the BBC Documentary Department had established the formidable reputation long enjoyed by British television documentaries. It is probably true to suggest, therefore, that while the period up to 1955 can be characterized as exploratory, the following period is marked by an increasing confidence and a more intuitive understanding of the potential of television's contribution to national culture and the circulation of information which enlivens it. This is true both of producers and of critics in whose writings an understanding of the specificities of televisual form became more evident through the decade.

Not only was radio the major source for television programming and scheduling , but also many successful radio programmes were transferred more or less directly to the screen. Hence the popular radio sitcom *Life with the Lyons* appeared on television screens intermittently from June 1955, while still continuing on radio. Here the established radio audience was invited to see as well as to hear the comedy and, according to the Audience Research Department, 'many of them . . . think it even more fun to see "these old friends" on television'[6] and 'hoped they would return to the screen as soon as possible "and for a much longer run" '.[7] The magazine *Woman* reported favourably on another light entertainment programme, *Songs for the Asking*, noting that 'It's *Housewives Choice* all over again, only visual'.[8] Drama, concerts, and variety shows all transferred easily from radio to television, but gradually the special requirements of television technology modified their forms. The different quality of attention required of viewers began to have an effect, first on the form and subsequently on the content of programmes. In particular the close-up was more satisfactory than the crowded long-shot and this was reflected in the privileging of material which allowed it, with the important exception of the Outside Broadcast spectaculars covering state occasions and national sporting rituals where the (then) astonishing sense of 'being there' was allowed by television's capacity for instantaneity.

The evolution of television drama presented different problems since, unlike documentary which was typically shot on film, it was generally performed live to camera—'repeat' performances later in

6 WAC VR/55/319, 29 June 1955.

7 WAC VR/55/390, 10 Aug. 1955.

8 *Woman*, 29 Oct. 1955, p. 16.

the week being precisely, in the days before videotape recording, a fully repeated performance. Here television drama took the live theatre for its model and during the fifties much discussion took place about the relation between live theatre and 'theatre of the air'. The question concerned whether or not access to 'theatrical' performance on television would engender an appetite for theatre, or whether it would 'kill' live theatre: powerful arguments and evidence supported both propositions. Additionally the BBC's Drama Department was engaged in protracted and difficult negotiations with the actors' union, Equity, particularly over the issue of repeat performances, and over videotaping technology when this became available towards the end of the decade. Initially drama, or theatre, on television was conceived primarily in terms of the single play supplemented by imported 'film' drama.[9] However, as transmission hours were extended and, after 1955, audiences were the subject of competition between rival broadcasters, other dramatic forms emerged.[10] These were the series, the serial, the sitcom, and the 'soap'—all with precedents in radio broadcasting and the print media. The boundaries between different forms of drama became blurred, as did the address to different audiences and the appropriate departmental responsibility for one or another type of drama. Despite their evident construction *as* drama, the sitcom *Life with the Lyons*, the proto-soap *The Grove Family*, and the serial *Dixon of Dock Green*, for example, were all produced by Light Entertainment. Here, perhaps, is one of the most compelling arenas in which to observe the opposition between 'giving the public what it wants' and 'public service' or, as Ien Ang has put is 'giving the public what it needs'.[11] The opposition between 'serious' and 'popular' drama was compounded by another distinction between 'classic' and 'contemporary' writing: securing and training adequate numbers of writers to fulfil television's increasingly voracious demand for all forms of drama was a continual problem. By the early sixties television drama was often the focus of public, not to mention parliamentary, discussion of broadcasters' output. Television's responsibility for cultural decline or democratic dissent frequently occupied centre stage, as it were, as new and younger writers seized the opportunity to present politically controversial material to unprecedentedly huge audiences.[12]

---

9 The note 'A Television Film' in the published programme announcement generally referred to imported, made-for-television American material. Cinema films were transmitted too, but these were subject to many constraints from a cinema industry which considered television as an unequivocal threat to its existence.

10 Series dramas was produced before 1955—notably the first six-part series of *Quatermass* in 1953—but the continuing form became increasingly widespread after 1955.

11 Ang (1991: 40).

12 The University of Reading's *The Wednesday Play* project, and esp. M. K. Macmurraugh-Kavanagh (1997*a*, 1997*b*) deal explicitly with these questions.

The ground was prepared for this development in drama by the increasing prestige of current affairs output, particularly following the demise of the 'fortnight rule' (see below, Chapter 2) in 1956. Within the BBC current affairs was the province of the Talks Department and followed models established in radio while also drawing on those current in the print media's editorial discussions. *Picture Post* (1938–57) the weekly magazine of photojournalism edited until 1950 by Tom Hopkinson, for example, offered features in which propositions were often demonstrated visually, through photographs, on topics very similar to those which later became the purview of current affairs programming. The magazine's demise, in 1957, was directly linked by its proprietor, Edward Hulton, to the growth of television.[13] Newsreels, a staple feature of wartime and post-war cinema programmes, also offered a visual commentary on the news and special events of the day, anticipating the characteristic current affairs programme in both its content and its magazine format, and these cinema newsreels, too, barely survived into the sixties. The news itself was handled separately from current affairs. In the BBC the news was given *in sound only* on television until 1954, since the presence of the newsreader in vision or, indeed, any supporting pictorial material, was thought to jeopardize the authority and, more significantly, the impartiality, of the spoken word.[14] Commercial television maintained this conceptual separation between news and current affairs. Sole responsibility for national and international news coverage was given to Independent Television News, and their output networked to the regions, whereas current affairs programming could be, and was, produced by all the companies. This attitude to 'the news' left the field open for current affairs producers to develop a more discursive approach to matters of current concern, and consequently to realize television's potential as an agent in democratic participation. The magazine format, employed by both *Picture Post* and cinema newsreels, was the preferred mode for current affairs output in both the BBC and commercial television. Sports coverage, too, employed this mode except for the more extended Outside Broadcast coverage of significant national sporting events such as the Wimbledon tennis championships, the cricket test matches, or the Oxford and Cambridge boat race. In this field, too, the special characteristics of television had substantive effects on both the extent and nature of the sports themselves as well as for viewers' and spectators' relation to them. In time some sports, such as snooker, developed a national importance deriving almost entirely from their special affinity with television technology.

13 Hopkinson (1970: 20).

14 See Thumim (1998: 91–104) for further discussion of this issue.

Consideration of the sources, or models, from which early television programming derived invites discussion of the question of *genre* in television. Like cinema, television production and broadcasting entail complex, costly, and collaborative processes which oscillate between the poles of industry and commerce on the one hand, and the arts and politics on the other. This is the matrix within which broadcast content and its meanings for audiences exist in a constant tension between the exigencies of the marketplace and the more philosophical conceptions of individual and national identities. The huge number of different interests invested in the various stages of the process all require some means of defining the product, or of distinguishing between already existing products. The concept of genre, which allows the categorization of discrete entities, thus introducing order, is crucial to all these interests but operates differently for each of them. At a meta-level, for example, it might be argued that the whole of televisions' output is, in itself, a genre among other twentieth-century forms of culture and communication. While this would undoubtedly be helpful in distinguishing between, say, television and cinema, or the print media, or the live theatre, it is less than helpful in distinguishing between the range of material *on* television. Similarly a distinction might be made amongst classes of, say, drama available on television, in the theatre, in cinema, and, indeed, in literature—such as the epic, the thriller, or the melodrama: if the object is to explore the contours of a dramatic genre across different media this would be a good starting point but, again, if the object of study is the forms and orders specific to television there would be drawbacks to this line of approach.

In terms of the organization of production *within* television broad distinctions were made between types of programming and, as I have suggested, these frequently derived from the institutional models established in radio—they pertained principally to the (quite new) task of producing and transmitting a more or less constant flow of material for an indefinite period. Different kinds of output required different pre-production organization and for managerial reasons it often made sense to distinguish between them on these grounds. Hence the separation between performance-centred light entertainment and drama which, though it also purveyed live or recorded performance, had writing at its core. Hence also the separation between news, by definition requiring a speedy, almost daily turnaround, and current affairs or documentary in which more leisurely planning and production allowed for the in-depth assessment required. Current affairs planning typically allowed a minimum of a week, often considerably longer, while documentaries could easily be in production for several months. One might account for the initial separation between current affairs and documentary, for example, on the grounds that whereas the former was largely studio-based with some imported filmed material, the latter was almost entirely based on location filming. However, though this distinction might have made some sense in 1955, by 1960 current affairs programming routinely deployed all available techniques, including location filming, to produce its in-depth exploration of current issues. Because of the importance of instantaneity to early concepts of television Outside Broadcasts—defined entirely by production method—was a free-standing and very powerful department, though not one aligned to any particular genre of programming. The managerial clarity which such broad distinctions may allow, however, particularly in terms of resource allocation, is of little consequence to the audience in its judgements about what, and when, to view. In this case a distinction in terms of content is required. In order to guide audience choice and to secure audience loyalty the central feature of generic differentiation—that is to say, the simultaneous *sameness* and *difference* which it promises—must be clearly deployed.

Audience choice was guided by scheduling patterns which were predictable and, it was hoped, also bore some relation to the assumed domestic routines of putative viewers—hence *Children's Hour*, the *Nine O'Clock News*, the *Sunday Night Play*. The actual contents of such programmes might, and did, vary enormously, taking on quite different generic features. The practice of promising something similar in a particular programme slot—such as an early evening variety show or a mid-evening current affairs programme or an afternoon magazine—which would also always be different from the previous week's offering, became more and more central to broadcasting strategy in its aim to secure and maintain audience 'loyalty'. There are interesting tensions between the varying interests (as sketched here) informing generic differentiation, and this is particularly evident in the fluid and rapidly developing areas of factual programming and popular drama. Both of these, I suggest, were especially susceptible to a specifically televisual development, and hence evolved, as we might put it, with particular and fascinating speed during the period with which this study is concerned, 1955–65. Their evolution was informed by producers' increasingly intuitive understanding of television's possibilities and audience's increasingly sophisticated perception of televisual form. These two poles of the television operation, we might say, *produced* the mature institution of the mid-1960s. Accordingly the following chapters will consider aspects of these two major programming areas—both, of course, are far too vast to permit thorough coverage in one study. My focus will be on the emergent form *current affairs* understood very broadly and including the BBC's short-lived experiment with specific broadcasting to the daytime female audience, and on the popular drama which, after 1955, rapidly became the mainstay of both broadcasting systems: the licence fee-funded BBC and the commercially funded ITV.

Chapter 1 offers an overview of the main features of this formative period: the start of plural, therefore competitive, broadcasting in the UK and the discursive environment it produced. Chapters 2 and 3 will deal with factual programming and Chapters 4 and 5 with drama for the mass audience. In each case—factual and drama—the second of the two chapters will offer detailed 'case studies' of exemplary programmes, aiming in this way to deliver some idea of the 'look' of television in this far-off period. Because questions concerning women and the troublesome concept of 'the feminine' are particularly significant in the implicit tensions marking television's development, I pay particular attention to the presence—or absence—of such questions in the material I present. As I shall argue, these questions are crucial to an understanding of television after 1955 and further, I shall propose, they contribute to understanding of this vital cultural form's contribution to the radical change experienced in British society between the mid-1950s and the mid-1960s. The final chapter— 'Women, Work, and Television'—will return to the overarching question of television's place in public sphere discussion of cultural change in post-war, pre-women's movement Britain. To what extent, I want to ask, can the emergent television institution, in its heterogenous development, be understood not only to reflect but also to produce change?

1

The Formation of Television in the UK 1955–1965

September 1955 The year 1955 marks the start of the broadcasting environment which, in the late 1990s, was still a familiar one. But the radical changes consequent upon new digital technologies in the 1990s produced fluidity and unpredictability in the television institution, making a dangerous game of investment and planning. This is very much how the advent of commercial broadcasting was viewed in the mid-fifties: not only was the pattern of provision altering, but also conceptions of audience changed since now it was at the same time a body—the national public—to be served with information, education, and entertainment, and one whose possibly fickle loyalties must be secured. It is also important not to lose sight of the fact that at this time the audience was not yet a fully national one: the transmitter network was still under construction, and the cost of television receivers still precluded their purchase by many. For these reasons imperatives informing broadcasting policy had implications which spread beyond the exigencies of day-to-day programming and scheduling decisions, to the formation of the mass audience itself. Though the BBC was still regarded as, and considered itself to be, 'the voice of Britain', this could no longer be taken for granted. Indeed much of the debate which followed the establishment of commercial broadcasting focused precisely on the question of national culture as this was seen to be reflected, formed, and influenced by the increasing presence of television. Hence, for example, *The Listener* in its weekly 'Critic on the Hearth' page:

> At least three years ago I wrote of it here as a time-wasting social force. Nothing that has happened since causes me to brandish the charge with less confidence. On the contrary, the alarm arises from a belief that television is eroding our country's good sense with its ceaseless projections of loose notions and unrelated information.[1]

---

1 Reginald Pound in *The Listener* 19 Apr. 1956, p. 476.

Since the first broadcasts from Alexandra Palace, London, in August 1936 the Reithian presumption that broadcasters' duty—if not their *raison d'être*—was to inform and educate audiences, while also entertaining them, had dominated television production. The British Broadcasting Corporation, the BBC, was charged with providing a service to the public:[2] they were licensed to make use of selected frequencies on the airwaves which, like other 'natural' resources, were to be administered by government on behalf of the people. During the Second World War this public service ethos took on a new significance as the BBC's radio broadcasts welded together civilian and service populations, constructing and presenting a united front in the face of wartime privations.[3] By the time television broadcasting resumed in 1946 the BBC was widely celebrated as 'the voice of the nation': though the appellation referred to radio, its import was unquestioningly accepted by the 'television service', then a relatively minor department within the highly organized institution.

As the austerity of the 1940s slowly and unevenly gave way to the expansion in employment and production which characterized the 1950s, the television service was also expanding. Popular memory ascribes great importance to television coverage of the 1953 coronation ceremony: though this was not the first State occasion to be televised,[4] it *was* the first to attract something approaching a mass audience. Sales of receivers rocketed, licence fee income followed, and BBC television earned public endorsement for its claim, along with BBC radio, both to exemplify and to disseminate 'Britishness'. By 1954–5 the television service was self-supporting for the first time; that is to say, the licence fees specifically required of those with television receivers produced revenue adequate to expenditure, and 'in terms of "box office" results, sound broadcasting and television are at present running neck and neck'.[5] In the early 1950s in Britain television *was* the BBC, its public service brief jealously guarded and this new form of broadcasting carefully monitored by means of regular 'Listener Reports' both for the appropriateness of its content and for its success in satisfying audiences. But as the television audience expanded and the post-war consumer boom took hold, the one-nation consensus necessary to wartime survival was superseded by an emphasis on the virtues of competition. Television, like other forms of production, it was argued, would profit from the stimulation of a plural broadcasting

2 Licensed in its 1927 Royal Charter.

3 Calder (1982: 413–22).

4 King George V1's 1937 coronation had been televised, though on this occasion cameras had not been permitted inside Westminster Abbey but were located on the processional route.

5 Keesings Contemporary Archives, vol. x 1955–6, p. 14444, 24 Sept.–1 Oct., BBC Reports and Accounts for 1954–5, paras. 3 and 6.

environment in which the BBC would have to compete with other broadcasters for audience attention. This proposition, debated through the early years of the decade,[6] resulted in the 1954 Television Act, the establishment of the Independent Television Association, the ITA, and the commencement of commercially funded broadcasting in September 1955.

The ITA, charged with the administration of independent television, held its first meeting in August 1954, and just over a year later their first broadcasts were on the air.[7] Agreement on the term 'independent' to designate commercially funded television represented something of a victory for its supporters and was regretted by those who feared that, by implication, the BBC's own independence from Government might appear to be compromised. Within the BBC the advent of 'the competitor' was regarded with a mixture of alarm, curiosity, and excitement. As one internal memo asking for policy guidance put it: 'My instinct is to attempt a story on it: however if the rules of war apply, it might be thought that this would draw attention to the opposition and thus damage the Cause.'[8] Complicated arrangements for monitoring ITV output were hastily put in place, and the pros and cons of this expenditure evaluated against the requirements of production as an autumn schedule to withstand the competitive onslaught of commercial broadcasting was planned.[9] ITV's debut was accompanied by a chorus of welcomes in the national press, and preceded by frantic—not to say heroic—activity in building transmitters, contracting the companies to produce material, securing advertising, and persuading the viewing public to have their one-channel receivers retuned. In its first editorial *TV Times* suggested that:

> Television is at last given the freedom of the air. The event is comparable with the abolition of the law that kept motor-cars chugging sedately behind a man with a red flag.
>
> Now it's the 'go' signal, the green light for TV, too—with no brake on enterprise and imagination.
>
> So far, television in this country has been a monopoly restricted by limited finance and often, or so it has seemed,

---

6 esp. in the 1951 Beveridge Report, commissioned in 1949.

7 The ITA comprised ten appointed members chaired by Sir Kenneth Clark, charged with the duty of overseeing the introduction and operation of commercial television in accordance with the provisions of the 1954 Television Act. They received an annual government grant of £750,000 and were intended to arbitrate complaints and disputes, and to ensure competition between the companies. Their first act was to appoint Robert Fraser to the executive post of Director General (Sendall 1982: 36–62).

8 WAC T32/1191/1, 12 Aug. 1955, memo from Michael Peacock to the Head of Television Talks.

9 WAC T36/28, 27 May 1955.

restricted by a lofty attitude towards the wishes of viewers by those in control.[10]

Adrenalin flowed, and a stream of features, news items, and analyses in the *Radio Times*, the *TV Times*, and the national press monitored the ensuing contest—for this is certainly how it was regarded during the first few months. *Picture Post* ran a special issue (24 Sept. 1955) headlined 'Television's Big Week', claiming that 'it is no exaggeration to say that this is the most important event in British entertainment since the war' and offering, under the title 'Let Battle Commence', comparative assessments of BBC's serial *The Grove Family* with ITV's American import *I Love Lucy*. The cover of the issue featured Lucille Ball rather uncomfortably sandwiched between the two male leads from the British drama. The *News Chronicle* (22 Sept. 1955) announced a monthly Gallup Poll survey of audience reaction, promising to publish 'the verdict on who is top of the month' in various categories which, in its attempt to cover all eventualities, recalls *Kinematograph Weekly*'s efforts to assess and monitor popularity in the cinema.[11]

Over the next few months considerable attention was paid, within the two broadcasting organizations and in the press, to the effective consequences of a plural system for British television. Perceived shortcomings in the BBC, such as 'stuffiness' and paternalism, were measured against perceived pitfalls of a commercial system dependent on the advertisers' need to secure large audiences and the companies' need to secure their profits. Thus 'public service' was considered in opposition to 'giving the public what it wants' and both concepts were subject to more or less detailed analysis. In the competitive spotlight of 1955 the celebration of the nation was invoked by both sides as the goal and duty of broadcasting. George Barnes, under the headline 'BBC Television: A National Service' wrote in the *Radio Times*, 'The BBC has always considered it a duty to make its Television Service completely national both in range and character. Television must reach into every home that wants it, and events must be televisable wherever they occur.'[12] Barnes was here

---

10 *TV Times*, 22 Sept.–1 Oct. 1955, p. 2.

11 These were to be: Outstanding TV actor of the year; Outstanding actress; Author of the best original play or serial; No. 1 personality of light entertainment; Producer of the most successful regular programme; Leading personality in TV music programmes; Foremost commentator in current affairs or news programmes; Outstanding personality of women's TV; Best camera team on outside broadcasts; Advertiser who screens the most entertaining and imaginative commercial spot. The poll was an interesting amalgam of those deployed apropos cinema box office performance at the time, recalling both Josh Billings's annual pronouncements in *KineWeekly* and *Picturegoers*'s annual poll of its readers. The *News Chronicle* invited its readers to suggest their 'top' in each of the television categories and the annual result was computed from these monthly returns.

12 *Radio Times*, 16 Sept. 1955, p. 3.

exploiting the fact that whereas by 1955 the BBC transmitter network was almost complete, ITV's was still under construction and hence ITV was available at this early date only to those homes within reach of their first transmitter in Croydon.[13] The *TV Times*'s end-of-year reflection on its first few months of operation quoted this exceptionally anodyne assertion from Sir Robert Fraser, Director General of the ITA: 'I believe in Independent Television in Britain—because I believe in Independence, because I believe in Television, and because I believe in Britain.'[14] Like Barnes for the BBC, Fraser was appealing to both patriotism and individualism. Such discussion rests on assumptions about who 'the public' is: while some commentators were content to evoke the democratic body more or less ingenuously, others—notably the broadcasting organizations themselves—explored it more fully through various forms of audience research.

Competition extended beyond evaluation of programming and quantification of audiences to the struggle to recruit, train, and keep personnel—particularly skilled technicians and writers, actors and presenters—and there was considerable movement of technicians, engineers, and production staff as well as performers from the BBC to the new companies. This was frequently noted and bemoaned in internal BBC memoranda, and publicly acknowledged by the Director of BBC Television, George Barnes: 'In the last six months 350 trained men and women have left us to serve the competitor. This is a severe test of efficiency, a painful separation from old friends, and a rueful compliment in that the competitor had to find well-trained staff and has sought them in the best place.'[15] One might add, here, that in 1955 the BBC was of course the *only* place where experienced personnel might be found—the only place in the UK, that is. Granada's energetic management recruited personnel from Canada, particularly to their drama and current affairs operations. The upper echelons of management were not immune: during the next few years many senior figures moved back and forth between the BBC and the ITA or the companies. Norman Collins was Controller of BBC Television from 1947 to 1950 and subsequently leader of one of the first companies, ATV. Kenneth Adam was the first chair of ITV's celebrated political discussion programme, *Free Speech*, from its inception in 1955, and was Director of BBC Television from 1961 to 1968. Sydney Newman, recruited from the Canadian Broadcasting Corporation, ran ABC's *Armchair Theatre* from 1958 to 1962, when he was

13 Twenty-two ITV transmitting stations became operational between Sept. 1955 (Croydon) and early 1963 (Strabane, Northern Ireland) (Sendall 1983: 3).

14 *TV Times*, 30 Dec. 1955, p. 5.

15 *Radio Times*, 16 Sept. 1955, p. 3.

appointed as Head of BBC Drama. Stuart Hood was Programme Controller at the BBC from 1961 to 1964, then moved to a senior position in Thames Television. Despite the undoubted stimulus to employment in the broadcasting industry as a whole provided by the advent of the second channel, the class, race, and gender composition of senior management remained more or less intact, dominated, as were most other arenas of public life in Britain, by the white, middle-class male.

Both the BBC and the ITA were agreed on the necessity to avoid what they saw as the pitfalls into which television broadcasting in the USA—despite some acknowledged successes—had fallen. Indeed once the initial excitement over competitive scheduling in the UK had worn off, debate about the quality and content of broadcast television frequently centred on British anxiety about American influence. This can be read, as it was at the time, as an aspect of the competition between Britain and the USA for cultural hegemony, which was to inform debates in the later 1950s about the 'state of Britain'.[16] There was much initial fascination, too, with the form and content of independent television's advertisements which were themselves often reviewed not only in the trade press[17] but also in the television criticism sections of the national press.[18] The novel conjunction of overt advertisement with established generic forms occasioned often withering criticism from those apparently affronted by the market's intrusion into the privacy of domestic space. The advent of commercial broadcasting heralded an influx of American product to British domestic screens as well as the introduction of market-led imperatives in scheduling strategy. Innovations in consumer technology, the commodification of popular taste, and the concomitant shifts in social power relations were all cited as evidence of the growing and unacceptable dominance of British culture by American values. In the mid-fifties, despite the secure hold on all forms of broadcasting by British establishment figures, independent television was popularly associated with the American example—an association welcomed by some and deplored by others.

| **What Is Television?** | Underlying the mid-fifties lobbying for the second, commercial channel, the subsequent negotiations about broadcasting hours, and all the various celebratory announcements of new stations, new programmes, and innovations in broadcasting technology emanating |

16 Hebdige (1988: 45–76).

17 e.g. *Commercial Television News* carried regular star-rated critiques of spot advertisements.

18 See Thumim (1995) for further discussion.

from both the BBC and the ITA, are some fundamental questions about broadcast television's relation to society. A 1955 *Picture Post* feature survey of work and leisure patterns compared Britain with the USA, noting optimistically that 'TV and Radio get good and growing audiences for serious down-to-reality programmes—TV in particular is widening horizons, particularly among housewives and young people. There has been a rise in civic and political consciousness.'[19] Not all commentators were so positive, but concerns about the wider consequences of television viewing also informed critical response to programmes: reviews at this time almost always carried such a subtext. On the surface might be a discussion of 'last night's viewing' but it was invariably a discussion pointed towards an assessment of the very existence of television, not yet taken for granted. Hence, for example, *The Listener* in its weekly 'Critic on the Hearth' page: 'Patient realism or impatient idealism: if television could help more of us to choose wisely between those alternatives of our present situation it might qualify for the respect which is still mainly evoked by its technical achievements.'[20] The BBC's mandate to inform, educate, and entertain was inevitably modified by its need, from 1955, also to *compete* for its audiences. The ITA, set up and partially funded by Government, was also required to maintain certain agreed standards and safeguards over programme content, a requirement strengthened after Pilkington's criticisms of ITV's performance between 1955 and 1960:

> We conclude that the dissatisfaction with television can largely
> be ascribed to the independent television service. Its concept of
> balance does not satisfy the varied and many-sided tastes and
> interests of the public. In the field of entertainment—and, not
> least, in light entertainment—there is much that lacks quality.
> It is these facts which largely account for the widespread opinion
> that much on television is trivial.[21]

Running in parallel, as it were, between the Scylla of public service ('giving the public what it ought to need') and the Charybdis of 'giving the public what it wants' were aspirations and assumptions shared by both sides. Most commentators were agreed that television's forte was its capacity for instantaneity, at that time often understood as synonymous with a kind of realist truthfulness. Even Bernard Levin's largely vitriolic assessment of 'A Week of Independent TV' closed with praise in these terms:

19 Fyfe Robertson in *Picture Post*, 2 Apr. 1955, p. 16.

20 Reginald Pound in *The Listener*, 19 Apr. 1956, p. 476.

21 Pilkington (1962: ch. 7 para. 201).

And here, at last, was pure television, television as it ought to be and yet might be. The people were real, and recognisable; there was an intelligent man, and a less intelligent man, and a still less intelligent man, and a member of Parliament. And the first three were very angry with the last and let him know it in their several ways. They argued, they shouted, they banged on the table, and the camera looked at them, and at the tea Mr Dodds had accused them of drinking to excess, and at their workaday clothes, while they for their part looked at each other and did not spend time gawping into the cameras for Aunt Cissie to see. For five minutes the screen looked in on life and came alive with an immediacy and a degree of reality that for the rest of the week was never even suggested.[22]

In this and other such commentaries there is excitement about the democratic advantage of wide and instantaneous access to public life in all its many forms: politics, cultural and sporting events, new ideas in science, technology, and marketing. There are assumptions about how people do, or should, spend their time, about domestic organization and routines, and about the disposition of power and authority both within the family and between the family and the State. All these combined to engender a self-conscious anxiety about national identity, about Britain's 'place in the world', and, most of all perhaps, about managing change. The advent of mass television both drew attention to and, it seems, in some cases also produced disturbances in British society: these disturbances centred on class, gender, and international relations as post-war Britain began to come to terms with a newly democratic egalitarianism and with the loss of Empire. Interestingly, and despite the mid-1950s influx of colonial subjects to the UK, the question of race relations was strikingly absent apart from a very few 'special' programmes[23] and occasional items on current affairs programmes which asked whether there *was* a problem. The consequence of television's need to be egalitarian in its appeal to the heterogenous audience was deplored by many commentators:

> Like the popular newspapers, BBC Television surrendered to the irresistible pressure of 'feminine interest' in the wedding at Monte Carlo and gave it priority of attention over the visit of the Russian leaders, which may turn out to be the more important event in the history of nations . . .
>
> These weightier matters apart, it was Cinderella week on BBC Television: the ex-bricklayer's daughter marrying her prince in

---

22 *Manchester Guardian*, 22 Oct. 1955.

23 e.g. of sixty-eight 'documentary and special programmes' broadcast by Granada between 1956 and 1965 only one, *The White Jungle (Coloured People in Britain)*, dealt explicitly with the subject of race relations. Granada Archive Box 1384.

Monte Carlo, the music publisher's daughter who is the Countess of Harewood amid the ancestral surroundings of her husband's family in Yorkshire.[24]

But televisual discourse was as much visual as it was verbal, a point noted by *The Listener*'s Reginald Pound in an astute aside to his commentary on the Budget broadcasts:

'Rab' Butler looked at us with a benevolent eye, in which the camera, tracking in close, let us see a gleam, as of preparedness for the martyrdom of public misunderstanding. The next night, there was Hugh Gaitskell on our screens, fluent, resolute, and over-acting. The problem for the parties is that we viewers are apt to be more attentive to mannerisms than to opinions.[25]

Here is a recognition that the images offered nightly on domestic screens could not always be contained by the narrative structures within which they were located—whether these be the structures of news, of drama, or of light entertainment. It is this recognition, I suggest, that produced considerable and widespread suspicion about the *effects* of watching television on various sectors of the population (especially children) as well as its consequences for the cultural 'health' of the nation in general.[26] Effectively this was a recognition that the nuanced meanings conveyed in the visual image—especially in the close-up view of facial expression—could not be adequately controlled. However, the implicit anxiety over this potential lack of control was displaced onto overt and explicit fears about the possible debasement of British culture through excessive American influence. This was to be found both in the content of imported drama series and in the generic models derived from American examples such as the quiz shows, game shows, and sitcoms which quickly and easily won large audiences. Kenneth Adam, then Director of BBC Television, in an assessment of US Television ironically titled 'Democracy of the Dial' warned:

Even London, according to *Variety*, that indispensable if often incomprehensible American magazine of show business, is 'applying the Minow touch to programme plotting'. A certain British television programme company which has an American subsidiary has announced a series on Sir Francis Drake, 'dialogue

---

24 Reginald Pound in *The Listener*, 26 Apr. 1956, p. 524.

25 *The Listener*, 3 Nov. 1955, p. 761.

26 T32/395 *Television's influence on Children*. This 1960 report of the BBC's Teenage Advisory Committee was recirculated in the newly formed Family Programmes Unit in 1965 by Doreen Stephens who noted in an accompanying memo that 'much of it seems to be as relevant today as when it was prepared'. See also Himmelweit et al. (1958).

and plots strictly on an adult level'; another called 'Khyber Pass', to be a 'Himalayan Gunsmoke'; and a third, 'atmospheric and period' entitled 'Terror'. . . . Swift and pervasive are American pressures, it would seem.[27]

The low cultural value ascribed to much broadcast material by journalists' criticism was often expressed in such terms as 'frivolous', 'light', 'distracting', 'mindless'—terms aligned with the feminine rather than the masculine in the parlance of the day. Though such epithets concerned content, the very habit of viewing also occasioned disquiet:

> Television has not, whatever the more extravagant of its supporters may say, risen to the status of an art: but it is obviously a most important medium of entertainment. Yet I am convinced that if the theatre or the cinema served up stuff like this to their patrons for even a few weeks there would be an outcry. Why, then, are the pavements not bright with the shards of cathode ray tubes? It can only be that there are a number of people who are sufficiently stupid to derive pleasure from such programmes, and that the Independent Television companies have decided that these people shall constitute their audience, framing their programmes accordingly. No other hypothesis can possibly explain the existence of programmes like 'The Adventures of Colonel March', 'Inner Sanctum', 'Gun-Law', 'People Are Funny', 'Take Your Pick', 'You've Never Seen This', 'Four-Star Playhouse', 'Dragnet', and 'The Scarlet Pimpernel'. The aim, then, is too low: but that we could have forseen. What we could not have known was how poor the quality of the arrows would be.[28]

The passivity of the viewer in front of the television screen was regularly deplored. Since, in patriarchal discourse, passivity is aligned with the feminine we might speculate that fears about the effects of mass television viewing centred on the potential feminization, or *emasculation*, of viewers, quite apart from their pollution through exposure to material of dubious cultural worth. Hand in hand with the excitement of participating in the development of the institution, it seems, was a fairly pervasive unease about its potentially demoralizing effect on audiences and therefore, by extension, on the electorate. In its 1962 Report the Pilkington Committee summarized its view of the purpose of television: 'by its nature, broadcasting must be in a constant and sensitive relation with the moral condition of society. Broadcasters are, and must be, involved; this gives them a

27 *The Listener*, 22 June 1961, p. 1081.

28 Bernard Levin in *Manchester Guardian*, 31 Dec. 1955.

responsibility they cannot evade.'[29] This responsibility for the 'moral condition of society' is one that patriarchy has conventionally allocated to women and the femimine, classically held responsible for society's moral failures. In this 'constant and sensitive relation' broadcasters' evasion of responsibility—their failure adequately to discharge their moral duty—renders them, in Pilkington's view, liable to the same condemnation to which women are invariably subject in situations of 'moral panic'. We should recall that the report's principle criticisms were explicitly levelled at the commercial broadcasters rather than at the BBC, hence commercial broadcasting is here aligned, by implication, with negative aspects of the feminine.

Transmission

By 1955, as we have seen, the BBC network of transmitters was more or less complete. Their capital investment programme concentrated on developing regional production facilities, on the one hand, and focused, on the other hand, on the newly established Eurovision link through which programming was to be exchanged at a pan-European level. In a *Radio Times* feature[30] Paul Rotha introduced his television film *The Challenge of Television* (September 1956) in which the international possibilities of television were explored and celebrated, 'more than thirty countries' having contributed to the film. But while the BBC was consolidating its local operations and beginning to consider global possibilities, ITA was launching their entirely different organization from one transmitter serving the London area. As Norman Collins of ATV recalled:

> While the Croydon transmitter was being built and the mast was climbing section by section upwards, film stages at Wembley and theatres at Walham Green and Wood Green were being feverishly converted into TV studios. And while Outside Broadcast vans, studio cameras and control room apparatus were being delivered at a speed which left visiting Americans aghast, more than 1000 staff (considerably less than half of whom, by the way, came from the BBC) were being engaged and trained for their new jobs.[31]

During 1956–7 ITA and the companies planned to begin transmissions from the various regional production centres. The plans, however—and the contractual arrangements between ITA and the companies, as well as those between the companies and their potential

---

29 Pilkington (1962), ch. 3, para. 42.

30 *Radio Times*, 31 Aug. 1956.

31 *TV Times*, 30 Dec. 1955, p. 8.

advertisers—assumed that it would be possible for ITA transmissions to share BBC facilities across the counties. In the event this proved technologically impossible, and the companies were faced with delays to their agreed start dates while the ITA and the Post Office negotiated with each other and the many other relevant authorities for new sites on which dedicated ITA transmitters might be built.[32] This had consequences for the 'reach' of the regional ITV stations, thus for their expected revenue and immediate financial viability.[33] Granada, for example, under the energetic and prescient management of Sidney Bernstein, had expected to serve both Lancashire and Yorkshire from the BBC transmitter at Holme Moss on the Pennines. In the event, however, two transmitters had to be built, at Winter Hill—serving Lancashire, Cheshire, and parts of Staffordshire, all to the west of the Pennines—and at Emley Moor on the east, serving Yorkshire, and Granada was thus deprived of the Yorkshire audience. The historian of independent television, Bernard Sendall, suggests that ultimately the new arrangements were beneficial since they produced a bigger northern audience for ITV in total.[34] However, this was certainly not clear to the companies at the time since, with no licence fee security, they were subject to the hesitations of investors and experienced serious financial hardship during these first two years. One consequence of all this was evident in programming policy: faced with financial crisis, the ITV companies privileged programming which reliably secured large audiences. This decision fulfilled the worst fears of opponents who had assumed that the commercial imperative must result in low-grade light entertainment and cheap imported material. Another consequence was that the ITV companies began to lobby for relaxation in the regulations concerning the permitted hours of transmission.

From 1936 the BBC had transmitted around twenty hours a week, and at the post-war resumption the PMG authorized transmissions between 3.00 and 4.30 p.m., and 8.30 and 10.00 p.m. to which were added occasional Outside Broadcasts and regular morning transmission of stills or films for the benefit of retailers. During the later forties various events, such as the fuel crisis of 1947 when in February the television service was closed down altogether, disturbed the regular pattern of broadcasting but by 1950 the average weekly hours had risen to between thirty and thirty-five depending on the volume of Outside Broadcast sports. From September 1955 the PMG increased the permitted number of hours to a weekly maximum of fifty. This

---

32 Denis Forman (1997) suggests that BBC engineers were unwilling, rather than unable, to solve the problem.

33 See Sendall (1982) for the details of these events.

34 Ibid., ch. 14.

figure was arrived at through negotiations with ITA, who were concerned to maximize the hours during which they might broadcast the advertisements which were to sustain their operation and the BBC, who by then were averaging forty-one hours and were therefore obliged, if they were to compete effectively, to fund another nine hours of programmes each week. In regulating broadcasting hours two issues were at stake. First the total number of hours per week, which could be averaged over a longer period to allow for Outside Broadcast special events, such as state occasions and sports, and secondly the actual hours during which broadcasts were to be permitted.

While broadcasting hours were limited, first the evening prime time (8.00–10.00 p.m.) and the afternoon (3.00–4.30 p.m.) periods were used, the gap between them being gradually whittled down as transmission hours were extended, till eventually the 6.00–7.00 p.m. break in transmission became known as the 'toddlers' truce'. After childrens' television (5.00–6.00 p.m.) finished, it was argued, a one-hour break in transmission would allow parents (mothers) to get their children to bed before the evening's adult entertainment commenced. This arrangement suited the BBC, in continual financial difficulties as they attempted to meet the rapidly expanding demand for programmes from a licence fee income which never seemed quite enough. But ITV programming was financed by the sale of advertising space on air, so both the enlisting and the maintaining of 'channel loyalty' were crucial. Audience research studies[35] showed that viewing figures built up steadily from the mid- afternoon onwards and that therefore the 6.00–7.00 p.m. slot was a potentially lucrative one in terms of advertising space, and if filled might also secure the evening audience. From early in 1956 discussion ensued about the domestic routines of audiences, about children's bedtimes, the preferred time of the evening meal, even the preferred place in the home for the television set. The BBC dragged its heels, in no hurry to jeopardize its investment in prime-time programming because of the necessity to fill another hour in the early evening. This was a necessity to which it felt obliged because of the competition between channels for viewers.[36] Finally, in October 1957, the principle was accepted by the PMG that broadcasters could choose their transmission times subject to the

35 The ITA commissioned studies in 1956, and these showed the percentage of sets in use during one-hour periods between 3.00 and 11.00 p.m., in summer and winter. Between 5.00 and 6.00 p.m. 44%/57% sets were in use, and between 7:00 and 8.00 p.m. 53%/67% sets were in use. Hence the presumption that between 6.00 and 7.00 p.m. at least 50% of the potential market was being lost to advertisers.

36 The licence fee doesn't seem to have been in jeopardy, but this wasn't so clear to the BBC's administration at the time who keenly felt the need to compete in and win the ratings war with commercial broadcasting in order to maintain their right to the licence fee which all receiver-owning households had to pay.

weekly maximum of fifty hours.[37] The necessity to fill the 6.00–7.00 p.m. slot while still keeping within the allotted fifty hours per week had knock-on effects on scheduling and programming. The significant feature for my argument is the assumed relation between scheduling and domestic routines combined with the explicit attention to the female audience which marked discussions of viewers' domestic lives. The engagement of the female audience was thus central to at least two aspects of the emergent institution: women's support was assumed to be crucial in embedding habits of viewing into domestic routines, and the majority of early advertising was for small domestic consumables typically purchased by women—items such as soap powders, convenience foods, and the plethora of new appliances coming on to the domestic market in the later 1950s.

The Audience   Throughout the 1950s television broadcasters were as much concerned with *building* their audience as with serving or satisfying it. In the immediately pre-war period the BBC had experimented first with technology, then with programme content as, simultaneously, the groundwork of television's managerial systems began to be established. Following the war, the 'Television Department' of the BBC looked forward to an ambitious schedule in which regional broadcasting centres would be developed, the transmitter network extended to cover the entire country, and, as the goal of this effort, a truly national audience secured. The BBC's wartime experience in building a national radio audience naturally informed their conception of what a national television audience might be, but the exigencies of wartime—as well as those of immediately post-war austerity— became increasingly irrelevant in the expanding economy of the 1950s. The fundamental similarities between radio and television— broadcasts from a central point being received in individual, mainly domestic, environments—perhaps obscured the much more significant differences. Two such differences have a particular bearing on the broadcasters' understanding of their audience. First the quality of attention required to receive a broadcast in vision on a small screen— at that time typically eight-inch—precluded, for most viewers, their engagement in any other activity at the same time. Thus, rather than being a pleasant accompaniment to domestic tasks or familial interactions, attention to the screen inhibited these: watching television was an activity in itself, substituting for other leisure pursuits. Secondly the high cost of receivers and the short range of transmitters necessarily limited the audience to those within range who could

---

37 The prohibition on Sunday broadcasting before 2.00 p.m. or during the irreverently tagged 'God slot' (6.00–7.00 p.m.) remained in force, however, for another twenty years.

afford a set. In practice, in the late forties and early fifties, this meant the affluent middle classes of south-east England. As the transmitter networks spread north and west during the first part of the decade so too did the audience, initially in the urban centres and later, as the power of the transmitters was augmented, to more remote rural areas. The task of building the audience, then, was complicated by the fact that its constitution was continually changing. By 1955, when commercial broadcasting commenced, the BBC was able proudly to boast that 'BBC Television is now within easy reach of 92 families in every 100' and to acknowledge that

> The population may consist of men and women but so simple a division does not separate highbrows and lowbrows, rich and poor, young and old. All these sections overlap each other and the job of a national service such as ours is to give as many of them as possible programmes to their taste as often as possible.[38]

The independent companies faced a rather different set of problems. On the one hand their task was, arguably, made easier by the fact that the habit of viewing was well on the way to becoming an established part of British domestic life, and that BBC programming had already provided a basis, as it were, against which the ITA and the companies could measure themselves, choosing whether to emulate or innovate, or to do both. On the other hand the huge financial outlay required by both the transmitter-building programme and all the start-up costs associated with programme production made it imperative that the biggest audiences be secured as fast as possible in order to attract the advertising which generated revenue. The latter problem was compounded by the fact that initially broadcasts could only be received within reach of the first transmitter at Croydon, and that all existing television receivers had to be retuned by industry technicians before ITA broadcasts could be received. New sets did not present problems, and the onset of commercial television gave a boost to the market which also benefited the BBC since they received additional licence-fee income.

It is interesting, though perhaps not altogether surprising, to note that the BBC and the ITA thought not in terms of an audience for television per se, but rather of their own audience: channel loyalty was jealously nurtured and guarded, with consequences for the development of scheduling patterns and in particular the concept of the 'peak hour' slot. Both broadcasting organizations, as well as the majority of television critics and commentators, found the temptation to make disparaging comparisons irresistible. The Director of BBC Television

---

38 Sir George Barnes, BBC Director of Television Broadcasting, *Radio Times*, 16 Sept. 1955, p. 3.

at the time, Sir George Barnes, for example, attempted in his *Radio Times* article appearing in the week before ITA transmissions began, to belittle the significance of this event: 'the starting up of an alternative service for a few hundred thousand viewers in London does not affect either the duty or the practice of the service which supplies those who are out of range of commercial television and, indeed, those who do not want it.'[39] One consequence of this attitude was that the period of the most rapid expansion of the viewing habit, of transmission hours, and of programme production—that is to say, the period with which this book is concerned, 1955–65—was also characterized by a competitive ethos which turned on matters of taste, class, and domesticity. Each institution was summarized, in popular discourse, by epithets thought to characterize their intentions and performance: hence the BBC was 'stuffy', 'paternalist', 'priggish', whilst ITV was 'vulgar', 'brash', 'slick'. This is not to ignore the fact that there was substantial admiration for and approval of the output of both 'services', simply to note the tendency to reductive discussion. However, despite such celebrations and denigrations the period is also striking for a generally felt excitement and curiosity about television and what it might bring to the cultural and political life of the nation. Those who welcomed it tended to embrace plurality and the diversity it appeared to promise, while those who deplored it blamed commercial broadcasting for what they conceived to be the deleterious effects of television as a whole.

The broadcasters themselves were naturally concerned to resist the homogenizing consequences of reductive discourse. Despite public pronouncements about 'the audience', both organizations were all too aware of the heterogeneity of audiences. Their conceptions of differing constituencies informed scheduling practices and generic development of programming, resting on a combination of assumption, guesswork, and audience research: it is one tricky but intriguing aim of this study to uncover some of these formative conceptions. Early differentiations of the audience entailed the recognition of special groups defined by gender or familial status—hence 'women', 'children', 'infants'—a differentiation which assumes the centrality of the dominant group who are not-children, not-women. This was expressed as much in scheduling as in programme content: morning programmes for infants and women, afternoon programmes for women, 'children's hour' in the late afternoon. Other, and later, differentiations concerned the recognition of 'special interest' groups whose professional or leisure pursuits might profitably be catered to in programming. In this case the special group was not thought of as entirely separate but rather to constitute a part of the dominant

39 Ibid.

audience. Hence special interest programming was not disposed according to time-based scheduling assumptions about daily routines but in terms of content, as a percentage of the total output. News and current affairs, some documentary, and light entertainment formed the staple, central programme material; sports, various types of music and drama, and religious broadcasting were the major special interest categories. In addition to these two major differentiations was a rather different third, regional broadcasting, which became more significant towards the end of the period when, to borrow the industry's own phrase, full penetration of the potential audience/s had been achieved. Here the local was acknowledged and celebrated and here too Griersonian objectives for a mass media form were most nearly realized through networking (ITA) and 'regional offerings' (BBC).[40] Class as a differentiating factor was rarely, if ever, mentioned explicitly but was nevertheless a constant presence underlying the competitive war of words between supporters and detractors of the rival broadcasting systems as well as in criticism of particular programming. Roughly speaking, commercial television came on the air at the time when the middle-class dominance of the early fifties BBC audience began to give way to an audience more nearly corresponding to the actual demographics of the whole population. The rise in employment and consumer spending, coupled with the relative drop in the cost of receivers, put ownership or rental of a television set, by the end of the 1950s, within reach of most. Since at the time advertisers were still more concerned with audience volume than with income-based differentiations within it, ITA's promise to 'give the audience what it wants' posed a real threat to the dominant middle-class, public service project of the BBC with their brief to inform and educate, while entertaining their audiences. By the early sixties, when ITA's transmitter network was more or less completed, there was a television audience that roughly corresponded to the national population, hence the very term 'television audience' becomes one of questionable usefulness unless specified as *an* audience *for* a particular programme or genre.

The importance of 'knowing' the audience in whose interests programming decisions were made was recognized, and audience research was an increasingly significant endeavour as broadcasters struggled to reconcile competition in the schedules with budgetary constraints. Here again, of course, different interests were to be served, differing uses made of researchers' assessments. The competition between the BBC and the ITA extended to critiques of the different audience research methods employed, but the invalidity

---

40 John Grierson in promoting British documentary cinema in the 1930s had thought that democracy would be well served by simply showing 'the people' to each other.

of comparisons drawn between data with differing methodological bases was also acknowledged. Bernstein proposed that the BBC's Audience Research operation could be commissioned to do similar research for the companies, suggesting that

> This joint organisation will save controversy and statistical innuendoes between the BBC, the PC [Programme Contractors] and advertisers.
> It will save disparaging attacks on one or both television systems.
> It should develop into a comprehensive research organisation of all aspects of television, and the information it gathers will be invaluable to producers and others working for either system. Using one method of measuring all aspects of television will, in the end, be more reliable.[41]

Not surprisingly, given the competitive climate of autumn 1955, the BBC declined to make its expertise available to the new companies. Their failure to think beyond the immediate moment, however, has deprived future historians of what would have been an invaluable and fascinating resource, given that only the BBC's Audience Research included verbatim critiques from viewers about programmes as broadcast. TAM and Nielson[42] data was restricted to statistical information. The Director General of ITA, Robert Fraser, noted early in 1956 that despite differences in TAM, Nielson, and the BBC's methods of obtaining audience statistics, in fact the figures were compatible: 'Fortunately . . . [there is] now an astonishingly close correspondance between the Nielson and the BBC Audience Research figures. We seem to have emerged from the bore of having to resolve serious statistical inconsistencies.'[43]

The BBC had established its Audience Research Department in 1936[44] which, in addition to occasional detailed reports on general questions, routinely provided short reports on all types of programme based on the responses of a 'viewing panel'. These reports offer an estimate of the total audience for the programme in question, expressing this as a percentage both of the whole adult population and of the 'TV viewing public'. In order to serve the purposes of audience research, from 1957 to 1958 the television viewing public was split into 'Band 1' (those who received only Channel 1, the BBC)

---

41 Sidney Bernstein paper 'Proposal for Television Research to cover BBC and ITA Programmes' 7 Oct. 1955. Granada Archive Box 0947.

42 Nielson is name of Market Research Company dominating the field in the USA.

43 'The ITA Audience', 21 Feb. 1956 paper by DG Robert Fraser. ITC Library 21 (56).

44 This was initially known as the Listener Research Department.

and 'Band 3' (those who could receive both channels 1 and 9[45]) and therefore had a choice of programmes. From this time, too, the programme(s)-available on the other channel were indicated in the report, thus a sense of the actual choices being made by viewers is available. In each report the actual number of respondents from the viewing panel who had seen the broadcast was given, and an 'appreciation index' was calculated from their numerically expressed assessment of the programme and the numbers thought to be watching. Though this was an undoubtedly idiosyncratic calculation it did at least have the merit of consistency, so that producers could quickly discover whether their work had been judged better or worse than previous examples, and managers could evaluate the popularity of generically different output. In addition each report gave verbatim quotes from respondents which amplified the numerical assessments and enlivened the reports, building an invaluable resource for today's researchers in the 'snapshot' of the (now) historical television audience's responses. Compared to the size of the television audience, however, the viewing panel was relatively small,[46] and though 'distributed over the UK roughly according to population density'[47] and taking care also to note differences such as age, gender, and occupation, it offered, as its opponents were quick to point out, only the roughest of estimates as far as audience volume was concerned. The *TV Newsletter*[48] assessed eight possible methods of audience research including the two routinely employed by the BBC, finding these to be unrepresentative and subject to bias.[49] Following the July 1954 passage of the Television Act, an article in *TV Newsletter* explored the constitution of the television audience for the benefit of potential investors and advertisers. Based on two large-scale surveys[50] it reported differentiations of the audience in terms of sex—48.5% men: 51.5% women—noting additionally that

> over 80% of women in the TV audience are housewives;
> 4 out of 10 viewers are over 45 years;

45 ITV in the London area was to be found on Channel 9: in other areas the Channel number might differ.

46 According to David Adams in the *TV Newsletter*, 1/5 (Nov. 1953), 'the BBC uses 3600 volunteers to cover 60 programmes weekly'; BBC references in various Audience Research reports suggest rather smaller numbers on particular viewing panels e.g. 650 (WAC:VR/59/41), '700 present members and 320 retired members of the viewing panel' (WAC:VR/60/606).

47 WAC file no. VR/59/41, Jan. 1959.

48 *TV Newsletter* began publication during 1953 when the debate about the possible advent of commercial broadcasting was at its height, and appeared to be addressed as much to potential advertisers as to broadcasters.

49 *TV Newsletter*, 1/5 (Nov. 1953).

50 Hulton, covering 13,000 adults over 3 months from Jan. 1954; and Radio Luxembourg, covering 16,200 adults and 1,300 children in one week in July 1954.

of the three age groups, the coverage is greatest in the 30–44 group;

6 out of every 10 viewers belong to the lower and middle classes. Television's coverage is still much greater in the upper income groups than in the lower—although every year it is brought nearer the proportions of the population as a whole.[51]

It noted also the preponderance of viewers in southern England but asserted that 'in terms of the percentage of viewers who watch television sometime during an average evening' the coverage was more or less identical in the south, the Midlands, and the north of England.[52] When ITV came on the air two methods imported from the USA were used—TAM and Nielson—both of which depended on mechanical recording of sets in use, and neither of which yielded qualitative material about what viewers actually thought of what they saw. But the BBC was concerned to demonstrate proper use of its licence fee, hence gathering data to justify its continuance, whereas the ITV companies required harder data concerning the advertisers' potential market: so long as the sets were on, programme content was a relatively minor detail. The BBC also used its reports routinely to give programme makers feedback on their work.[53]

Hence by the middle of the fifties there was a rapidly expanding television audience, and an uneasy but nevertheless widely understood recognition of the central importance the medium was to play in shaping national culture. Equally important, I suggest, was the recognition noted above, and explicitly pointed out in the *TV Newsletter*,[54] that women were of crucial importance in this audience.[55] They ordered the domestic routines into which television viewing must be inserted and they were the primary purchasers of the consumer goods whose advertisers provided the funding for the second channel. But at the same time there was a deep-seated ambivalence about the consequences, for British culture, of television viewing as a routine element of daily life[56]—viewing not only of the

---

51 *TV Newsletter*, 1/11 (Sept. 1954), pp. 6, 18.

52 Ibid.

53 All available reports are filed at BBC written archives at Caversham under VR = Viewer Research, but in addition copies are frequently to be found in the production files relating to specific programmes, and are also quoted in production and planning meetings, memoranda, and so on.

54 vol. 1/8 (May 1954), pp. 7–9, 'in Britain both the BBC and commercial groups are out to have TV appeal to women. This account describes how NBC ordered *Home* into their range.'

55 This is noted, apropos the American audience, by Spigel (1992) amongst others. The early tie-ins between 'women's programmes' and women's magazines, in Britain, suggest a similar pattern.

56 Spigel (1992: 76) notes, apropos the US context, anxieties expressed about the possible disruption to women's domestic routines that might be caused by excessive television viewing. A similar anxiety is evident in the UK.

deeply suspicious commercial channel but also of the BBC—evident
not only in the 1962 Pilkington Report but in much contemporary
criticism. In such commentary television is frequently located at the
low, or soft, end of the scales by which cultural value was measured by
its self-appointed arbiters. This is reminiscent of the value-laden discourse of cinema critics of the late 1940s, noted by Ellis.[57] It seems
there was thought to be something inherently passive, possibly even
duplicitous, about the new medium. But, as Streeter and Wahl have
argued, the equivalence of 'the audience' with 'the consumer' in
which both are idealized in discourse, is resonant with patriarchy's
mischievous idealization of the feminine.[58] All—the audience, the
consumer, the feminine—are necessary to the enterprise of which
they are the object, are 'served' by the enterprise, but, crucially, lack
control of the enterprise. In the cases of the television audience and
of the consumer the enterprise is the marketplace, in the case of the
feminine it is the maintenance of a social order in which women
can be depended upon to perform certain designated tasks of which
men may enjoy the benefits while retaining overall social control,
hence power.

While much contemporary discourse proposed television as a
debased and therefore, by implication, a feminized form, the same
discourses idealized the television audience as consumer. A typical
cover of *TV Times* in January 1956, for example, showed a three-
generation family beaming happily from a TV-screen-shaped frame.
The cover story, 'The Jones join the ITV Family', describing their careful purchase of a new, seventeen-inch, ITV-receiving set, elided their
pleasure in consumption—referencing their 'neat, semi-detached
house . . . in Wembley', 'their new 10 h.p. family model car', 'the warm
red carpet in the corner of the room where two toning colours
meet'—with their satisfaction with ITV programmes, including the
commercials which they found 'amusing and interesting'.[59] Here is
the family, icon of the nation *and* of the television audience. And
women were addressed directly, their attention actively solicited in
such articles and in TV commercials, as well as being represented on
the screen itself. Hence the unstable matrix of contradictory definitions of women and the feminine so characteristic of this period.

All broadcasters were agreed that they did, indeed, have a responsibility to their audiences. Where they differed was in defining
'responsibility', and, indeed, in defining 'the audience'. At the heart
of the broadcasting operation is the relation between viewers and
programmes, but this is not a relation that comes automatically with

57 Ellis (1975).

58 Streeter and Wahl (1994: esp. p. 249).

59 *TV Times*, 30 Dec. 1955, p. 3.

the technology. The audience must be constructed and defined, and this construction and definition must be seen to be done. Though viewing was conceived as a largely domestic, if not an entirely private affair, *viewers* were in the public domain. Privileging the instantaneity of television's images, asserting the temporal equivalence of the seeing and the thing seen, was the preferred strategy in most of the early construction of audiences. Viewers, it was suggested, were able to *be there* at events from which all previous generations had been excluded—for example at the 1958 State Opening of Parliament:

> It was really wonderful to be able to see the pageantry and procedure of the State Opening of Parliament; television has certainly enabled us to take part in events which are part of our history...
>
> A most memorable occasion which cannot help but have impressed viewers both in this country and on the Continent. It gave everybody who saw it an insight into an event of which they have heard so much, but never appreciated in its true magnificence.[60]

This sense of participatory pleasure, undoubtedly experienced by viewers enjoying the work of the Outside Broadcast Unit, was drawn upon in establishing another trope of early television; that is, the direct address to camera, in close-up, of the location reporter or studio announcer. This is the figure providing the link between viewers in their homes and the 'pro-filmic event' before the television cameras. Here the ubiquitous use of the plural pronoun, *we*, elides the spatial separation between viewers and location or studio event. The face, or head and shoulders, of the announcer, seen framed in an eight- or fourteen-inch screen, is near enough to life-size and seems to be looking straight at *us*: hence a community is suggested, a community experiencing together whatever is to follow. The most celebrated example, one which also embraced a substantial temporal elision, is that of the BBC announcer Jasmine Bligh when she proclaimed the recommencement of television broadcasting in 1946 after the long 'break' of the Second World War by smiling into the cameras on the terrace of Alexandra Palace in London as she said 'Hello, remember me?' The close-up was widely regarded as the paradigmatic televisual image: partly, no doubt, because of its relative clarity on the small, low-definition screens of the day, but also because it asserted the *presence* in the domestic arena of the men and women before the camera.

The business of constructing the television audience continued throughout the fifties, but as the decade wore on, audience size

60 WAC file VR/58/588, 28 Oct. 1958.

increased, and transmission hours were extended, it became increasingly important to recognize and cater to differences within it. As I have suggested, these were conceived partly in terms of assumptions about the timing of domestic routines, and partly in terms of interest groups. Daytime viewing, apart from occasional outside broadcasts of sporting events or state occasions and the morning test transmissions, was regarded as the province of women and children. The BBC generally dedicated the afternoon slot to programming specifically addressed to women at home, preceded by the long-running infants' *Watch with Mother* and followed by the late afternoon *Children's Hour*. ITV did much the same, initially locating its women's programmes in a late morning slot but subsequently broadcasting them in the afternoon. Children's television, *Tea-V Time*, competed directly with BBC children's programming. Both the BBC and ITA also designated early evening as 'family viewing' and the latter part of the evening as 'adult' viewing. Such programming assumes that infants and toddlers will be asleep at certain times in the day; that older children will return from school in time for 5.00 p.m. viewing and will be in bed by the middle of the evening; and that women at home are housewives/mothers performing predictable tasks. These are, of course, reasonable assumptions and they were carefully checked by audience research.[61] The point here, however, concerns the broadcasters' assumption of a substantive relation between *family* routines and television viewing in which broadcasting practice entered into a symbiotic relation with a normative concept of the family. The broad differentiations of the audience indicated here were expressed in scheduling and programming decisions and reinforced by programme announcements and features in the *Radio Times* and *TV Times*. Mary Hill's announcement of the first ITV women's programmes in September 1955 exemplifies the carefully judged assumptions about domestic routines and viewers' interests characteristic of such material:

> Most women that I know, having got a husband and schoolchildren away between 8.00 and 9.00 in the morning, whisk round the home dusting and tidying—and usually pause to draw breath and have a cup of tea or coffee around eleven.
>
> By this time a baby is fed and, we hope, settled down to sleep and the toddler deposited in the pram or play pen.
>
> Surely the woman at home, like any other worker, is entitled to, and needs, a mid-morning break? And like any other worker she will get through the quicker and the better afterwards if she takes it. . . .

61 e.g. 'Timing and Frequency of Programmes for Women, Children and Infants', Feb. 1950, VR/50/94; 'An Enquiry about Afternoon Television Programmes' 2 Nov. 1955, VR/55/516; and 'Women's Programmes on Television' 1959, VR/59/364; all at WAC.

If you are one of those who just can't sit still there are
lots of odd jobs that can be done while viewing—from
ironing or polishing brass or silver to peeling the apples for
lunch...

Most women today have held down jobs before they married.
Most of them admit they get attacks of depression when they
are alone in the house all day. So above all we plan to bring *real*
people to 'Morning Magazine'—the famous and the not so
famous. People with charm and gaiety to make us smile; people
from other countries to widen our horizons; people who are
doing worth while things to inspire us. But because women are,
above all, concerned with their homes and families, there will be
practical programmes too.[62]

In such ways the assertion of contiguity between broadcasters and
viewers, central to the initial construction of the audience, was con-
solidated through the nurturing of particular groupings of viewers
whose necessary tasks and daily routines were thought predictable.

Finally the audience was secured through the practice, increasingly
widespread after 1955, of *representing* viewers themselves on screen.
Wild shots of crowds at sporting events and state spectaculars come
into this category, and are probably the first examples of it. But in
the latter part of the fifties the studio audience for popular drama
or light entertainment offered viewers 'at home' the sight or sound
of their equivalents *on* television: the audience's representatives
were an essential ingredient of the spectacle. A refinement of this
development—though that is hardly the word used by contemporary
commentators—was the quiz or game show in which members of
'the public' (aka 'the audience') became the protagonists, central to
the programme's format and indeed the main attraction. A regular
host would conduct events, but camera, and thus audience, attention
was focused on the participants who were endlessly the same yet
always different. This programming strategy, in addition to narcissist-
ically binding audiences into programmes—rather like Lumiere's
operatives did in 1896, when they showed locally shot footage to
new cinema audiences in cities around the world—had the great
advantage of being cheap. Given the need to fill transmission hours
with reliably popular programming, and the financial constraints of
most broadcasters during the latter part of the fifties, the ubiquity of
such programmes is hardly surprising.

All these endeavours—constructing, defining, and representing
the audience—have in common the general project of first establishing the British television audience as an entity and then securing the

62 *TV Times*, 22 Sept.–1 Oct. 1955, p. 14.

loyalty of discrete sections of it. The latter must take account of viewers' readiness to view and their ability to do so: they must want to see the programme and it must be available to them at a time when viewing is possible. Hence broadcasters' careful attention to scheduling and to their discovery and acknowledgement of viewers' various tastes and interests. In addition, and in recognition of the responsibility owed to their audiences, most broadcasters sought to develop tastes and interests in their audiences by offering material thought *in itself* to be laudable because of its cultural value, or its democratic or practical usefulness. And here, of course, is where the values of broadcasters' senior management were most likely to inform production policy. BBC Talks and Documentary Departments' output, particularly in the area of current affairs, is one example, and ATV's early sixties foray into high culture, *A Golden Hour*, is another. Bernard Sendall, Deputy Director General of ITA (later IBA) from 1955 to 1977, wrote to Lew Grade about one of these:

> whilst, of course, the first two 'Golden Hours' were a great tour de force, they do as an institution have the drawback of seeming to be a sort of Palladium Show for the culture snobs. Indeed, if I may say so without seeming to be critical, Palladium Show techniques ill become some of the splendid artistes whom you presented on the last occasion.
>
> Is there any chance of breaking right away from the Opera House and massive OB atmosphere and doing an equally worthwhile job in the studios, with or without a live audience?[63]

The Palladium Show—*Sunday Night at the London Palladium* (ATV, 1955–67; 1973–4)—was a highly successful and widely popular televisual version of the music hall/vaudeville review including a series of song and dance spectaculars, comedy sketches, and the occasional circus-based act, linked by an 'MC' presenter. It was reminiscent of theatrical performances popular during the 1950s at seaside resorts, and catered to a similarly middle- to low-brow audience. In his evident unease with *Golden Hour*'s appropriation of this format for 'high' culture, Sendall references 'culture snobs'—an accusation typically levelled at the audience for BBC arts programming—while simultaneously applauding ATV's success in securing such illustrious performances for ITV. In the wake of the Pilkington Report, with its own culturally snobbish denigration of ITV's output, Sendall's recognition that though the content was welcome the form was inappropriate is a significant one. ITV could and should compete with the BBC at all cultural 'levels', but its experiment here is

---

63 29 Aug. 1963: ITC Library file no. 5081/2/10.

compromised by the inappropriately 'low' cultural form through which 'high' culture was purveyed.

Advertising Practices

Commercial broadcasting depended by definition on advertising revenue: as in the USA advertisers were, effectively, 'sold' an audience for their product, the rates they paid being dependent on the predicted size and demographic likely to be viewing. This accounts for the exclusively quantitative assessments of audiences for particular programming undertaken by all except the BBC's Audience Research Department which, as we have seen, attempted also to discover qualitative response to programming. Legislation for the second channel and its controlling body the ITA was fairly specific about the permitted placing and timing of advertisements, refusing, for example, many practices then common in the USA such as product placement or programme sponsorship. Advertising magazines, however, were allowed until the 1962 Pilkington Report proposed that they should be banned. Advertisements punctuated both programmes and schedules on ITV, and though the BBC did not carry overtly commercial messages nevertheless it similarly punctuated its schedules with programme announcements and, sometimes, trailers.

The question of advertising, which turns on the degree of influence television material may be thought to exert on its audiences, is a fascinating one. It is at the heart of the passionate debates of the early fifties over the possible consequences of commercially funded television, but it is also, in its widest sense, implicated in the very concept of public service broadcasting's brief to educate and inform its audience since all—advertising, education, information—involve some suggestion to viewers that they might think or act in a certain way. Once the 1954 Television Act had been passed debate centred on the manner in which advertising might acceptably be grafted on to British television. As Sendall noted:

> the anxieties . . . about television financed by advertising . . . were but a part of the great debate about the power and influence of mass communications which . . . was bound up inextricably with fundamental beliefs about the nature of liberty in a free, democratic society . . .
>
> Parliament found it necessary to ensure in the Television Act that so far as possible commercial television was insulated from control by commercial interests over the information supplied and opinions expressed in its programmes.[64]

---

64 Sendall (1982: 98).

American models were examined and, generally, deplored and some practices were consequently forbidden, such as sponsorship of programmes or direct product placement. In general 'spot' advertising was favoured and the length, frequency, and siting of such spots made subject to the control of the ITA. The ITA set up an advisory committee in January 1955, whose report *Television: The Viewer and the Advertiser* laid down basic principles concerning the ethics and content of television advertising which were to inform practice for the next twenty-five years.[65] Various 'safeguards' were agreed, such as the prohibition of advertising within two minutes of any programme presenting the royal family, or of religious programmes, and various classes of goods or services were excluded altogether. Advertisements promoting matrimonial agencies, fortune tellers, and moneylenders, for example, were forbidden, as were cures for smoking or alcoholism—whereas the advertising of both tobacco and alcohol was permitted. The majority of spot advertisements were for food, domestic and cosmetic products, or small consumer durables, hence the principal address was to the (presumed) female controller of the domestic purse: the first 'commercial break', on the evening of 22 September 1955, consisted of two one-minute advertisements: one for Gibbs SR Toothpaste and one for Cadbury's Drinking Chocolate. *Commercial Television News* carried routine reviews of advertisements and a complete listing of those actually broadcast on each day,[66] and at the commencement of commercial broadcasting much of the press commentary included reference to the novel advertisements. The *Liverpool Daily Post*'s television critic, writing about the launch of Granada's service, devoted nearly one-third of his review to the spot advertisements which had punctuated the evening:

> Fifteen minutes after the network opened, Northern viewers were broken in gently to their first experience of an advertising spot. I say gently, because this initial experience comprised a little tour of a chocolate factory which was not so different from the tour of the television transmission factory which Mr Quentin Reynolds was rather too earnestly conducting. Only the tour of the chocolate factory was shorter. I noticed, by the way, that they did not give the signal white flash we get on screen in London before the advertising spots come on and when they go off. Omitting it gives the viewer less of a feel of that natural break which is supposed to occur for advertising on commercial television, but leaving the signal out can be clever, at first, at any rate. At one point in the

---

65 Sendall (1982: 102).

66 *Commercial Television News*, 20 Apr. 1956, pp. 4–11.

variety show last night, only experienced viewers of the commercial channel promptly grasped that a lady who at first appeared to be the next turn was in fact about to project a soap powder.[67]

At the start of commercial broadcasting advertising magazines, or ad-mags, were also permitted, and it is in the discussion of these that some of the more subtle anxieties about television's potential influence are apparent. Here the familiar format in which several separate but related short items were linked by a presenter—or 'host'—and/or through a consistent *mise-en-scène*, was adopted. *Jim's Inn* (A-R, 1957–63), for example, had Jimmy and Maggie Hanley as a couple running a village pub in which they discussed the prices and quality of various domestic products with their customers.[68] *Man Alive*, also by A-R, was bylined 'Pounds, Shillings and Sense Series' and was principally concerned with the domestic interior: 'John Horsley has finally got down to decorating and furnishing his cottage. However, his daily help, Mrs Phipps, played by Nora Gordon, insists upon supervising the way he spends his money.'[69] *About Homes and Gardens* (ATV, 1956) was another example and various others dealt with holidays (*Where Shall We Go* (ABC TV, 1956), *Over the Hills* (A-R, 1956–7)), furnishing (*What's New* (A-R, 1957)), and shopping (*What's in Store* (ABC TV, 1956), *Slater's Bazaar* (ATV, 1957–9)). The format was in many ways not so far from the BBC's early fifties afternoon women's programme *Shop at Home* as well as the later *Look and Choose*, and certainly had much in common with the factual elements of both the BBC's and ITV's magazine programmes for women. The problem seems to have been assumptions about the supposed difficulty, for the audience, of distinguishing between information or opinion disseminated by partisan advertisers and that offered by the (presumed non-partisan) presenters of other magazine programmes. In the early and financially precarious days of commercial television these magazines were a welcome contribution to both programming and revenue but as the companies became more secure their scheduling at the beginning of peak early-evening viewing—typically at about 7.00 p.m.—was resented. The Pilkington Report recommended their prohibition, mainly on the grounds that distinctions between programmes proper and advertising magazines were blurred, and that the recurrent appearances of the ad-mag 'host' produced a 'friendly figure' whose endorsement of the product, though scripted and paid for, 'appears

---

67 *Liverpool Daily Post*, 4 Apr. 1956.

68 Vahimagi (1994: 65).

69 At 7.15 p.m., 18 Apr. 1956, *TV Times*, 13 Apr. 1956, p. 18.

honest': 'they give the impression of having, on the most sensible and homely grounds, decided to recommend this article rather than that'.[70]

Pilkington's prohibition rests on fears about television's power to influence its audiences, hence also on fears about the gullibility of the audience and the fragility of the beloved notion of impartiality or objectivity in the face of conflicting claims. Though it may seem to be stretching the point, I find the demise of the fourteen-day rule (see below, Chapter 2) which strengthened the power and status of broadcasters, and the banning of advertising magazines because they might not easily be recognized as such, to be two sides of the same coin. If broadcasters were to be trusted with public discussion of issues crucial enough to concern Parliament, the argument ran, it follows that television broadcasting must not be debased by muddying the generic clarity of its programme boundaries. There's an uneasy paternalism at work here, in which acknowledgement of the democratic good of free speech and of open (though preferably well-informed) debate was locked in a kind of tension with the awful possibility that viewers might not understand the issues correctly—that is, in line with the hegemonic consensus.

Contemporary Criticism

Press criticism of television broadcasting, after the flurry of interest following the advent of commercial broadcasting in 1955, is more striking for its absence than for features of its content. Some of the broadsheets had daily television reviews, as did also some of the tabloids, but none of these routinely ran to much more than half a column: that was in response to up to ten hours' broadcasting daily on each of the two channels. By 1960 the *Daily Telegraph* still carried only occasional reviews, mainly of 'serious' drama, on their Arts page. The *News Chronicle* had a regular column 'Last Night's TV', and the *Daily Mirror*'s 'Telepage' carried reviews of the previous night's fare and 'previews' of 'tonight's' viewing in which the emphasis was frequently on individual female performers and on quiz shows, light entertainment, and popular drama with occasional references to *Panorama*. Where criticism did exist, it responded in the main to the emergent genres of news and current affairs or to 'quality' drama, references to popular drama and light entertainment being mostly in rather negative asides betraying the assumption that such things were not worth any column space. The *News Chronicle*'s television critic James Thomas, for example, couched his positive review of a BBC programme with a typical dig at ITV: 'No-one can say that the BBC is

---

70 Pilkington (1962), ch. 8, para. 259.

not fighting to win back their supremacy on a Sunday evening in the face of the sustained lowbrow attack of Lucy, Trinder and Jackson.'[71] There were notable exceptions, particularly Peter Black's 'Teleview' in the *Daily Mail* and Bernard Levin in the *Manchester Guardian*, both of whose writing suggests, in very different ways, a genuinely speculative interest in the new medium and a willingness to consider it on its own merits. Irene Shubik, writing with the benefit of hindsight, acknowledged this paucity of serious criticism as a problem for the television dramatist—one that did not face those working in cinema or the live theatre:

> The television critics . . . are predictably divided. A certain
> number, in the popular press, purport to be representatives of the
> people: 'Mr Joe Average' reacting; others, usually on the 'class'
> papers, take a more professional approach as critics of the art
> or craft of television-making, though few have any practical or
> inside knowledge of that field. Knowing that their criticism can
> make no difference to the audience figures, coming, as it does,
> after the event, some critics seek to be more columnists than
> critics and concentrate on their copy rather than the programme
> itself.[72]

It is true to say that unless there was some obviously wider significance—such as Granada's coverage of the 1958 Rochdale by-election and its implications for the future of democratic politics—the assumption seems to have been, as Shubik implies, that television's very ephemerality rendered it unsuitable for public comment. John Osborne commented memorably on this in a 1971 *Guardian* interview: 'Millions might watch television, but on the other hand, last night's television was even deader than yesterday's newspaper because you couldn't even wrap fish and chips in it.'[73]

Public concern with the fact of expanding audiences and increased consumption of broadcast content came to the fore during the Pilkington Committee's deliberations and following its Report, but here too television's ephemerality and its supposedly low cultural worth is constructed as problematic. The profit motive is universally regarded with suspicion—despite (or perhaps because of) the historically parallel growth of the 'free market'—and the BBC's output thought to be contaminated by the unfortunate necessity to compete for audiences with commercial providers. At stake, it was felt, was national cultural identity, often obliquely referenced by the anodyne term 'taste', as the journalist Monica Dickens deploys it in a 1960

---

71 *News Chronicle*, 3 Dec. 1956, p. 3.

72 Shubik (2000: 162).

73 Osborne, quoted in Shubik (2000: 163).

Woman's Own article about children's television viewing: 'you may hate westerns and gangster plays as much as I do [but] to try to ban them only makes them more attractive . . . teach them good taste. Teach them morals. Teach them to recognise the second-rate, and not to take seriously the cruder entertainment that is offered.'[74] There are undertones here of Hilde Himmelweit's distinction between the discriminate and the addictive viewer, also made in terms of that all-important group for the nation's cultural future, the child audience.[75] The important question of how viewers, any viewers, were supposed to discriminate, to 'recognise the second-rate' if the majority of popular programming was either ignored or routinely denigrated by critics, is rarely addressed. Yet the very popularity of such programming with audiences would seem to have called out for a measured critical response which addressed the programmes rather than, as Shubik noted, the journalists' preoccupation with their own copy to which the material of television seems often to have been at best a convenient 'aside'. Writing about the global impact of just such programmes as were deplored by Monica Dickens—'westerns and gangster plays'—Richard Paterson has noted the perennial gap between critical regard and popularity with audiences.[76] The earliest serious critical engagement with popular television drama came in the 1960s when such series as *The Avengers*, *Dr Who*, and *Z-Cars* began to attract recognition: in general this followed in the wake of attention, both positive and negative, to some of the ABC's *Armchair Theatre* or the BBC's radical *Wednesday Play* productions, which insisted on their active relevance to contemporary social problems.

---

74 Monica Dickens in *Woman's Own*, 9 Jan. 1960, quoted in Oswell (1999: 71).

75 This distinction is proposed in Hilde Himmelweit et al. (1958), and discussed by Oswell (1999: esp. 77–81).

76 Paterson (1998: 60).

2
Factual Programming

Generic Delineation Today's television audiences 'know' what news is, have a clear expectation of what they might find in a current affairs programme, and a pretty good idea of the general types of intention informing documentary. In all cases it is the programme makers' approach to their subject matter, rather than the specific details of programme content, about which the audience has prior 'knowledge'. Most viewers would probably also acknowledge that though the boundaries between these ubiquitous forms are permeable ones, nevertheless the working assumptions which have informed both schedule announcements and critical discussion for the past fifty years rested on a widely held consensus about what distinguishes them. But this consensus has been arrived at pragmatically, as it were, as a result of five decades of 'custom and practice': it was not so clear to television managers and programme makers in the mid-fifties and neither could it be, they assumed, to contemporary audiences. At the start of the twenty-first century these generic descriptors seem once again to be losing their clarity—for example as a consequence of the widespread deployment of so-called 'reality TV'.[1]

Writing with the benefit of hindsight, John Corner offers useful insights into the complexities of both generic differentiation and audience activity in deriving meanings from such texts, suggesting that in topical, fact-based television, viewers are engaged as *witnesses*, 'for television does not constitute particularity through *description*, but seeks to *image* it for our direct response'.[2] The tentative distinctions essayed by commentators in the 1950s, however, privileged *intention* and *approach* over the analysis of form or, indeed, of the nuances of readerly activity ascribed to audiences. Most such discussion is to be found either in the television reviews of the broadsheet press from the mid-fifties, or in the pragmatic managerial memoranda guiding the expanding broadcasting services. Documentary

---

1 A current (Feb. 2004) example is particularly confusing. *Regency House Party* (Channel 4) involves ten male and ten female participants (all single), in period costume, living in 'regency' style for a specified period, their encounters with period technologies and customs, as well as with each other, being filmed for transmission. Is this to be understood as game show, documentary, costume drama, or history programme?

2 Corner (1995: 31).

producer Robert Barr, for example, in a 1951 paper to the Controller of BBC Television, attempted to articulate the distinctions between Talks, Documentary, and Drama because 'In lining up writers and directors for the new series I have found so many people so impossibly vague about the relationship of TALKS–DOCUMENTARY–DRAMA that I feel a clear definition of documentary is necessary.'[3] Whereas in a TV talk 'expert opinion or information is conveyed directly from the authority to the viewer' and 'the appeal is to the intelligence', documentary, Barr suggests, offers a *report* in which the intention is 'to make people feel as well as think. Its appeal is to the emotions'. He is less than clear, however, about the distinctions between drama and documentary and his claim that 'Drama is the easiest to define: its purpose is to entertain. Of its nature it deals in fiction',[4] might well be refuted or at least qualified. Paul Rotha, Head of BBC Documentary in the mid-fifties, acknowledged the centrality of *intention* to the documentary producer and celebrated the special advantages of television in securing his putative aims: 'To those who still believe that documentary has a specific social job to do, this mass access to audience and quick answer is of paramount importance. It is something new in documentary experience.'[5] Noting the twin sources of British documentary practice in the BBC Radio feature and the pre-war State-funded film units, he considers both the funding arrangements for television and its access to audience to be immensely advantageous to the documentarists' project. In his report on a visit to the Regions made earlier in 1954 he summed up his impression that 'Public attention in the Regions was fully alive to Documentary's appeal. There was certainly no need to fear being serious.'[6] Both Rotha and Barr were committed documentarists, and we should understand their comments as polemics intended to secure documentary's place in the broadcasting environment. There was, after all, a BBC department dedicated to documentary production—though it did not have its own film unit. Rotha recalls that 'the very small Documentary department in TV was guided mainly by McGivern, along with his other duties, until in 1953 a Head of Department was appointed.'[7]

The Talks Department was a rather more powerful one and as it expanded it tended to overlap with both News and Documentary. In a sense documentary—central as it became to British television's reputation for excellence, and despite its complex relation with

3 WAC T/16/61/1, 3 Aug. 1951.

4 Ibid.

5 Rotha 'Television and the Future of Documentary', 25 Oct. 1954, WAC T16/61/1.

6 Report of H.Doc.Tel's visit to the Regions, 10 May 1954, WAC T16/61/1.

7 WAC T16/61/1, TV and the Future of Documentary, p. 9.

drama—is a more straightforward generic descriptor than current affairs. In the latter, broadcast television's direct engagement with the contemporary political process was overtly acknowledged both by those like Grace Wyndham Goldie in the BBC and Sidney Bernstein at Granada, who welcomed current affairs broadcasting as an extension to democratic debate, and by those like the Labour MP Patrick Gordon-Walker who feared the usurpal of parliamentary privilege by unelected broadcasters. Documentary, by contrast, was typically conceived and executed over a much longer time span. The film-maker would pitch his or her (invariably his) idea to the Head of Documentaries or of Talks (these days the Commissioning Editor) sometimes, though not always, in response to a call for a particular subject. Though the subject matter might well reference contemporary concerns, it did not generally engage with current news stories—though these no doubt *prompted* many documentary projects. A 1957 memo from Leonard Miall, then Head of Talks, reporting on the various projects with which his producers were engaged, began by emphasizing the time required for documentary production:

> documentaries . . . take between eight and ten weeks to produce (three weeks editing, two weeks shooting, two weeks scripting, and one to three weeks research and thought, dependent on the subject), and it is essential to keep a flow of major programmes in the pipeline . . . producers in the department must have time to think[8]

It was in the permeable boundary between news and current affairs that women found opportunities—or made them, as Adams, Stephens, and Goldie did in the BBC—and for this reason current affairs, in all its generic fluidity, perhaps offered a more promising terrain for women than that bastion of masculinity, the newsroom itself. Goldie met some opposition in maintaining a special unit devoted to current affairs, as this note to her superior, Leonard Miall, indicates:

> I feel that you have never been very enthusiastic about the continued existence of the current affairs unit, and so it is difficult for me to maintain it against what I feel is your own real wish that it be dispersed . . . nevertheless I am reluctant for it to be dispersed on two grounds
> —because . . . the group works better as a group than they would individually
> —because we should be forced to create a current affairs unit very soon if we dispersed one now. With the increasing emphasis on

8 WAC T31/164/2, 13 Nov. 1957.

topicality, sound broadcasting have had to create a unit to deal specially with current affairs[9]

Much current affairs programming aimed, like Grierson's intervention into documentary film practice in the 1930s, to *present* 'the people' to each other. Within the BBC the Documentary Department's series such as *Special Enquiry* (1955), as well as the Talks Department's topical magazine programmes like *Panorama* (1953–) and *Tonight* (1957–65) concerned themselves with *the state* of Britain *today.* Similar material was produced by the independent companies; for example, A-R's *This Week* and *The Dan Farson Show* and Granada's substantial production of what it termed 'current affairs and documentary', not to mention its innovatory coverage of the Rochdale by-election in February 1958. The institution of television itself often figured problematically in these programmes' discussions of contemporary Britain: from the start, it seems, British television was marked by a virtuous self-consciousness and its practitioners took their responsibilities very seriously indeed. Running through both public and private discussion of the scope and limits of broadcasters' interventions into contemporary debate is a considerable uncertainty— perhaps not acknowledged as such—about the 'nature' of the developing institution.

The development of serious—which means *hard*—current affairs programming such as the BBC's *Panorama* and *Tonight*, A-R's *This Week*, and from the early 1960s Granada's *World in Action*, retained enough of the magazine format with its variety of tone, changes of pace, and mixture of items, to secure a heterogenous audience. Indeed, a memo from Goldie to the Panorama team in November 1956 at the height of the Suez crisis cautioned against a third successive week devoted exclusively to the crisis since this might alienate the audience, and affirmed the intention to maintain *Panorama*'s mixed diet of items.[10] The generic fluidity implicit here was clearly understood as a positive virtue, one which was further developed in *Tonight* and brought to a head—some thought taken too far—in the celebrated *That Was The Week That Was* (BBC, 1962–3). But it is based in an acknowledgement that television's address—in the days before terrestrial channels 2, 4, and 5 not to mention the satellite and cable explosion of the 1990s—must secure the broadest possible audience for programmes intended to fulfil the informative aspects of the broadcasters' mandate, and that this might be done by utilizing a range of forms within the same programme.

---

9 WAC T 31/164/2, 1955–8, undated memo from Wyndham Goldie to Miall.
10 WAC T32/1191/3, 13 Nov. 1956.

BBC Talks Department

Although after 1955 there was a variety of programme providers, the commercial companies' idea of television was necessarily based on the existing examples of the BBC and the major American companies: Bernstein and Forman, for Granada, looked closely at both in determining the pattern of their provision. A closer look at the history of the BBC Talks Department and its emergent hierarchy of programme forms, expressed in resourcing, scheduling, and personnel, will illuminate some of the constraints and assumptions underpinning the development of factual programming.

The concept of 'Talks' originated in the very earliest days of the BBC's radio operation: broadly 'Talks' seems to have covered all subject matter and forms *not* accounted for in other more obvious generic or departmental divisions such as Drama, Light Entertainment, News, and Outside Broadcasting. Hence 'Talks', in radio, were just that: a disembodied voice giving a talk on a subject of interest. When television broadcasting recommenced after the Second World War, the managerial structure of the relatively small 'Television Department', as it was initially called, not surprisingly reflected that of the by now well-organized radio broadcasting operation. But Television Talks soon began to expand its field of endeavour: not only was the 'expert' commissioned to offer his or her informed views on topics of general interest or current importance, but other ways of presenting factually based, topically interesting subject matter were devised. When the question of special-interest audience groups was considered, the Talks Department was thought to be the most appropriate to the task of developing subject matter and programme forms which would cater to such groups—hence the topical commentary on current affairs for peak-hour audiences, as well as the afternoon programming addressed to women at home. The 'Women's Programme Unit', as it came to be called, quickly became a specialist section under the aegis of Talks, competing with other sections for resources. Talks as a whole had recourse to the services of the Outside Broadcasts Department, for which they were in competition with both Sports and News; and like all departments they competed for the services of the film unit. There were frequent ambiguities concerning the boundaries between documentary and talks productions. Talks also required close liaison with News over breaking stories which might warrant a more in-depth coverage than News could provide.

But in the early fifties none of these developments were yet apparent, and perusal of the relevant archival material suggests a far more tentative and speculative approach than the bare managerial facts imply. Already by 1949 Cecil McGivern, then Head of Television programmes, was aware that

It is becoming more and more difficult to keep as two separate sections the Talks and Documentary sections.

As you know, it is my opinion that, unlike 'sound' radio, television talks and documentaries (the equivalent of 'sound's' features) should be combined in one section. So far, I have opposed this fision [*sic*] because of the fact that, had they been joined, it would have been inevitable, up to now, that the present H.Tel.T., Mrs Adams, should have taken over both sections.[11]

McGivern blocked this structural development on the grounds of his perception of an individual's (Mrs Adams) shortcomings. His memo went on to detail these: she wouldn't be capable of administering a 'large section', she had no experience of documentary production, she mistrusted 'showmanship' which McGivern considered central to documentary, and, perhaps most damning of all, the existing team of documentary producers (all men) had refused to work for her. He concluded:

At present I am still keeping the two sections separate, but there has recently been considerable overlapping of programmes, with resultant difficulties. Very soon, as television progresses, the artificial separation will appear ludicrous.[12]

Was McGivern's decision based on his own (and the documentary producers') gendered prejudice, or is this an example of a pragmatic approach to difficult managerial decision making? The case can be argued either way, and is one example amongst many of the tentative and frequently ambiguous developments in BBC programme hier- archies, not to mention the expression of such nascent hierarchies in terms of personnel considered 'appropriate'. Whatever the answer, Mary Adams remained Head of Talks and the two sections remained separate. The issue was clearly still current two years later, as H. Rooney Pelletier's 1951 'report' indicated:

I recommend the fusion of the Talks and Documentary Sections because they are both aspects of the same thing i.e. the presentation of facts and ideas to an adult audience. Distinctions between them are mostly theoretical. For instance: Talks do not use actors, Documentaries do; Talks present experts or personalities, Documentaries do not; Talks produce simple programmes, Documentaries are elaborate. These distinctions are more and more difficult to apply. Half a dozen programmes in the last three months prove this to be so.

---

11 WAC T31/164/1, 4 Oct. 1949.

12 Ibid.

The functions of the Talks-Documentary section would be

a) To produce any kind of programme not already the concern of another unit.
b) To provide refresher courses and a training ground for new personnel.
c) To develop new forms of television.[13]

The distinctions to which he refers are practical rather than theoretical ones and the revealingly broad list of 'functions' suggest a producer's desire to escape bureaucratic definitions. He goes on to acknowledge, but also to marginalize, the suggestion that a division of responsibility informed by content might make sense:

> I like H.Tel.T.'s [Head of Television Talks] plan to divide the Talks section into units concerned with subjects like international affairs, medicine and science, fine arts and women's interests. However this scheme should not interfere with the greatest need which is for Talks-Documentary producers capable of giving professional presentation to almost any subject.[14]

The need for training and for a ready supply of new personnel was a constant theme in many memoranda—Pelletier's suggestion that an element of the brief for the envisaged 'Talks-Documentary' section should be 'to develop new forms of television' also captures the impatient excitement of many of his contemporaries. His suggestion for possible subject matter may seem a little conservative today, but we must nevertheless acknowledge his foresight since the majority of these subjects have, in fact, become staples of mainstream television in subsequent decades:

> I recommend more consistent television coverage of a greater variety of subjects. For instance:
> Agriculture and country matters generally.
> Regional interests, primarily urban.
> Simple Topography.
> Religion—the Easter experiments showed what could be done.
> Operetta and musical plays—outflank the Anglo-American bans by using Continental sources, notably French and Austrian.
> Reportage—not the news reporting of Newsreel but up-to-date documents on current topics i.e. 'Document of meat', 'Anatomy of a Strike', 'Bricks and Mortar', etc.
> Adolescent interests—basically adult editions of Children's programmes plus items on sport, dancing, films, travel, discussion etc.

13 Report on Television Talks and Documentaries, WAC T31/164/1, 20 Apr. 1951.
14 WAC T31/164/1.

Literature—add to plays and book reviews. Why not a series of Television biographies? Poetry must find a place, possibly helped by music and dancing. A series on great illustrated books: Bewick, missals, Morris' Birds, Turner, Leonardo, etc.[15]

In the event, though Talks was organized into more-or-less specialist sections as demand for its productions increased, Documentary and Talks were not combined. Rotha, with his commitment to the documentary per se, would certainly have approved the distinction between the two. The consequence was an increasing focus, within Talks, on current affairs as an expanded version of news coverage and, as the decade wore on, as the locus for television's most direct interventions into the political issues of the day. Perhaps with hindsight, a distinction between the outputs of Talks and Documentary can be made on the grounds that whereas Talks in its current affairs output tended to *respond* to topical issues, Documentary attempted to *introduce* new issues to the domain of the topical: in other words Talks dealt with items on the existing agenda for public discussion whereas Documentary proposed new ones. In both sections, as the memoranda quoted above and others indicated, the function of producer was an increasingly powerful one. Adams in a 1951 memorandum concerning future staffing requirements in Talks outlined the necessary qualifications for a producer as 'a good cultural background' probably including a degree, particularly for the specialist subject areas; she emphasized the importance of personality, 'social savoir-faire', and the 'understanding of social backgrounds from whatever cultural or economic level speakers are drawn', and of 'quickness, resourcefulness and initiative'. Her outline concluded: 'The work is strenuous, and candidates should have physical stamina. On the whole, men are more suitable for jobs as producers (at any rate in the present developmental state of the television service).'[16] Adams's reference to gender is noteworthy: a career broadcaster with as much experience as any, she nevertheless participated in the prevailing consensus over gender-specific attributes and capabilities. In assessing the significance of McGivern's, Adams's and others' approach to personnel, the historian—feminist or not—must take account of such contemporary assumptions. Though these may seem anachronistic in the twenty-first century we are obliged to acknowledge their pervasiveness in the 1950s. In this light the articulation of gender specificities as having a bearing on managerial decisions may be seen as a first step, as it were, in disputing the consensus. As we shall see, similar objections were made to female personnel in Drama—both as technicians and as writers. The challenge, albeit implicit

15 WAC T31/164/1, p. 2.
16 WAC T31/164/1, 18 July 1951.

rather than explicit, to the gendered specificity of the new working roles available in broadcasting, gathered weight during the following ten years. Such challenges—or contestations—as I shall argue, may be understood as an important contribution to hegemonic struggles in the field of gender politics, culminating in the women's movement of the later 1960s.

In 1957 the Talks Department had forty-one staff—not including those engaged in Women's Programme Unit productions. Of these forty-one only five were women: the Assistant Head of Talks, Grace Wyndham Goldie; two producers, Wilcox-Bower and Dove;[17] and two production assistants, Thomas and Judah.[18] Amongst the five temporary contract staff and the six 'attached' for training there were no women. Of these forty-one, twenty-three had come from BBC Sound Broadcasting and twenty were graduates of Oxford or Cambridge universities. The three female producers included two Oxford graduates and one documentarist from the National Film Board of Canada and CBS (Bower).[19] An exchange of memos between Leonard Miall, then Head of Talks, and Controller of Programmes Kenneth Adam, offers insight into the kinds of projects currently engaging Talks' personnel. Bower was working on an *Eye to Eye* and a *Commonwealth Magazine*, and Dove was fully engaged in the production of an *Arts Magazine*. Each of the two female production assistants was assigned to one of the current affairs magazines, *Tonight* (Judah was one of five PAs on this programme) and *Panorama* (Thomas was one of four PAs on this programme).[20]

Adams had been 'brought in to deal with Talks'[21] in 1938 and was responsible for establishing the Women's Programme Unit in the early post-war period, later becoming an Assistant Controller of Television. Goldie, Assistant Head of Talks in the latter 1950s, Head of Talks from the early 1960s, was a considerable force in the development of current affairs programming. Unlike Adams, who had herself brought Goldie in to the BBC as a Talks producer in 1948,[22] the latter was not noted for her encouragement of female entrants to the field. Perhaps *because* of her primary commitment to current affairs and to the development of political journalism on television as a significant part of the democratic process, she operated rather like male newsroom journalists in the print media who typically expected their female colleagues to write *as women* while they themselves wrote as

17 Of twenty-three producers three were women.

18 Of seven production assistants two were women.

19 WAC T31/164/2, 18 June 1957.

20 WAC T31/164/2, 29 Oct. and 13 Nov. 1957.

21 Briggs (1985: 170).

22 Ibid. 272.

journalists.[23] Goldie certainly privileged the talented group of young men to whom she offered opportunities in the early development of current affairs broadcasting—who came to be known as 'Grace's boys'—and many of whom went on to occupy illustrious positions in the broadcasting hierarchy of the future.

Two other factors, less obvious at the time perhaps but strikingly clear with the benefit of hindsight, are probably rather more central to the question of gender balance in current affairs production. As the Talks Department developed its characteristic genres and programme forms, and established its increasingly central *place* in the confident BBC of the 1960s, it became identified with current affairs. As News coverage developed—particularly after 1955 when in-vision presentations became the norm—the potential for duplication and consequent competition over stories increased. By 1955 it is true to say that the dominant activity in Talks was the production of current affairs programming, a development for which the energetic Goldie rightly claims credit.[24] The 1957 memos detailing current 'effort', as it was termed, not only show that current affairs programming dominated Talks output—well over half the Department's staff was directly engaged with current affairs—but also constantly refer to 'documentary' production as a staple part of their routine work.

ITV News and Current Affairs

Women as producers, writers, and presenters were similarly marginal to ITV's early factual programming, though there were exceptions. Caryl Doncaster was the first editor of A-R's *This Week* and Liz Sutherland, having joined Granada as a researcher on quiz shows in 1958, graduated to trainee producer in 1959. After a spell working for drama on *The Army Game* she joined the new *World in Action* team, as she recalls:

> In September 1962 I heard that Tim Hewat was setting up a new series and I volunteered to work on it. Tim made it very clear that I would spend all the time in the office typing scripts and transcripts and I could not, repeat not, expect to go out with the film crew. Two months later I was with him and a full crew in Hamburg! It was the start of *World in Action*.[25]

Despite Hewat's warning that she would be based in an office in a largely secretarial role, she did join the crews on location on this and many subsequent occasions—but this is the early 1960s and her

---

23 Steiner (1998).
24 Goldie (1977).
25 Finch (2003: 256).

achievement (aided by her evident tenacity) was still unusual, to say the least.

The commercial companies which began broadcasting from September 1955, collectively known as 'Independent Television', were able to design their operations with the benefit of the BBC's necessarily more evolutionary experience. The legal constraints under which they operated—the ITA guidelines to franchise applicants—were in many ways even more stringent than the obligations enshrined in the BBC's charter. These guidelines had been developed between the 1954 passage of the Television Act permitting commercial broadcasting on the second channel and the commencement of broadcasting a little over one year later. This period coincided with the emergence of the current affairs debates taking place within the BBC, hence the White Paper preceding the Act was informed by these debates as well as by the anxieties accompanying the prospect of commercial use of Britain's airwaves. The National Television Council, formed on 18 June 1953 to lobby against commercial television, and the Popular Television Association, formed in July to lobby in favour, both busily set about securing support for their causes and putting their arguments to Parliament, to the press, and to public meetings around the country.[26] It was in the light of such public scrutiny that the commercial companies laid their programming plans including those for news, current affairs, and documentary broadcasting. Granada and A-R, for example, were concerned to demonstrate their innovatory freshness of approach in order to distinguish between themselves and the BBC, and ITV generally aimed to characterize BBC news and current affairs output as 'stuffy' and 'highbrow' in order to lure viewers to their own, supposedly more accessible, offerings. If Granada was (eventually) somewhat more open to female participants in current affairs production, perhaps this can be seen as a later example of innovatory thinking contra the BBC model. In the highly charged, competitive climate of the mid-1950s the BBC made its own efforts to rise to the challenges posed by its unwanted competitors—for example, from the summer of 1955 newsreaders were, at last, in vision, and *Panorama*, which began in 1953 as a fortnightly arts magazine programme, was transformed in 1955 into a weekly magazine focusing on topical issues, two days before ITV began broadcasting.

During the frenzied discussions at the ITA, which held its first meeting five days after the successful passage of the 1954 Act, the question of how television news was to be handled was high on the agenda. Indeed in the very early 1950s when discussions about the very possibility of a second, commercial channel began, it had

26 Briggs (2000: 63–91).

not been 'considered to be fitted to broadcast political or religious programmes, both of which are expressly denied to it'.[27] The ITA considered various options before general agreement on the establishment of a separate company, Independent Television News, which was to be jointly and equally owned by the initial four commercial companies with the proviso that new contractors would be able to join it.[28] This company would be the provider of all national news, the programmes being networked to regional broadcasters. ITN Ltd was incorporated in May 1955 with Captain Brownrigg RN, the General Manager of A-R, as its chairman and Aidan Crawley as its first Editor-in-Chief. Crawley had been an RAF fighter pilot, a German prisoner of war, a Labour MP from 1945 to 1951, and had subsequently become a well-known television figure in the BBC public affairs programme *Viewfinder* and various special programme series.[29] ITV's national news was to be networked from a single source, while local coverage was the responsibility of the appropriate regional contractor.

The ITA in its January 1955 report envisaged national bulletins 'delivered in vision by personality newsreaders' and this informality was, indeed, recognized as being in contrast to the BBC's far more formal style—their bulletins having been delivered in sound only until the summer of 1954. BBC Television News was first broadcast at 7.30 p.m. on 5 July, presented by Richard Baker as an 'illustrated summary of the news'. Vahimagi notes, however, that 'even when TV news arrived in its own right, it was a cautious compilation of stills, interviews, maps and newsreels' and that 'it was another year before 'the BBC put newsreaders into vision'[30] because of the fear that the newsreaders' facial expressions might unduly colour viewers' understanding and hence inadvertently pollute the news. While BBC newsreaders remained anonymous, ITN's policy, following the American practice with which Crawley was familiar, was to stimulate a relationship of trust between the named newsreader and his audience. Newsreaders were, at this time, exclusively male though Crawley's initial team did include two women reporters, Lynne Reid Banks and Barbara Mandell—later to become one of the first women newsreaders. Robin Day, at that time a young barrister, was personally selected by

---

27 Hood (1980: 63–4).

28 The intial four companies participating in the formation of ITN in March 1955 were ABDC (later ATV), A-R, Granada, and Kelsley-Winnick. The latter pulled out before transmissions began but ITN had already been incorporated (4 May 1955) and their place was eventually taken, after some difficulties over financing and over the agreed form for ITV news, by ABC in March 1956. Sendall (1982: 86, 140–1).

29 Ibid. 85–7.

30 Vahimagi (1994: 43).

Crawley[31] to be one of these first ITN newsreaders and he quickly earned a reputation as a talented and formidable exponent of the new television journalism, as Michael Tracey notes: 'in 1957 ITN's Robin Day landed a world exclusive in an interview with Egyptian leader Nasser that was noted for its journalistic sharpness'.[32] The *News Chronicle*, commenting approvingly of ITN's coverage of the 1956 Hungarian uprising, noted that ITN was 'now a formidable competitor which furiously collects film where the BBC too often makes do with words'[33]

It was not only in news, however, that ITV's early programmes were innovative. Though, as Wegg-Prosser suggests, the genre 'current affairs' had not yet been invented,[34] Granada and A-R, at least, certainly had plans for such programming which they, like Goldie at the BBC, presciently understood to be crucial to the establishment of television's democratic centrality. Granada was particularly energetic, introducing weekly programmes such as *What the Papers Say*, *Youth Wants to Know*, and *Under Fire* from 1956 as staple elements of their schedule in addition to what were listed as 'specials and one offs' of which, in 1956, there were nine. These included titles such as *Polio 1956*, *Burgess Story* and *Suez*.[35] *What the Papers Say* had a journalist presenter giving a review of the week's events as reflected in the national press; *Youth Wants to Know* assembled 'prominent experts' to be questioned by a group of young people; and *Under Fire* also had a 'panel of experts'—this time London-based experts—questioned by a panel of northern (i.e. Granada region) audience members. On ATV *Free Speech* revived elements of the BBC's earlier 'current affairs' or, as it was then termed, 'topical' provision *In the News* and *Press Conference* (both the result of Goldie's pioneering efforts). The US publication *Variety* noted in its summaries of ITV's first week's output that *Free Speech*, which was 'a direct pinch from the BBC TV program *In The News* . . . got off to a flying start with a heated discussion of the Burgess-Maclean incident, allowed because Parliament is in recess and the 14-day ban does not therefore apply',[36] concluding approvingly that it was 'a highly controversial and lively feature'. In all these programmes discussion on topical issues took place between a (politically balanced) group of prominent individuals such as, for example, Michael Foot, Robert Boothby, and the historian A. J. P. Taylor. As Sendall notes, 'One of the things which ITV discovered

---

31 Sendall (1982: 124).

32 Tracey (1998: 71).

33 *News Chronicle*, 9 Nov. 1956.

34 Wegg-Prosser (2002: 195).

35 Granada Archives Box 0978.

36 *Variety*, 5 Oct. 1955.

early, when budgets were tight, was that if you could bring people together in the studio and create an event or happening in which these people participated, then you could engage and hold your audience by the sheer drama of what was going on'.[37]

This was (relatively) cheap programming, providing both 'controversy' and 'drama' and satisfying at the same time the audience expectation for immediacy—seeing and hearing faraway debates as they happened and thus enjoying the illusion of participation—and the ITA's claim that it provided for democratically responsible use of the public airwaves. Perhaps the most important and celebrated of ITV's early contribution to the emergent genre was A-R's *This Week* which ran continuously from 1956 until 1992 and was similar in format and content to the BBC's revamped *Panorama*. Wegg-Prosser suggests that with these two programmes, broadcast respectively on Friday and Monday evenings, 'television's exploration of "current news" became recognised as a new genre: "current affairs" '.[38] In her analysis of *This Week*'s earliest output, for which Caryl Doncaster as A-R's Head of Features was responsible, Wegg-Prosser notes a trend 'towards the serious and away from the light-hearted' resulting in a production paradigm which was 'more masculine in tone and more heavyweight' and resulting also in Doncaster's removal from control of the programme which passed to Peter Hunt (1958–61) and later to Jeremy Isaacs (1963–5). The acute critic Bernard Levin, however, had noted Doncaster's achievement with approval, referring in his summary of television output in its first full year of plural broadcasting to 'Miss Doncaster's admirable news magazine, a programme which straddles comfortably the yawning gap that separates being fundamentally serious and being delicate in style'.[39] Levin here acknowledges the 'fundamental seriousness' of the programme while also recognizing that there is no necessary opposition between seriousness and what he terms 'delicate in style', a point often lost on less subtle critics. Though the programme was evidently addressed to both men and women, the majority of production staff and guest reporters were men; when women were deployed, as Mary Hill (presenter of ITV's daytime programme for women) was for the 28 December 1956 edition, it tended to be for the more explicitly lightweight elements of the programme, Hill's contribution being a piece on 'Fashion for the next year'.

By 1960, when the Pilkington Committee was collecting its evidence, Granada's 'Documentary, including current affairs, talks and discussions' output had fallen from 11% in 1957, the first full year of

---

37 Sendall (1982: 352).

38 Wegg-Prosser (2002: 201).

39 *Manchester Guardian*, 22 Dec. 1956.

operations, to 8%.[40] Taking Granada as exemplary of the commercial contractors, Pilkington's conclusion, that the ITA 'had misconceived its relationship with the programme contractors; that it saw itself as an advocate of them; that it excused and defended rather than controlled them'[41] and that ITV output was unsatisfactory, seems to have been harsh. Despite the slight fall in this type of output between 1957 and 1960, with hindsight the current affairs output sketched above was generally both innovative and well received. The reasons for Pilkington's harsh judgement lie partly in the constitution of the Committee and also, no doubt, in echoes of the heated antagonisms of 1953–4, which preceded passage of the 1954 Act. The fact that by 1960 the ITV contractors had recovered from their initially precarious financial situation and were making handsome returns on their investment may also have been an issue. Following Pilkington's Report the ITA, now the IBA (Independent Broadcasting Authority) was strengthened and henceforward 'used its powers to "mandate" certain programmes such as *World in Action*, *TV Eye* and documentary programmes. Mandated programmes must be included in the schedules at specified times and cannot be put on at times when there will be very small audiences.'[42] Granada, as we have seen, having assembled its production team in 1962, began transmission of the long-running current affairs series *World in Action* (1963–98) in 1963. Over the next decade they frequently crossed swords with the regulator (now the IBA) over the issue of impartiality. Granada interpreted the guidelines to mean that 'balance' could be achieved *between* or *across* programmes whereas the IBA held to the notion that it must be achieved *within* each programme.[43] Nevertheless their robust and often contentious journalism kept current affairs in the public eye, satisfying, one might think, the Pilkington Report's requirement that the independent television companies fulfil the public service element of their contracts.

Women's Programmes

The producers of women's programmes, in the fifties, faced a difficult task. Their audience was defined partly by its ability to watch television during the afternoon, partly by assumptions about its interests as

---

40 These percentages of total transmitted output include programmes networked from other providers. The figures do not include News (6.2% and 6.4%), and can be compared with Light Entertainment (21.5% and 14.2%) and Sport (9.9% and 7.7%) both of which show a similar reduction. The compensatory rise in output is most marked in the categories Drama Series (1.7% and 12%) and Welsh programming (0% and 7.1%). Granada Archives Box 1384.

41 Hood (1980: 77).

42 Ibid.

43 Goddard (2003).

defined by gender. Those working in this section of the BBC's Talks Department, as well as those producing equivalent material for ITV, were in a double bind. They must produce programmes appealing to conventional 'women's interests' in order to secure their audiences, yet the very notion of programming explicitly defined by the gender of its audience must also have raised the possibility of refuting conventions which limited the horizons of that audience. The conventions which limited women's aspirations to take their full place in democratic public life were themselves informed by the interests of patriarchy, apparently reasserting its hold on gender definitions after the upheavals caused by wartime displacements. Thus convention upheld the myth of the hierarchical family, while experience indicated that this was indeed a myth. Producers of programming for women, answerable to a masculine establishment, must uphold and reinforce the myth, but in gaining the respect and attention of their audience they must also address their audiences' real experience. Added to this dilemma were questions of class—as the audience expanded so, too, its class composition broadened to include a majority of working-class families—and of resourcing rarely adequate to the production of high quality programming. These problems go some way towards explaining the uneasiness which often characterized both production planning and the published announcements about programmes. Both are marked by a tension between a desire to be useful (public service) and to be entertaining (giving the audience what it wants) and factual, news, and drama programming were all subject to justification in both terms. As Mary Hill, the editor of A-R's women's programmes, asserted: 'the woman at home, like any other worker, is entitled to . . . a mid-morning break'.[44] Here the woman as domestic worker was invoked, as she was also in the many information-based programmes such as the BBC's *About the Home* and ITV's *Hands about the House* in which instruction, information, and discussion all centre on particular domestic responsibilities. But the probable desire for relief from such concerns was also acknowledged, hence news, some repeated evening programmes of general interest, and episodic drama all found their place in afternoon scheduling. It is significant that by the mid-sixties the tension between 'needs' and 'wants' had been differently articulated and that, in the BBC at least, programming was defined by its content rather than by its intended audience, apart from the special case of the child audience. By this time, too, there was a general consensus, confirmed by the Pilkington Report, that the early evening period was for 'family viewing': the concept of the 'family' audience certainly included the woman at the family's centre whether or not she was able, in practice, to view at this time.

44 *Radio Times*, 16 Sept. 1955, p. 3.

At the very beginning of the fifties Mary Adams had suggested to Cecil McGivern that the BBC Talks Department might produce afternoon programmes for a putative female audience.[45] By September 1955 all programming had been revised to meet the challenge of commercial television and transmissions were extended through the 4.00–5.00 p.m. gap. The new 'Afternoon Viewing' arrangements were the subject of a half-page feature in the *Radio Times* (23 Sept. 1955) giving programme details and concluding with a piece of prose designed, it seems, to assert both continuity of viewing and contiguity between programme 'hosts' and female viewers 'at home'.

A regular series of afternoon tea dances is planned. Every week a new hostess will announce for you.
A 'Model Club' will enable you to show models you have made, and among stars soon to come in are . . .
The programmes will be international and up to the moment, so if you are at home between four and five, switch on.[46]

The 'you' in these pieces is the female viewer. By April 1956, however, though the time slot was maintained, programming appeared to be much more specifically linked to the presumed domestic/familial responsibilities of women. A similar diet was offered by commercial television: in a typical weekday afternoon, the *Teatime Magazine* included fifteen minutes each of 'helpful suggestions for redecorating', 'news and views of the film world', 'behind the scenes' with the Household Cavalry at Knightsbridge Barracks, and an episode of the serial *One Family*.[47] But by May 1960 this pattern had begun to break down.[48] The BBC still carried some programming specifically

---

45 In Jan. 1950 there were *Your Wardrobe* and *For the Housewife* from 3.00 to 3.30 p.m. on Monday and Tuesday, both followed by short documentary/information films. The next four days (Wednesday–Saturday) had a pre-recorded (and often imported) film, usually a drama about one hour long, in this time slot. By April 1955 the afternoon slot was occupied by *For Women*, *Family Affairs*, and *About the Home* on Tuesday–Thursday: these were magazine programmes lasting about an hour, though *Family Affairs* was 30 minutes long, being followed by another 30-minute programme *In Town Tonight* highlighting current entertainment events in London. The 3.00 p.m. slot on Monday carried *Fabian of Scotland Yard* and *In the News* (a studio discussion chaired by Malcolm Muggeridge) both of which were repeated broadcasts first aired in the evening schedules for the general audience. On the whole Friday afternoon programming was not specifically addressed to women, though the address to *mothers* was maintained via the toddlers' *Watch With Mother*.

46 *Radio Times*, 23 Sept. 1955.

47 (18 Apr. 1956), in *TV Times*, 13 Apr. 1956, p. 18.

48 e.g. 22–8 May 1960: on Monday there was *Your Turn Now* (2.45 p.m.) described as 'home made entertainment from the TV theatre, London', and *Keep Fit* (3.15–3.30 p.m.), following *Watch With Mother*, now at 2.30 p.m. On Tuesday *Watch With Mother* was followed by a half-hour item on dogs, and *Cookery Club* (3.15–3.30 p.m.). Wednesday's *WWM* was followed by *The Wednesday Magazine* (2.45–3.30 p.m.) and the pattern repeated on Thursday with *Family Affairs* (2.45–3.15 p.m.), a magazine programme of items about children and the home, and a fifteen minute episode of a serial (3.15–3.30 p.m.).

addressed to women in the early afternoon but the particular slot now varied from day to day, and the overall amount of time was significantly reduced. Here is clear evidence of the gradual marginalization of such programming since, as many *Panorama* memoranda indicate, a dependable time slot was regarded as imperative in securing and maintaining a programme's audience. One reason for the reduction in Women's Programmes is clearly the increased transmission of schools broadcasts. By June 1961[49] there were no programmes addressed to women except *Watch with Mother*, now broadcast in the morning. The afternoon slots were entirely taken up with Outside Broadcast sport (cricket and horse racing). From 1964, as we have seen, there were no programmes specifically addressed to women.

The content in these programmes fell into fairly clear groups. Predictably these were broadly concerned with the kitchen and garden (practice, management), with the domestic environment (consumption, crafts), and with childcare and healthcare. In addition there were frequent items of more general interest within the magazine programmes *Mainly for Women*, *About the Home*, and *Family Affairs*.[50] Within these groups there was considerable variety. In programmes focusing on the kitchen and garden, items on cooking appeared with the greatest regularity taking, early in the decade, a rather didactic tone. The *Radio Times* announcement for *Cookery Lesson no. 5*, for example, promised: 'Philip Harben explains how carbon dioxide gas brings about the aeration of flour. Marguerite Patten demonstrates the principles involved when making soda gingerbread and doughnuts.'[51] Later in the decade there were items such as *Cookery for Busy Mothers* (1 June 1955), and *Foreign Cookery* (24 Nov. 1955). But there were also items not so directly related to the details of recipe and procedure, though still within the realm of the kitchen/garden such as *Raising Poultry for the Table* (7 Apr. 1950), *Bee-Keeping* (1 Aug. 1950), *Hygiene in the Kitchen* (2 May 1950), *The Design of Food Containers* (26 Oct. 1955), and *Refrigeration* (9 June 1955). In the succession of these sampled items we can note the shift from a middle-class audience at the end of the forties austerity to a wider audience primed to receive the new consumer durables of the fifties. The second group of programme contents concerned these new consumer durables in the context of the domestic environment. They ranged from the *Shop at Home* series in 1950–1 in which various new consumer goods were

---

49 On the evidence of the *Radio Times* for 10–16 June.

50 e.g. an item on the British iron and steel industry (1 Aug. 1950); a ten-minute film of life and customs in India (31 Aug. 1950); an item on the world budgerigar championships (24 Nov. 1955); as well as rather more predictable pieces on the lives of exceptional women. The *Women of Today* series profiled, amongst others, radio and television performer Gladys Young (3 Aug. 1950) and film critic Dilys Powell (31 Aug. 1950).

51 *Radio Times*, 2 May 1950.

discussed, often in association with specialist councils[52] and/or (in 1951) the Festival of Britain displays of consumer goods, to programme items which were specifically concerned with home-making in the decorative/aesthetic sense.[53] There were regularly items on dressmaking and alterations, on crochet, tapestry, and other practical skills, for example on 24 November 1955 'Eleanor Summerfield, instructed by Frank Preston, puts up a shelf'.[54] Items concerned with safety in the home also come into this category.[55] The third programming category dealt with childcare and family healthcare: the various stages of baby and childhood all attracted special attention[56] and there were 'problem' forums, much like those in women's magazines or the 'special topics' which appeared from time to time in *Picture Post*. *Family Affairs* (25 May 1955) had a panel with Dr Winifred de Kok, an educational psychologist James Henning, Revd Arthur Morton Director of the NSPCC, and John Watson, a children's magistrate, discussing problems sent in by viewers. A similar format was employed in *Mainly for Women* (26 Oct. 1955), with the same panel of 'experts'. Thus the content of programming specifically addressed to a female audience, to women 'at home', began the early 1950s with a tentatively 'open' moment in which serious attempts were made to use the opportunity afforded by broadcast television to consider cultural and political events and ideas in relation to female experience— with the conscious aim of *broadening* that experience. In the autumn of 1956, however, the *Manchester Guardian* headlined a short piece about the BBC's new women's programmes schedule as 'TV Service for Housewives',[57] and by the end of the 1950s this open moment had been closed down, as it were, and such dedicated programming as remained, firmly and unequivocally located women in the domestic context alone. It is significant to recall the widening *class* address which characterized the same period as the audience gradually extended to include the whole demographic variety, dominated by the then-so-called working classes.

Doreen Stephens, BBC Editor of Women's Programmes from April 1954, knew her audience and recognized also the constraints within

---

52 Examples are *1: Aluminium* (18 July 1950); *2: Electrical Goods* (1 Aug. 1950); *3: Rubber* (29 Aug. 1950).

53 e.g. *Prints for the Home* (5 May 1950) and *A Room of Their Own* (26 May 1950) dealt with nursery fabrics and furniture.

54 *Radio Times*, 24 Nov. 1955.

55 e.g. *Accidents to young children* (14 Sept. 1955), and *Danger in the home: poisons* (18 Apr. 1956).

56 e.g. *New Babies* (1 June 1955), *Teaching Reading* (14 Sept. 1955), *Adolescence* (20 Apr. 1955), *The Teenager's Skin* (18 Apr. 1956), and *Yours by Choice* (26 May 1960) about adoption.

57 *Manchester Guardian*, 15 Nov. 1956, p. 9.

she was bound to operate. She was responsible for the production of forty-five minutes of programme on four or five days a week, for the production teams and support staff and for liaison with the Regions and the Outside Broadcasts Department, both of which occasionally supplied material to the various magazine programmes. By 1956 she had established a well-organized schedule in which a particular segment of the audience was addressed on each day of the week and within these weekly slots thematic concerns made a fortnightly or monthly appearance.[58] Tuesdays, for example, were devoted to younger women with the magazine *Your Own Time* which included items on fashion, current affairs, and the arts, and was

> Designed especially to help the young married woman who is tied to her home by domestic responsibilities to maintain a pride in her appearance despite the budget limitations by increasing her knowledge of current taste in the fashion and beauty fields; to keep her in touch with the outside world of affairs, entertainment, literature and art, and to establish a background of information and taste to which any new developments can be compared.[59]

The assumption here is that the 'young married woman' will be at home whilst her unmarried sister was unlikely to be watching television in the afternoon—as McGivern had pointed out[60]—raising the question whether the 'female audience' was in fact conceived as comprising exclusively mothers and wives.[61] Fridays were aimed at 'older' women, *Twice Twenty* being

> A magazine for the older woman, from great-grandmothers to those whose children are growing up and who thus find themselves with time to spare. It will include new interests and

58 *Look and Choose* appeared fortnightly and offered a 'consumers report' on new domestic goods, in the same Monday slot, other offerings were *Come to Tea with Elsie and Doris Waters* whose 'guests include people of general topical interest and professional performers'; *Success Story* which featured 'women with successful and interesting achievements to their credit, but who are not well known'; *Male Opinion* which comprised 'a panel with three or four men with a woman chairman and a woman guest, who has special knowledge of the subject in question'; and *Signs of the Zodiac* 'an entertainment item in a light-hearted style'.

59 *Radio Times*, autumn 1955, probably Doreen Stephens.

60 '20% of our audience consists of women with jobs . . . this 20% consists largely of youngish women—who are probably not very interested in many of the domestic subjects', WAC T32/362, 18 Mar. 1952.

61 *Family Affairs* on Wednesdays aimed to help 'in tackling the problems and enjoying the delights of family life' with 5–15-minute reports once a month on health, schools and careers, problems, 'the frills of family life' which included parties, play activities, family photos, and 'general interest' items such as 'My Family Life' with Mrs Jack Hawkins, or with a Mrs Howard, mother of ten. On Thursdays *About the Home* offered 'practical information on all matters relating to running a home' including cookery, 'house welfare' (what we would now call DIY or home improvement), a shopping guide, and various general items including complaints to manufacturers, pets, and dressmaking.

activities, and items designed to encourage women to discover that 'life begins at forty' and to regain confidence and seek new interests outside as well as inside their homes.[62]

These magazines included topical and current affairs material alongside the specifically practical, information-based content which aimed to serve the particular audience segment. Commercial television followed the BBC's example in scheduling programmes for women with similar content. Initially the *Morning Magazine* edited by Mary Hill was broadcast from 11.00 a.m. to 12.30 p.m. but by April 1956 ITV had followed the BBC's scheduling and *Teatime Magazine* was on air from 4.00 to 4.45 p.m. followed by the children's *Tea-V Time* from 5.00 to 6.00 p.m. However, Granada, at least, did not have a department devoted to production for women though they were acutely aware of the importance of gaining and keeping their afternoon audience which they presumed to comprise children, housewives, and pensioners. A September 1956 memo concerning their programme *Sharp at Four* (21 Sept. 1956–15 Feb. 1957) noted that

> We are now selling two minutes of advertising between 4.00 and 5.00, and I think 'Sharp at Four' could obtain fairly high ratings if the programme is designed to appeal to the four groups of viewers available at this time, namely
> 1) children below school age (from 4.00–5.00)
> 2) children at school age (from 4.30–5.00)
> 3) Old Age Pensioners (from 4.00–5.00)
> 4) Housewives (from 4.00–5.00)
> ... I think it is most important that any programme designed for housewives should be as 'audible' as possible with some musical segment to ensure a housewife being able to keep track without having her eyes glued to the set all the time.[63]

Here women's multiple domestic roles are acknowledged in programme planning, as is also the pensioners group which, interestingly, never appears in BBC production memoranda. Although the *TV Times* matched the *Radio Times* in soliciting a specifically female domestic audience, the companies were more concerned with ensuring sets were turned on early and that programming appealed to as wide a potential audience as possible.

All these concerns, about the domestic space, the care of family members from the cradle to the grave, and about the informed and creative management of goods and services, are familiar ones. We are accustomed to such concerns being attributed to the realm of the

---

62 *Radio Times* for autumn 1955, probably Doreen Stephens.

63 18 Sept. 1956 memo from J.C.R to S.L.B., Granada Box no. 1333.

'feminine'. It is also true that these concerns *are*, precisely, the 'servic-ing' role—they constitute it—allocated to women in patriarchal order. Programmes dealing with science, medicine, and documentary/current affairs, of which there were a considerable number, were invariably scheduled in the evening though occasionally one might be repeated in an afternoon slot, particularly in the early 1950s. The content of women's programming both acknowledged and participated in the variety of responsibilities allocated to women in the patriarchal economy of Britain in the 1950s, while also separating these concerns from factual programming addressed to the general audience. As I have suggested above, the audience for women's programmes was increasingly defined as wives/mothers *not* employed outside the home, despite the growing numbers of women, married and unmarried, in the workforce. Though in many respects afternoon television for women delivered content similar to that typically found in women's magazines, the latter were far more likely to acknowledge the full range of female experience—albeit segmented by the class address of the various publications. But women's magazines were produced within a publishing structure dealing specifically with female reader-ship whereas television programming for women had to compete with all other programming for funding, scheduling, and personnel. As the scale of the television enterprise enlarged and pressure on resources intensified, it was *always* the afternoon programming which had to give way: the afternoon audience of women at home was clearly of secondary importance—this is marginalization in practice. The question remains, however, whether or not the decision to abandon a direct address to the female audience was a progressive move, for women. It is worth recalling that BBC Radio's *Women's Hour* (7 Oct. 1946–), which had provided both personnel and programme ideas to fifties women's television, continued—and continues—to occupy a daily weekday slot. This radio magazine privileges a female audience while being by no means confined to a patriarchal model of what may be appropriate to that audience, and continues to be a lone model of progressive and varied broadcasting by and for women, one which also attracts a substantial male audience.[64]

An important factor informing the precarious and often uncertain address to women in the latter fifties was the synonymity of the tele-vision audience with the marketplace. The production not only of television receivers themselves but also of the many other domestic goods and services consequent on the economic expansion of the period depended on a marketplace thought to be heavily influenced, if not entirely controlled by, women. Hence the address to women in

---

64 Roughly one-third of BBC Radio 4's audience is male, and this has been the case 'for ever' (Marion Greenwood, BBC Radio 4 Press Officer, Feb. 2004).

many of the early commercials and hence also the imperative to secure, particularly among women, the habit of television viewing as central to domestic routines. As the *TV Newsletter* noted in a 1954 feature article about American television's address to women and, specifically, NBC's magazine *Home*:

> *Home* is ... 'the most practical television programme ever designed for women'. It is an ingenious and efficient adaptation of all that woman's magazines have been offering to readers and advertisers. In Britain both the BBC and commercial groups are out to have TV appeal to women. This account describes how NBC ordered *Home* into their range.[65]

It might be argued that it was the success of this endeavour to secure the support of a female audience which allowed, from 1964, for the cessation of programming addressed specifically to women whose loyalty could by then be depended upon, and whose interests could therefore be submerged into those of the general audience. Though, famously, the BBC did not (and, at the time of writing, does not) carry advertising, many of the 1950s women's programmes dealing with consumer durables came pretty close to it—arguably functioning as a critical forum for the evaluation of available products, rather along the lines of the Consumer Association's *Which?* magazine which commenced publication in 1957. On ITV there was some afternoon programming for women following the BBC model, and we should note also that much if not most of the early advertising was more or less specifically addressed to the powerful domestic consumer—usually conceived as female.

Television and Politics

Running through the programmes' planning, their discursive reception, and, not least, through Pilkington's assessment of the first five years of plural broadcasting in Britain, is an increasing anxiety about the relation between the content, address, and control of television programming and the meanings of democracy. Television was by the early 1960s unequivocally the major source of information about current affairs, chief amongst which were politics, both national and international. What part should it play in the articulation of political questions, and how could speakers in this mass forum, this new public sphere, be held accountable? The complex matrix comprising television, politics, and democracy was recognized by the eternally self-conscious programme planners and producers in both the BBC and ITV working to explore and establish new forms. Certainly an

65 *TV Newsletter*, 1/8, 1 May 1954, p. 7.

almost crusading commitment to securing regular and large audiences for current affairs programmes was seen not only as an antidote to supposedly dubious and anodyne entertainment but also as a positive and crucial contribution to the democratic process. As a memo from the BBC's Head of Talks, Leonard Miall, in relation to a current House of Lords debate noted:

> [Nevertheless] it is vitally important for the informed electorate that the television service should retain important and responsible programmes dealing with current affairs which can be presented in a lively manner to attract a mass audience, for the mass circulation newspapers do not concern themselves much with politics, economics and international affairs.[66]

In soliciting audiences for items concerned to confront the uses and abuses of political power, programme makers thought themselves able to hand power to the democratic citizens who constituted their audiences. Contemporary discussion about coverage of elections is of interest in this context, as is also the question of the Fortnight Rule, finally abandoned during the Suez crisis of 1956. The Fortnight Rule dated from 1944 when there was 'an informal understanding between the BBC and the Government' that 'precluded the broadcasting of talks, discussions or debates on any issue being discussed in Parliament or for two weeks before such a Parliamentary debate was to take place'. It was formalized in a Notice from the PMG on 27 June 1955[67] but nevertheless came under increasing attack from broadcasters and was the subject of discussion both in and outside Parliament. Parliamentary records allow delightful insights into the deep suspicion with which commercial television was viewed by the British establishment, for example Patrick Gordon Walker (Lab), speaking in the House of Commons in November 1955: 'This is going to be settled by the people who broadcast, and among these is commercial television. This alters the situation. If it were only the BBC I could understand some argument for a gentlemen's agreement, but with commercial television we are, by definition, not dealing with gentlemen.'[68] The matter came to a head during 1956, precipitated by public discussion of the Suez crisis, and in December of that year the rule was suspended.[69] Coincident with the Suez crisis which so directly engaged the British people and Parliament was the 1956 Hungarian uprising against Soviet domination, brought to British

---

66 WAC T32/1191/7, June 1960.

67 Briggs (1985: 385).

68 *Hansard* for 30 Nov. 1955, quoted in Sendall (1982: 239).

69 The suspension was agreed for an 'experimental period' of six months, and was confirmed in July 1957—or rather it was decided to continue it indefinitely.

television screens by both ITN and *Panorama*. The contrast in public access to visual information on these two events was striking, as the *News Chronicle* noted: 'While the iron curtain was so briefly raised, TV brought home a window on another world, but on the Suez issue the curtain hardly budged. The 14-day rule stilted both channels.'[70] At issue in what may now seem a rather parochial, if not arcane, debate about the pros and cons of the rule was the question of whether domestic viewers ought to be privy to the views of unelected individuals on matters of such national importance that they were to be the subject of debate between elected representatives of the people, at Westminster. Hence the real question was the scope of broadcasting's participation in informing—or forming, as opponents of the change claimed—public opinion. Proponents of the freedom of speech lobby won the day, and this had important consequences for the standing of current affairs.

Abandonment of the Fortnight Rule marked an important acknowledgement of audiences' and producers' rights to engage 'directly' with issues of the day—to bypass Westminster's formulations. This represented a considerable achievement for Goldie amongst others who had been attempting to persuade politicians of the central importance television could, and would, play as an extra-parliamentary forum for national debate. Though the effective jettisoning of this increasingly unpopular and inhibiting rule was broadly welcomed in the press, there was nonetheless still unease expressed about its real consequences, many fearing that Westminster politicians would not so easily give up their priviledged control of public debate. The *Manchester Guardian* echoed much of the broadsheet coverage when it suggested that 'the limitation of political broadcasting, far from upholding the dignity of Parliament, has merely weakened it' and warned that 'mere withdrawal of the formal rules will be a doubtful gain if the intention of the party leaders is that the same result shall be brought about by informal pressure.'[71] Despite such suspicions I would argue that the abandonment of the Fortnight Rule did have the direct effect of enhancing the status of broadcasting as a whole. In an earlier *News Chronicle* article headlined 'Eden Tells Top Tories Jump on the TV Bandwagon', Ian Trethowan concluded, 'But viewers are also voters—and TV should be the enemy, not the ally, of those who want to insulate the public from the tiresome responsibilities of democracy.'[72] Henceforward, in its news and current affairs provision at least, television was recognized—and expected—to be a 'serious' contributor to the public sphere, a recognition which further fuelled

70 *News Chronicle*, 9 Nov. 1956.

71 *Manchester Guardian*, 19 Dec. 1956.

72 *News Chronicle*, 23 Oct. 1956.

the anxieties of those commentators who saw it as a dangerous pollutant of British cultural life.

The abandonment of the Fortnight Rule (aka the fourteen-day rule) and the rapidly developing acceptance of television as an appropriate forum for political discussion gave the green light, as it were, to coverage of British politics with a capital P, that is to say party and election politics. Here Granada was in the vanguard with its coverage of the 1958 Rochdale by-election, though we should note that Goldie had long been lobbying within the BBC for such coverage. She had been allowed to put on a programme in the 1950 general election which delivered results as they came in, but not, as she had wished, to deploy the airwaves for pre-election discussion. Apropos the summer 1955 general election, which occurred before ITV broadcasting began, Sendall notes that apart from formal party election broadcasts 'the BBC followed their established practice of ruthlessly excluding from their programmes everything that could conceivably be held to influence opinion on election issues . . . radio and television avoided the election campaign like the plague'.[73] It was not until Rochdale in 1958, however, by which time there was a more genuinely national television audience, that television broadcasting participated fully in the campaigning preceding the vote and the 1959 general election was the first to be fully covered by television. As Sendall puts it, 'in February 1958 there came the breakthrough in political broadcasting with their [Granada's] local coverage of the Rochdale By-Election, which alone made possible the extensive national and regional coverage by both ITV and BBC of the 1959 General Election'.[74] Granada's plans were hard-won, Labour and Liberal candidates agreeing to participate while the Tories held things up as they sought clarification over the legalities of the proposed coverage. Subjects to be covered and questions to be asked had to be agreed with all the candidates beforehand. Planning and negotiations were reported and mulled over in the national press and the two broadcast programmes, keenly and critically watched in the Granada region and reported on in ITN's national bulletins, were regarded as a major success which would transform the conduct of democratic politics in Britain. Barrie Heads, who had joined Granada in 1956 as Head of Research in the Outside Broadcasts Department, recalls:

> Early in 1958 a by-election fell in Rochdale, a few miles north of
> Manchester. At this time no by-election had ever been covered
> on TV, a piece of insanity on which we consulted constitutional
> lawyers—and then spent many hours arguing with the political

73 Sendall (1982: 255).

74 Ibid.

parties and with the ITA. Eventually the politicians and the TV regulators were won over. We made a series of outside broadcast programmes about the election, none of them especially interesting but it was a historic series paving the way to modern by-election and party political coverage.[75]

The 'two simple programmes', as Sendall describes them, 'changed for all time the character of the British electoral process'.[76] In one the three candidates discussed the election issues in a live broadcast chaired by a stopwatch-wielding Brian Inglis (assistant editor of *The Spectator*) whose task was to ensure that each candidate had exactly the same amount of airtime, and in the second they were interviewed by three journalists from national newspapers: one Labour, one Liberal, and one Tory. Granada had originally planned for five broadcasts, including one of a public meeting in which the candidates would be questioned by local voters, but at the last minute the three candidates unanimously agreed that two would be sufficient since they feared that, as Liberal candidate Ludovic Kennedy put it, 'this was developing into more of a show than electioneering'.[77] At issue in the legal advice sought by the Tories as well as in broadsheet comment was the question of exactly what the term 'balance' should mean in the context of election broadcasting, and both lawyers and newspaper editors went back to the BBC charter and the 1954 Television Act in support of their interpretations. In the event balance appears to have been achieved by means of the stopwatch and the careful selection of journalists, a proposed programme with local journalists having been jettisoned on the grounds that there was no local socialist newspaper. Both ITV and BBC profited from Granada's pioneering efforts in their coverage of the 1959 general election but even then current afffairs programmes such as *This Week* were taken off air for three weeks before the election—anxieties about inappropriate influencing of the electorate being, clearly, still a factor. By the time of the 1964 and 1966 campaigns, however, the habit of broadcast discussion and debate had been established and current affairs programmes were broadcast throughout the campaigns.

Television and Ethics   In a House of Lords debate in June 1954 Lord Reith expressed his opposition to the advent of commercial television, saying that 'it was sad that the altar-cloth of one age had become the doormat of the

---

75 Heads in Finch (2003: 195).

76 Sendall (1982: 351).

77 *Daily Mail*, 5 Feb. 1958.

next'.[78] In the BBC of the early 1950s documentary producers were beginning to articulate 'the belief that a proper, even necessary function of TV is to examine the condition of society'.[79] Whereas television's hesitant steps towards the central position it was to occupy in democratic politics were guided, sometimes impeded, by reference to existing legislation, its place in the far broader project of exploring and shaping culture and society was developing through custom and practice. Reith's 'altar-cloth', though it may have been inspiring, was less likely to fill the function of examining 'the condition of society' than the more familiar and ubiquitous 'doormat'. As the place of current affairs in the schedules of both BBC and ITV was secured, so also the always permeable boundary between current affairs and documentary became a more and more porous one. Socially contentious issues, whether or not they appeared in daily news bulletins, came to seem appropriate subjects for the preferred current affairs format of round table discussion by 'experts' as well as for the in-depth presentation offered in documentaries or, as they were often described, 'special programmes'. Such issues were explored in drama, too, particularly and explicitly in the hands of people like Sydney Newman whose avowed aim was to bring to the small domestic screen new writing dealing with concerns exercising contemporary audiences. The perenially difficult distinction between drama and documentary was one often seized on by critics; for example, L. Marsland Gander, reviewing in the *Daily Telegraph* the BBC's documentary about prostitution *Without Love*, asked, 'was this true documentary, drama, or a blend of both? All connected with a programme ought to decide precisely what they are trying to do. If they are trying to entertain, that is one thing. If they are seeking to inform, that is another.'[80]

As the decade 1955–65 wore on, such programmes elicited passionate responses (for and against) in the print media, in viewers' letters, and in the BBC's routine audience research. Indeed, with the benefit of historical distance, we might come to understand better what were the most contentious issues for the viewer/citizens of the period by gauging the strength of feeling from the volume and tone of the responses elicited by programmes. Underlying much of these commentaries are questions about what was fit subject matter for public discussion, how it should be approached, and what constraints were commensurate with the need for decency, appropriateness, and of course 'due impartiality' and 'balance'. Here are concerns about the

---

78 House of Lords Official Report, vol. 188, cols. 270, 394, 30 June 1954, quoted in Briggs (2000: 88).

79 Tracy (1998: 74).

80 *Daily Telegraph*, 17 Dec. 1956, p. 8.

moral and ethical bases for television's contribution to society and increasingly in such discussion, if not directly on television itself, partisans for and against contentious issues sought to air their concerns. The *Manchester Guardian*'s TV critic, Bernard Levin, was in no doubt about television's potential:

> The great strength of television . . . is in its ability to present the actual and the immediate. This must not be interpreted too narrowly: it embraces far more than newsreels and reporting outside broadcasts, and relays of sporting events. A political discussion, for instance . . . or a documentary about life in East Anglia or a feature on road safety . . . all these come well within my definition . . . Now, when the screen is filled with . . . a real television play that is properly designed for its medium, the effect is one of far greater intimacy and verisimilitude than is ever possible in theatre or cinema. How much greater, then, is this effect when what one is seeing is . . . the drama of life.[81]

There are some tricky terms in play, here. Levin's open-minded recognition of television's ability to convey 'the drama of life' begs most of the more detailed questions which exercised programme planners about the boundaries between drama and documentary, documentary and current affairs, current affairs and news, and, indeed, between all of the above and advertising. One of the ways in which many critics and viewers responded to the new medium was by seeking to establish generic ground rules with which to order their subsequent judgements about effectiveness, fitness for purpose, or truth to reality. Not surprisingly this often led to the substitution of a discussion about appropriate form and method for one responding to the content of the item, as in Gander's *Daily Telegraph* item, quoted above. This is a familiar evasive technique in criticism but its ubiquity in this period does point to real uncertainties about just how to respond to the flood of material emanating from domestic screens. While macro-questions about the overall effect on culture, taste, and democracy were ones which, quite properly, concerned the Pilkington Committee and its many advisers, micro-questions about how a particular programme should be understood concerned all viewers, particularly when, as must often have happened in this exciting decade, they were confronted with a programme which didn't quite fit any mould they were yet familiar with. In the case of the former group, recourse was had to existing canons of cultural worth, compromised though these might be, but in the case of the latter there simply was no generally accepted canon. This uncertainty might account for the growing importance of 'anchor' men or presenters with whom viewers could quickly identify and on whom they could subsequently depend for guidance, such as Cliff Michelmore of *Tonight*, Richard Dimbleby of *Panorama*, Dan Farson of *This Week*, and Farson again as lead presenter in many social investigation series for A-R such as *Out of Step*, *People in Trouble*, *Keeping in Step*. It also accounts for the success of serial drama and, more broadly, for the great significance attached to stable scheduling arrangements whereby viewers quickly learned what type of programmes they might expect at certain times.

There is a cacophony of different voices to be discerned, from a disingenuous assumption that ITV's only possible motive for anything was a cynical desire for profit to be had by duping its huge working-class audiences into dependence on a diet of cheaply produced, mindless, and repetitive 'package' drama, quiz shows, and light entertainment, to the equally unsubstantiated assumption that serious, quality programmes in whatever genre would only appeal to the educated minority and that the task facing programme makers was to extend this minority by whatever means they could. An internal memorandum from the BBC's Director General headed, pre-Pilkington, 'The BBC: Past and Future' and writing about the relative audience share of commercial and public service broadcasting, asserts that

> We would be in grave danger, in my opinion, if we had secured a 50:50 average, because in doing so we would have made our output indistinguishable from that of ITV. There may be 40% of the public who normally stay with the commercial programmes. There are perhaps 25% who stay normally with the BBC. The remaining 35% switch from one to the other. There is no doubt however that the significance of the 25% far outweighs that of the 40%. The greater part of the educated, thinking and articulate public is numbered in the former.[82]

Eric Maschwitz, BBC Head of Light Entertainment Television, in a memo to the Controller of Programmes gathering material for submission to the Pilkington Committee, and citing recent satirical revues featuring Michael Bentine and Ron Moody, claimed that

> one is, I feel, justified in believing that popular taste in LE is improving under the influence of BBC Television. Commercial TV dare very seldom risk such adventures into the 'avant garde'; its peasant audience does not respond to adventure of this kind (which in any case is hard to present amidst a welter of advertisements). I could argue convincingly in front of any

82 WAC T16/326/1, 30 Dec. 1959.

Committee that the BBC has successfully introduced a mildly 'cultural' note into Television Light Entertainment and should be allowed to develop this[83]

These two fairly typical examples of BBC management's arrogant and defensive view of its audience are in marked contrast to, say, Granada's trust in its audience's interest witnessed in their innovatory coverage of the Rochdale by-election, say, or of their live coverage of the 1962 TUC conference. But they are also, fortunately, in contrast to the instincts of programme makers and producers in both BBC and ITV—noting that there was substantial and more or less continuous transfer of personnel between the two—who were thoroughly engaged with the challenges television posed and the opportunities it offered for exploring contemporary Britain, for developing new communicative forms, and for getting issues onto the agenda for public discussion. Race relations, homosexuality, prostitution, unmarried mothers, teenagers, venereal disease, the contraceptive pill: these and other contentious and difficult subjects were examined in a variety of documentary series and one-off specials from both BBC and ITV. Granada's *Searchlight*, for example, specialized in the investigation of 'social scandals', producing fortnightly reports between March 1959 and September 1960 including programmes on venereal disease, the contraceptive pill, and homosexuality.[84] There were Granada Specials on polio (13 July 1956), the death penalty (25 June 1957), asian flu (20 Sept. 1957), and mental health (28 Jan. 1959) and their series *A Case to Answer* was particularly explicit in its intention to stimulate public discussion, as Denis Forman's June 1956 list of subjects suggested. The programmes were to propose a contentious and topical argument, for example

(a) That the police have undue influence in Magistrates Courts (20 June) . . .
(f) South Africa. That the present government of the Union of South Africa is a disgrace to the Commonwealth (this is to be researched immediately and to be used when South Africa is in the news).[85]

A-R had contracted Dan Farson, initially as part of *This Week*'s reporting team, who subsequently made a reputation for investigative

---

83 WAC T16/326/1, 4 Oct. 1960.

84 This subject had been approached earlier, in a 5 Sept. 1957 Granada Special *Homosexuality and the Law* presumably timed to contribute to discussion surrounding the 1957 Wolfenden Report whose findings eventually led to the decriminalization of male homosexuality.

85 Granada Archive Box 1333, 8 June 1956.

reporting in the social field with programmes such as *Out of Step* which looked at minorities and the later *Keeping in Step* which 'showed that majorities can be just as odd as the minority: we included the Stock Exchange; Winchester; Harrods; and the Guards'.[86] Historical hindsight might question the term 'majority' as applicable to these subjects—'exemplars of the dominant in British society' might now be a more appropriate appellation. Farson recalls of *Out of Step* that 'we started with that wise old man A. S. Neill, the headmaster of Summerhill, the school where pupils could do as they liked. We filmed witches; vegans; scientologists; and men who believed in flying saucers'.[87] His sixteen-minute programme on British nudists (2 Oct. 1957, 10.30 p.m.) 'leapt straight into the top ten ratings, even at that late hour' and generated substantial press coverage including a front-page piece in the *Daily Herald*. This series was followed by *People in Trouble* offering in-depth interviews in order to illuminate subjects such as 'the meths drinkers of Whitechapel; midgets; disfigurement; epilepsy; suicides; and illegitimacy'.[88] In later reminiscence about this productive period in his television career, Farson suggests his growing awareness of the moral ambiguities of such programmes: 'After twenty six programmes we called a halt. Our *power* on the screen was becoming sinister, enabling us to cover *any* subject in the guise of the 'dogooder', in order to achieve sensational television.'[89] He also developed, through trial and error, a sense of the televisual which recalls Levin's critical response: 'The *interview* is pure television; so is visual information . . . so is the *event*, large such as the Coronation or Churchill's funeral, or small as show jumping or a village Harvest Home.'[90]

The BBC demonstrated a similarly developing confidence in its output. The *Special Enquiry* series produced a rare example of a programme dealing with the question of race relations in Britain, *Has Britain a Colour Bar?* (31 Jan. 1955, 8.30–9.15 p.m.), which, according to their Audience Research, was well received and indicated that

> the majority opinion was that the programme was well timed, well conceived and well compiled and while presenting the matter frankly and courageously nevertheless did justice to both sides of the problem

and noting also, as Farson was to discover, that

86 Farson (1975: 50).

87 Ibid.

88 Ibid. 48.

89 Ibid. 50.

90 Ibid. 51.

the interviews with people who have actually come up against the problem were amongst the most interesting parts of the programme, viewers being impressed by the Mayor of Lambeth's 'good sense', the 'politeness' of 'the coloured people', despite 'one or two viewers [who] resented the 'unnecessary remarks' made about English husbands by the white wife of a coloured man.[91]

A 'documentary' about unmarried mothers, *Woman Alone*, made a year later, was similarly welcomed, viewers congratulating the BBC

on having the courage to tackle so delicate a subject in such a bold and imaginative way though a 'small group' thought 'too rosy a picture of the treatment of unmarried mothers was given': and some others said knowledge of welfare organisations such as those described would serve only to encourage 'unmarried motherhood'.[92]

Whereas Farson's programmes and the BBC *Special Enquiry* deployed material easily defined as documentary since it entailed footage of *in situ* interviews, real locations, and so forth, it is a little harder in the case of *Woman Alone* and the subsequent and much more contentious *Without Love* (13 Dec. 1956, 9.15–10.30 p.m.), about prostitution, to accept this categorization since in both these programmes actors were deployed to play exemplary roles, the roles being 'based' on actual cases. As one BBC Audience Research respondent commented,

'This type of programme is very difficult to analyse. We can hardly classify it as entertainment, but we admit that it certainly was a valuable piece of moral education, especially to the adolescent' though another disagreed: 'since there was nothing in it to indicate how the average person should think (or act) in the face of this problem, it had much better be left to the attentions of the authorities concerned'.[93]

Nevertheless the appetite for factual information about contemporary society was clearly stimulated through such experimental and often formally innovative material which frequently, if implicitly, demanded both thought and engagement from its audiences—a demand evidently resented by the second respondent cited above. Press response to this programme was similarly polarized, the *Manchester Guardian* noting neutrally that 'the BBC felt it right to put on this serious programme because it was about something which

91 WAC VR/55/59, 17 Feb. 1955.

92 WAC VR/56/11, 25 Jan. 1956.

93 WAC VR/56/655, 9 Jan. 1957.

people rarely discussed but kept in the background, referred to only with a shudder or as a joke',[94] whereas the *Daily Telegraph* found it 'difficult to understand why the BBC should tackle this subject'[95] and the *News Chronicle*, hiding behind the drama/documentary question wrote that it was 'alarmingly naive . . . it was a play, well done. A documentary would have marched more fearlessly towards the truth', going on to take issue with production methods which had actors playing the prostitutes on location and no footage of, or interviews with, actual prostitutes. But by 1964 the *Daily Mail*'s television critic Julian Holland was able to write glowingly of the programme on divorce in BBC2's series *Marriage Today*:

> but no viewing last night, or for many, many a night has produced anything so compelling as BBC2's Marriage Today edition in which a couple, quietly, haltingly, told separately the story of their divorce . . . A horrid, nasty story of two people's estrangement— never did their versions of what happened come within miles of each other—it had the cold beauty of truth . . . Television itself is a spy and a snooper. But sometimes it has a poetic eye.[96]

Two different ethical dilemmas emerge in the responses to the programming noted here. The first one concerns what is appropriate for mass broadcast dissemination to a heterogenous audience and here there is an emergent sense of the social benefits to be had from articulating precisely the plurality of opinion that moral problems elicit. While many felt that prostitution, for example, was an utterly unsuitable topic and an embarrassing one to confront in a mixed-age family context, others welcomed the opportunity that television offered for airing the subject, referring particularly to its potentially salutary effect on adolescents. The other, in many ways far less straightforward, dilemma concerns the production practices deployed in the making of programmes. This has continued to bedevil television criticism, at issue (as with the anxiety about advertising magazines) being fears about the audience's ability to distinguish between 'truth' (documentary veracity) and 'falsehood' (fictional reconstruction). Here is the critical opposition between *realism* which allows for many ways, including scripted performance, of arriving at the heart of a subject in order to reveal its complexities and to suggest its relevance to contemporary debate, and *naturalism* which requires a scrupulous and transparent fidelity to the perceived surface of things, people, and events. The latter privileges description, while the former provokes analysis, often deploying polemic to achieve its ends. It seems that

94 *Manchester Guardian*, 15 Dec. 1956, p. 5.

95 *Daily Telegraph*, 14 Dec. 1956.

96 *Daily Mail*, 8 Oct. 1964, p. 3.

then, as now, many programme makers as well as their audiences slipped uneasily between these two critical modes in their production and reception, respectively, of programmes confronting head-on the ethical and moral issues of the day. Ken Loach's 1966 BBC *Wednesday Play*, *Cathy Come Home* and Peter Watkin's 1967 *The War Game* remain perhaps the most celebrated examples of the creative deployment of both modes, that in itself being one of the factors exercising current and subsequent critics and audiences in the voluminous discourse accruing around these two programmes. Each drew on drama, documentary, and investigative current affairs techniques to offer both information and entertainment which, then as now, defied easy generic categorization but was nonetheless—perhaps consequently—highly influential in informing, stimulating, and steering public debate on these two crucial issues: the provision of housing and the proliferation of nuclear arms.

Around the time of the Pilkington Comittee's work and the publication of their report—that is to say, roughly from 1959 to 1961— public discussion of television was polarized around the competing, and *therefore* necessarily opposed, services delivered by the BBC and ITV, though some writers on television made attempts to position themselves outside the arena, as it were. Irving Kristol, in a *Manchester Guardian* piece headlined 'Democracy and Mass Culture', saw little difference between the two:

> Instead of the stuffy establishment of yesteryear there is commercial television à l'Americaine and a BBC television that is scarcely to be distinguished from the commercial variety

and both, in his view, presented a dangerous threat to democracy. He concluded:

> In the measure that people are encouraged to believe that what they want coincides with what they ought to want; in the measure that the mass medium conceives it as its function to pander to 'the prejudice, ignorance, and silliness' of its audience—in just such a measure is the moral fibre of democracy corrupted.[97]

The elite's distrust of 'the mass' manifested in Kristol's pretentious prose reappears in a *Daily Mail* feature rehearsing the arguments for the location of the third channel: 'But will this give the viewer what he wants . . . or only twice the number of programmes aimed, like the present ones, at the mass audience?'[98] On the previous day the same writer made an interesting distinction between 'serious'

---

97 *Manchester Guardian*, 8 June 1960, p. 8.

98 *Daily Mail*, 20 July 1960, p. 8.

programming and 'entertainment', suggesting that competition between broadcasters had had quite different consequences for each:

> In serious programmes and news coverage particularly it
> [competition between ITV and BBC] has been a stimulus to both
> ... for example in the coverage of South Africa's racial crisis. But
> in entertainment it has worked a different way. . . . The war of the
> programme schedules began. Western was pitted against western,
> crime serial against crime serial, even parson against parson.
> American package shows were brought in to counter ITV's
> pulling power in home-grown show business.[99]

Here the apparently unquestioned opposition of the serious with the
entertaining is expressed not in terms of public service vs. commercial
broadcasting but in terms of genre. Serious programmes, we might
conclude from perusal of these and other contemporary commentary, are what the (discerning) individual viewer wants, and both
broadcasters provide this, their efforts being constantly sharpened
and improved by the healthy competitive climate in which they
operate. In the field of entertainment, by contrast, we are talking
about the 'mass' audience which somehow never seems to include the
discriminating viewer with whom every commentator identifies, and
here the same competitive climate results in a declining and homogen-
ous diet of popular drama compromised even further by its dilution
with 'American package shows'. It is refreshing to note, a few years
later, a much broader recognition of the positive heterogeneity in
programming in Kenneth Adam's post-Pilkington paper on television
and education which pointed to the 'almost nightly confrontation of
the expected and the accepted with the unexpected and the unac-
cepted'.[100] His remark, perhaps despite himself, appears to valorize
both innovatory subject matter and generic ambiguity as inevitably
stimulating to television audiences, noting also that 'It [TV] may
assist conformity through social contagion, but it also strips its viewers
of old concepts'. Following Pilkington's glowing endorsement of the
BBC's operation and the launch of the anticipated third channel in
the shape of BBC2, Adam was clearly able, in this paper, to rise mag-
naminously above the combative tone of earlier discourse and to talk
about television in general. His paper marks, for our purposes, the
'coming of age' of plural broadcasting in Britain: henceforth the television institution as a whole may have, and did, come in for criticism
of its supposed 'dumbing down' of taste and culture but this is less
and less likely to have been simplistically ascribed to a fundamental
difference between the fiscal systems sustaining the two enterprises.

---

99 *Daily Mail*, 19 July 60, p. 4.

100 Kenneth Adam, quoted in the *Guardian*, 3 Sept. 1964, p. 2.

Gender and   Current affairs broadcasting—bordering on the one hand on news
Veracity   and on the other hand on documentary—was, with the equally celebrated 'quality' drama output, widely identified with television's successful 'coming of age' in the 1960s. This is true of both public service
and commercial broadcasting which, as a consequence of their competition for audiences and their constant exchange of personnel,
exhibited a similar profile in their output if not in their managerial
systems. As Philip Abrams, writing in 1964, noted: 'the coming of
independent television increased the number of sources, but left
the theory of the system unchanged'.[101] Now 'current affairs', while
not necessarily precluding programming addressed specifically to
the female audience, was nevertheless conceived as pertaining to the
public sphere of democratic politics and, Goldie's guiding presence
notwithstanding, adopted an accordingly masculinist stance. BBC
Talks Department production staff were predominantly male, and
the two female producers were not engaged with current affairs items.
A similar situation prevailed in A-R's *This Week* where Doncaster
presided over a male group of producers and was herself replaced
by a man within two years of the programme's launch, despite its
acknowledged success. This fact, and Adams's ambivalence about
women in production—she supported many women entrants to
broadcasting, but her 1951 memorandum had suggested that producing was a job more appropriate to men than to women—may
be taken as evidence of a masculinist hegemony in current affairs
broadcasting. Linked to this—indeed, I'd argue, informing it—was
the growing confidence in the centrality of the broadcasting institution to British cultural and political life which countered anxieties
about the inherently emasculating effects of television viewing on
its audiences. Once television was fully established, as it was by the
mid-sixties—the 1962 Pilkington Report and the advent of the third
channel, BBC2, in 1964 being evidence of this—it seems that it must
also, by virtue of its public centrality, be masculinized.

An increasing uneasiness with women's presence—in power
behind the screen, as it were, as well as in vision on screen—can be
discerned in the daily minutiae of policy making as evidenced in
memoranda concerning programme personnel, both production
staff and potential subjects in the BBC and, perhaps to a lesser extent,
in the commercial companies. In the surviving ephemera available it
seems, too, that the uneasiness felt by production managers and policy
makers was not necessarily shared by the audiences for whom they
claimed to speak. It is particularly intriguing to note, in this context,
that at the very start of television broadcasting before the Second

101 Abrams, quoted in Heller (1978: 28).

World War, a BBC Viewer Research paper found that 'There was an overwhelming majority in favour of women announcers as opposed to men, the result being exactly opposite to that of sound's questionnaire on the same subject.'[102] As noted earlier, it was the female announcer Jasmine Bligh who famously introduced resumed television broadcasting in 1946 with the words 'Remember me?' Now it may be that the male voice was more clearly discernible by listeners to pre-war radio broadcasting because of its deeper pitch, and that since in vision this was compensated by the viewers' ability to see as well as to hear the announcer the marked difference in audience preference, discovered in the Viewer Research questionnaires, can be accounted for in this way. If this is the case, it must follow that the post-war marginalization of women as purveyors of broadcaster's on-screen authority had cultural rather than technical foundations, a proposition which tallies with other observable post-war cultural attempts to 'put women back in their place' following their high profile in the very public sphere of the wartime home front.[103]

It would seem, then, that there was a developing marginalization of programming addressed to women, an increasing reluctance routinely to admit women to senior positions, and a developing assumption that there was something inherently lightweight because distracting, thus not-serious, thus *inappropriate* in the very spectacle of a woman on the television screen where the gravitas of the screen was a necessary corollary to the intended content of the broadcast— as in news and current affairs. Three examples will deliver a sense of the gradual detachment of women from the egalitarian position that had seemed a possibility in the embryonic television hierarchy of the pre-war period. 'Mrs Knight *must* be balanced' is the closing line in an instruction from the Controller of Programmes, Television, to the editor of *Panorama* in January 1955.[104] At issue here is neither harmony nor aesthetics but an altogether more difficult value; that is to say, the achievement of the as yet undefined but *appropriate* tone for this programme which was in the process of claiming its place as the BBC's flagship current affairs programme. It is not clear from the memo whether Mrs Knight's views were too extreme, or whether her manner was overwhelming, or her voice too loud or too shrill: it could have been any of these, judging from the kind of memos that fluttered constantly between offices of the embattled BBC early in 1955. The memo also notes that she was to be 'cross-examined' by an interviewer who should similarly examine a person holding opposing views. In addition to *balance*, the notion of *cross-examination* is of

102 WAC T32/40/1, undated memo.
103 See e.g. Thumim (1992: 57–63; and 1996: 238–56) for discussion of this issue.
104 WAC T32/1191/1, 14 Jan. 1955.

interest, suggesting as it does a courtroom model in which the role of the jury was, perhaps, assigned to the audience. But the memo's emphatic instruction ('must' is underlined) draws attention to the proposed interviewee, prompting the question whether her gender is an issue in the question of balance.

A rather more explicit example is the November 1957 memo to the *Panorama* team, from Presentation Editor Clive Rawes, which confirms the notion that Mrs Knight's gender might have been a factor in her acceptability. Rawes was trying out some male announcers recruited from sound broadcasting and would therefore, he suggested, have little occasion in future to call on the services of three 'freelance actresses' (Polly Elwes, Pauline Tooth, Vera McKechnie) all of whom had been previously employed for this work because, he wrote, 'the television service is moving towards the position where its regular announcing team will comprise 3 or 4 men and probably only one girl'.[105] Apart from the ubiquitous demeaning of adult women in the opposition 'men : girl' there is a barely concealed unease with the female: 'probably only one', and no explanation for what clearly seemed a self-evidently appropriate policy decision—though it may not have seemed so clear to Elwes, Tooth, and McKechnie. In 1959 a similarly revealing memo was sent to Rex Moorfoot on the *Panorama* team. It concerned the ongoing production of cartoon puppets for use as a regular item on *Panorama*—anticipating *Spitting Image* (1984–96) by twenty-five years—a project which in the event was dropped. Three figures had been completed—De Gaulle, Eisenhower and Khrushchev, and two more were in production, Adenauer and Macmillan. Derek Holroyd, responsible for their production, wrote, 'thereafter the stock characters to be made would be Nehru, Nasser, Nkrumah and Mao-tse-tung, plus three symbolic characters—John Bull and Uncle Sam and a female figure to represent variously the UN, Peace, etc.'.[106] Despite the obvious point that these currently central figures on the world political stage *were* all men, it is the anonymity and flexibility of the lone female which is so striking here. Here is a disingenuous acknowledgement of the semiotic fluidity of the female, in patriarchy: the female figure can 'represent variously' according to the changing needs of the discourse. This, I think, is precisely why there is such discomfort with the presence of *actual* women who, outside the domains of drama and light entertainment, could not be so easily malleable because they must, as *actual* subjects, speak to the audience in their own behalf and become, as Messrs Michelmore, Dimbleby, and Farson did, guides to the interpretations of society, politics, and culture offered in, and mediated by, broadcast television.

105 WAC T32/1867/1, 11 Nov. 1957.
106 WAC T32/1191/6, 30 Apr. 1957.

3

Factual Programmes: *The Wednesday Magazine, Panorama, Marriage Today, Living for Kicks*

THIS chapter will explore in more detail what factual programming on television in the 1950s and 1960s actually looked like, focusing on particular examples: *The Wednesday Magazine* from the BBC Women's Programmes Unit; *Panorama* from BBC Talks; a six-part series *Marriage Today*, from BBC Family Programmes Department; and *Living for Kicks*, an investigative documentary made by Daniel Farson for A-R. In each case the programme is contextualized to give some idea of its production history and personnel and to consider particularly the ways in which women were represented on screen. Where possible, the reception accorded these programmes when they were first broadcast will be noted. The chapter aims, in short, to deliver a snapshot of the factual television routinely available in this formative period, and some sense of how it was received.

BBC Women's Programme Unit and *The Wednesday Magazine*   In the immediately post-war period the BBC's afternoon programmes were produced by the Talks Department. They were addressed, as we have seen, to a small, middle-class audience of women based in the south-east of England and presumed to be at home and at leisure. In line with the public service remit of the BBC, programmes dealt with matters considered to be both useful and enlightening to this audience. As the fifties progressed and audiences expanded, the programmes became known as Women's Programmes, constituting a section of the Talks Department to which the production team was answerable. Mary Adams was Head of Television Talks and negotiations between her and the Controller of Programmes, Television, Cecil McGivern, through the early fifties, resulted in Women's Programmes producer Doreen Stephens being designated Editor of

Women's Programmes from April 1954. The memoranda which detail these negotiations reveal some interesting and thoughtful consideration of the status, content, and, indeed, of the very advisability of such programming. At issue were questions of resourcing, scheduling, and appropriateness for the intended audience. A 1950 memo from Mary Adams touched on the first two:

> I should like to be able to offer a half-hour woman's programme on as many days in the week as studio practicalities permit. The staffing arrangements for such a proposal are now under discussion . . .
>
> I know your main concern is with timing, and on this question I imagine we must wait until the timing of the children's programmes is agreed. On the other hand, if the station is to be opened at a separate time for women's programmes, I imagine Silvey could go ahead and discover the optimum time for a half-hour programme put out on, say, three afternoons a week.[1]

R. J. Silvey was Head of Audience Research, and in 1952 he was asked to explore the potential audience for women's programmes scheduled in an evening slot. Both Adams and, later, Stephens seem to have been concerned with the 'ghettoization' of programming addressed to women, possibly alert to the desirability of including such programming in the mainstream evening schedules. But McGivern, advised by Silvey, resisted the idea of women's programmes broadcast during prime time:

> He [Silvey] states that about 20% of our audience consists of women with jobs. He also points out that this 20% consists chiefly of *youngish* women—who are probably not *very* interested in many of the domestic subjects covered in the afternoon programmes.
>
> He points out that there would probably be criticism of women's programmes in every transmission from
> a) part of the above 20%.
> b) a lot of the women who can watch in the afternoon.
> c) most of the men.
> . . . This confirms me in my own view that it is far too early to make such a move.[2]

McGivern's view that it was 'far too early' for such an intervention is intriguing: most likely his wording was designed to placate, but it does suggest that in 1952 the possibility remained open whereas, as we have seen, by 1960 virtually no special programming for women

---

1 WAC T32/330/1, 17 Feb. 1950.

2 WAC T32/362, 18 Mar. 1952.

remained at any point in the schedule. By this time, however, the television operation was wholly transformed by the presence of ITV and, as I shall suggest, the enormously popular soap operas entailed substantial narrative attention to female experience and concerns.

Though it was true that the majority of programming concerned topics related to the domestic responsibilities of the presumed audience, in the early fifties programme content drew on a wider field, explicitly raising questions which would today be defined as feminist. In 1951, for example, a fortnightly discussion programme *Women's Viewpoint* (alternative titles proposed were *Women Without Men*, and *For Women Only*) was announced by the (male) producer, David Bryson, as follows:

> A regular for-women-only discussion forum is something new in British broadcasting . . . Topics will include many public questions which have a special bearing on the home and family life, or on the 'position of women' (what our fathers and mothers would have called 'the Woman question'). . . . Will our afternoon viewers, who are predominantly women, like to view discussions confined to their own sex? Will some feminists discover a sinister plot to confine their sex to an intellectual zenana of the air, where they are much more concerned to break down the male grip on general discussion programmes? Will it be denied that there is a discussable 'women's viewpoint'? And more important will the spectacle of women discussing make good television?[3]

The programmes were twenty minutes long, broadcast at 3.00 p.m. The first had Dame Vera Laughton Matthews, Jill Craigie, Margery Fry, and Lady Violet Bonham Carter addressing this very question 'Is there a women's viewpoint?'. In a later programme the editors of *Woman* and *Vogue* confronted Craigie's criticism that 'women's magazines are escapist, unreal, and full of false values'.[4] In such discussions and the accompanying memoranda concerned with production and audience responses there is a clear acknowledgement of the tricky implications of programming specifically addressed to a section of the audience defined by gender, and of the presumptions being made about the interests of such a grouping. Later in the decade, however, the competition for the expanding audience—no longer restricted to the middle classes—obliged the BBC to forgo such subtleties.

McGivern acknowledged that Doreen Stephens's remit obliged her to undertake a broad variety of programme forms, as a 1954 memo to Mary Adams indicated:

3 WAC T32/363, 1951.
4 WAC T32/363, 29 May 1951.

At present, and as an experiment, Women's Editor is responsible directly to me . . . My own idea is that Editor, Women's Programmes has a separate field of programmes, though the content includes *various* programme categories and techniques. I would like full opportunity to be given for natural development. If this idea is correct, no doubt this small section will in time be given its own organiser. If, however, events show that Women's Programmes *naturally* fall into the field of responsibility covered by Head of Television Talks, we can easily adjust matters. Miss Stephens became fully operational on April 1st, 1954. I suggest I review this position in February–March 1955.[5]

Goldie, by then Assistant Head of Talks, thought the section too small to operate independently and, at that time, considered that the overlap in output of Talks and of Women's Programmes suggested their continued integration:

There is so much in common between Talks Department output and Women's Programmes output (numbers of personalities can be considered for either *Panorama* or *Leisure and Pleasure*, for instance) that an element of working together should be possible so long as the need for independence is fully appreciated.[6]

During the next few years staffing expanded as a result of Stephens's energetic and persuasive lobbying.[7] The resource question, however, was a continual problem and Women's Programmes were markedly underfunded relative to the allocations allowed for other departments supplying the more prestigious evening schedule. They were under-resourced, too, relative to other daytime programming such as that provided for Schools and Children's programmes. They had no dedicated studio, no routine allowance of film or technical facilities for pre-recorded inserts or location work, and a budget that was insufficient to finance experienced or high-profile guests or performers.[8] The Women's Programmes Unit was still being asked to propose and, less frequently, to supply programming for the evening schedules but when they did the lack of resources showed, as McGivern's critical memos indicated:

It had been done anxiously and lovingly, but alas! it remained amateurish, fumbling and far too weak for an evening

---

5 WAC T32/362, 26 July 1954.

6 WAC T32/362, 16 Aug. 1954.

7 See e.g. her reports and memos in WAC T16/597, esp. 24 and 30 June 1955.

8 WAC T32/1867/1, Oct. 1957 memo 'The main requirements for the future development and improvement of Women's Programmes', unsigned but probably from Doreen Stephens.

transmission period. Like the first attempt, it did little (in my opinion) for its main audience, the women at work who miss the afternoon programmes, and its doffing the cap now and again to the male audience would please very few of them, surely. . . . The commere, Roma Fairley, looked most attractive . . . but she obviously lacked the experience necessary to carry such a programme. She should be tried out thoroughly in the afternoon before being thrust into the fiercer spotlight of the evening transmissions.[9]

I realise more and more as I watch women's programmes that there is almost a complete lack of imagination and sparkle in the presentation. The aim is sound, the content good, the presentation *at its best* only competent—and it is not always at its best.[10]

By 1957, when the 'toddler's truce' had been breached, the costs of programming the additional early evening hour resulted in suggestions from BBC management that Women's Programmes should be cut, a suggestion which Stephens strenuously resisted:

Women's Programmes as they are now developing make a worthwhile and acceptable programme series for an important and specialist audience, whose goodwill to the BBC can have a great influence on family viewing and the attitude of their families to the BBC generally. Is it desirable to undermine a programme which is really good of its kind in order to follow ITV? Or if additional evening transmission time is essential, is the reduction of Women's Programmes necessarily the best way to obtain the required time?[11]

From then on, however, the future of Women's Programmes was insecure, despite Stephens's assertions that this programming was both valuable to its audiences and directly fulfilled the requirements of the BBC's Charter. As in so many other aspects of the early formation of mass broadcasting, contradictory imperatives and instincts were at work. The original intention behind Women's Programmes, expressed in Adams's 1950 memo and supported by McGivern, acknowledged a particular audience grouping—affluent, educated women at home in the afternoon—and aimed to cater to them with particular programmes. These were successfully developed and gathered their own momentum so that by the time commercial broadcasting began in 1955 Stephens had considerable authority and

---

9 Re *Home*, 17 Jan. 1955, 8.15–8.45 p.m.; WAC T32/191, 18 Jan. 1955.

10 Re *About the Home*, 7 Feb. 1955, 3.00–4.00 p.m.; WAC T32/1/6, 7 Feb. 1955.

11 WAC T16/597, 18 Sep. 1957.

responsibility which, like Adams, she used both to build on programming experience and to train new female entrants to the field. She never really managed to breach the evening schedules, however, for by the time she was equipped to do so another imperative, the fiscal predicament faced by all broadcasters as transmission hours were extended, was working against her. Since the daytime audience was relatively small and since competition for audiences required maximum 'effort', as it was termed, for the peak hour slots, the budgets for daytime programmes failed to match producers' expectations. Consequently their efforts were marginalized as, in McGivern's words, 'amateurish' and 'lacking sparkle' and these drawbacks were associated by default, as it were, with the female afternoon audience, notwithstanding the fact that they stemmed from poor resourcing. The low prestige associated with small audiences and inadequate budgets also militated against Women's Programmes being able to attract the strongest of the new entrants to broadcasting, as McGivern acknowledged in a 1958 memo: 'The staff needs strengthening...The recruitment of men producers might provide a certain toughness— but for obvious reasons few men are prepared to work in this special environment and with this limited horizon'.[12]

It was not only men whose ambition steered them away from this 'special environment': Goldie, for example, was not noted for her support of either women's programmes or female entrants to broadcasting, preferring instead to place her considerable abilities at the service of current affairs. As the television institution developed through the fifties so, too, did its internal hierarchies and, despite the consensual emphasis on the importance of the family and of woman's place at its centre, women and the feminine were increasingly marginalized. Senior management was dominated by men, many with a Services background—especially in the immediately post-war period—and so too therefore were agendas informing the allocation of resources to programmes. The heady and exhilarating climate of innovation which characterized the period was fundamentally masculine. So much so that women, too, more often than not colluded in marginalizing the feminine, acquiescing in language and value structures demeaning to women. Even Stephens seems to have accepted the proposition that female announcers were, somehow, second best:

At the Programme Board yesterday morning you reassured members by telling them that the less acceptable announcers, particularly women, would not now be appearing after 7.00 p.m. in the evening. If this means that Women's Programmes are to be subjected to undiluted introduction by Sylvia Peters then I must

12 WAC T32/1867/1, 2 Apr. 1958.

protest most strongly. I find her milk and water voice and face uninspiring and would prefer no announcement . . . I would prefer a good strong voice, possibly out of vision.[13]

Perhaps the most striking example of this pervasive masculinist hierarchy, however, is in the on-air slip made by announcer Mary Malcolm, gleefully reported in the *Daily Mirror*:

once, while testing the sound channel before the start of the programme 'Mainly for women' she said 'Good afternoon. Here is a programme mainly for morons' and this was accidentally broadcast.[14]

A substantial Audience Research survey of women's programmes and their audiences was commissioned in 1958, its report circulated in 1959.[15] Its summary revealed the disquiet with which the very idea of special programming for women was beginning to be regarded by the senior managers who had commissioned the report:

Though patrons of Women's Programmes include a disproportionately large proportion of mothers of young children, they do not differ markedly from non-patrons in respect of such things as marital status, educational background, occupational level before marriage . . . Nor did they differ markedly in respect of the one aspect of personality which was studied. There was no evidence to support the view that viewers of Women's Programmes were conspicuously more 'cabbagey' than non-viewers.[16]

Despite the fairly positive evidence of the report in terms of audience satisfaction with programme content and the size of the potential and actual audiences,[17] Women's Programmes continued to be subject to budget restrictions, and to rescheduling or cancellation in favour of sports and Outside Broadcast special events. Within a few years the Women's Programmes Unit had been disbanded and its personnel moved, with those from Children's Programmes, to the new Family Programmes Department formed in February 1964. This was 'one of the bigger production departments in the Television service, both in personnel and programme output, outside the four main production departments (Drama, Talks, Light Entertainment, Outside

13 Memo to Presentation Editor Clive Rawes, 28 Nov. 1957, WAC T32/1867/1.

14 *Daily Mirror*, 1 Nov. 1956, p. 3.

15 WAC VR/59/364, 1959. It is interesting to note also that a 1949 report, VR/50/1, did not once mention the gender differentiation of its respondents, though it did attend to differentiations by social class and age.

16 *Women's Programmes on Television*, p. 26. WAC VR/59/364, 1959.

17 Eight million potential, one million actual viewers on any one day.

Broadcasting)'.[18] Its output was divided into two categories, Adult and Children's, and as a memo from the Organizer noted:

> There are no longer . . . any programmes purely aimed at a Women's audience in the afternoon or at any other time. The programmes mainly now transmitted can be defined as features or documentaries of 'social interest' ranging from films such as *Two Town Mad*, and *Anatomy of a Street* on BBC1 to *Marriage Today* (BBC2) and Adult Education *Having a Baby, Running a Home*, and *Home Cooking* on BBC1.[19]

Thus the material implicitly addressed to women and previously typical of Women's Programmes afternoon schedule was now conceived as 'Adult Education' whereas in the 'social interest' category programming was addressed to a heterogenous audience though frequently, and significantly, it was *about* women, as in the 1964 six-part series *Marriage Today*. In this series, as we shall see, women were constructed as problematic figures, encapsulating if not provoking the social concerns of the day. Whereas in the relatively closeted broadcasting environment of the early 1950s there seems to have been the beginnings of a bravely speculative approach to questions of gender politics and their implications, by the end of the decade this had degenerated into low-cost, low-prestige, and ultimately dispensable programming considered to be of minor interest even to its disregarded audience. On the other hand the ten years of experience and training in dealing with women's issues in a mass-broadcast context produced many competent women producers who continued to make programmes and to maintain their presence in the post-Pilkington environment of the sixties. Despite the presence of a substantial minority of women in production, however, many of these programmes subscribed in their language, presentation, and implicit values to a masculinist orthodoxy which perceived women and the feminine as inherently suspect.

The Wednesday Magazine (BBC, 1958–1963)

The Wednesday Magazine was a weekly programme conceived by the Women's Programme production team at a point when their responsibilities still seemed to be expanding, and continued until the demise of such programming. The catalogue of the NFTVA carries one entry which, on investigation, turned out to be a seven-minute filmed insert of Spike Milligan preserved, presumably, on account of Milligan's

---

18 WAC T32/395, 20 Oct. 1964.

19 WAC T32/395, 20 Oct. 1964, para 2.

growing reputation rather than as an example of the magazine itself. The BBC's own archives are similarly barren: they hold one filmed extract which contained a very short, and rather stiff, interview of Margaret Rutherford by the magazine's presenter, David Jacobs, and a piece of film of an unidentified child's drawing with a voice-over commentary by the child. This is all that remains of a magazine programme which went out every week for five years and, for the production team, was one of their better resourced and more prestigious efforts. Some of the women producers who worked on the programme—for example, Monica Sims and Lorna Pegram—went on to make substantial contributions to the BBC's output in the sixties, Sims becoming Editor of Radio 4's *Woman's Hour* in 1964.

Between 1956 and 1958 Stephens had achieved a more integrated approach and the new *Wednesday Magazine* exemplified this strategy:

> I have given much thought to this balance between entertainment and information. At present 'Wednesday Magazine' sets out to strike a balance between the two. I think it is right to try to get 'the best of both worlds' on one day a week, but wrong to do it every day. . . . The popularity, for example, of 'Your Turn Now' which is only entertainment, and 'Tell Me, Doctor' and 'Family Affairs' which are Public Service programmes for information . . . emphasises this point.[20]

In *Wednesday Magazine* a broad spectrum of items was offered and, allowing for the severe resource constraints which impeded its development, there are clearly comparisons to be made with the much more successful and highly regarded current affairs magazine *Tonight* (1957–65, 1975–9). Indeed there was sometimes competition between the two programmes and Stephens made a point of viewing *Tonight* on Tuesdays in order to avoid duplication in the Wednesday afternoon programme. The difference was that the *Wednesday Magazine* approached its broad range of subject matter—some trivial, some profound, just like *Tonight*'s—with the particular concerns of the female audience in mind. The main compère was the popular David Jacobs, and an increasing proportion of the guests were also men, but the central concern was always a 'woman's angle' on the items in question. In an article for the BBC's in-house journal *Aeriel*, after pointing to her resource restraints and noting that Women's Programmes 'are not intended to be an extension of the general run of evening programmes done at a cut price rate' but are instead planned to include matters 'not generally covered in the rest of the television evening time', Stephens outlined the peculiarities of her audience:

20 Memo from Doreen Stephens, 25 Aug. 1959, WAC T32/1867/1.

The attitude of women to viewing in the afternoons is awkward for programme planners, for there are two diametrically opposed demands. A sort of Martha and Mary division. One from the women who, having neatly and efficiently tackled the home chores, sit down and want to be entertained, some with escape material and others with an appeal to their intelligence. The other is from the women who, if they sit down to watch television in the middle of the afternoon have a guilt complex at doing so. They prefer practical programmes which add to their knowledge and skill as housewives. There is a further hazard in the viewers who take the ironing, mending or other chores to the television and divide their attention between the two. . . . Afternoon viewers tend to watch on their own so all their reactions are very personal and there is no dilution by immediate contact with other points of view.[21]

Lorna Pegram had overall charge of the *Wednesday Magazine* and Monica Sims, Joyce Bullen, and Richard Gilbert alternately produced it. The best items from two week's programmes were recorded for a repeat broadcast on alternate Sunday afternoons. An Audience Research report in November 1960 documented viewers' responses to five recent programmes, offering rare evidence of the actual content.[22] In each programme there were six or seven items. In this five week period the items scoring the highest 'Reaction Index' according to Audience Research's calculation—that is to say, the items with which the viewing panel respondents were most satisfied—were 'Josephine Hunter in the studio with three homeless animals in search of adoption'; Pearl Binder in the studio talking about her recent visit to China and showing artefacts she had brought back; a studio interview with a sculptor, McDonald Reid, showing some of his work; Mme Jeanty Raven 'heroine of the Belgian Resistance' interviewed in the studio about her newly published biography; and Marghanita Lasky 'talking to a consultant psychiatrist and a member of Alcoholics Anonymous about women and drink'. Other well-received items dealt with a new, cut-price supermarket, a talk about 'slavery in 1960', an extract from the film *The Entertainer* and an interview with its star, Shirley Ann Fields. It seems clear from this spot sample that a broad range of topical items unlikely to find their way into the main news or current affairs programmes were introduced. It is also clear that the majority of items were studio-bound although there were small film inserts such as 'a film of a witches meeting' which was not much appreciated, or a 'brief glimpse of the Motor

---

21 Doreen Stephens, 25 Sept. 1958 article for *Aeriel*, WAC T32/1867/1.

22 The published programme announcements included no details of content.

Show' which scored even lower. Probably the supermarket item was on film, and extracts from current releases accompanying interviews with stage or screen performers seem to have been regularly included. The budget (£400 per programme in 1958) was almost double that allowed for the other afternoon magazines, but still too low to permit any elaborate sets or much location filming—hence the prevalence of studio items. Nevertheless the programme was cut as a consequence of the new administrative arrangements whereby women's and children's programming were to be produced by the Family Programmes Department. Nothing survives except the few memoranda quoted here, but the popularity and longevity of the topical magazine was already assured in *Tonight* and in the celebrated current affairs magazine *Panorama* which, though they did not directly privilege a female audience, were certainly addressed to an audience including women.

Panorama[23] *Panorama* began as a fortnightly half-hour arts magazine programme in November 1953, covering amongst other things book reviews, theatre, and cinema—though the last caused some anxiety as a 1953 memo to A. Miller Jones of the Panorama team indicates:

> your inclusion of film reviews in Panorama *might* make good television, but it would certainly help the film industry and we do not see why, in the reigning circumstances, we should go out of our way to help them. . . . C.P.(Tel) feels that to stage a film criticism without 'quotation from the films under review' would *not* be good television and should not therefore be attempted.[24]

The circumstances referred to were the efforts of the distribution branch of the film industry to limit television's access to cinema material in order to protect their own interests, since in their view cinema was under threat from television's increasing attraction to audiences. A longer term and less parochial approach might have recognized that a more united view of British culture across the arts could have strengthened British cinema production and exhibition in the face of the far more serious competition from Hollywood. Nevertheless this fragment from routine office correspondence indicates both the hesitant exploration of what was appropriate to television and the constant attention to ways in which the best interests of the new form might be furthered. The *Daily Mail* television critic, Peter Black, wrote nostalgically on the occasion of *Panorama*'s 200th edition in June 1960:

23 See Lindley (2003) for a thorough and absorbing account of this long-running programme.

24 WAC T32/1191/1, 8 Oct. 1953 memo from P. H. Dorte, Head of Films, Television.

aged viewers may possibly remember the early years of Panorama . . . because television was developing hourly all sorts of things used to turn up in the programme because it seemed the best place for them . . .

Panorama overdoes political affairs and underdoes social ones. There is too much about the world, not enough about living in it[25]

Black is lamenting here not so much the pre-1955 emphasis on the arts as the exciting unpredictabilty of the early programmes. The growing focus between 1955 and 1960 on Politics (with a capital P) was, he seems to say, at the expense of the much appreciated contextualizing of politics-and-society which had characterized the earlier part of that period. Be that as it may, by mid-1955, according to Michael Peacock, *Panorama*'s shift into the territory of current affairs was under way:

It was after the 1955 Election Results Programme that the idea of a weekly Panorama with Richard Dimbleby as anchorman was born . . . with Richard Dimbleby and with Malcolm Muggeridge, Woodrow Wyatt, Max Robertson and, six months later, with Chris Chataway we set out to explore the virgin lands of weekly television journalism.[26]

Leonard Miall, then Head of Television Talks and Documentaries, gives the credit for *Panorama*'s overhaul to Goldie:

When we decided to make Panorama a weekly programme in 1955 I asked my deputy, Grace Wyndham Goldie, to supervise its new look . . . It was she who first demanded that Richard Dimbleby should be the new anchorman, and before soon moving off to energise in turn the start of Tonight and then of Monitor she had firmly settled the guiding lines for Panorama's integrity in its coverage of current affairs, showmanship in its intelligent exploration of the television medium.[27]

Almost all the reporting and production personnel in the 1955 team were men, the only women being the studio floor manager Joan Marsden, and the production secretary Margaret Douglas, as Richard Lindley acknowledges:

Panorama had been given the go-ahead by a woman, Mary Adams, Head of Talks, Television. Under another, Grace Wyndham Goldie, the programme had become important. But for all that, *Panorama* remained for the most part a deeply male

25 *Daily Mail*, 4 June 1960, p. 6.

26 Peacock (1966: 96).

27 Miall (1966: 102).

preserve in which masculine beasts of the jungle prowled and postured while a few self-effacing secretaries and willing researchers indulged their roars and growls.[28]

Female personnel were being sought, however, as an advertisement in the 27 October 1958 *Evening News* indicates: fourteen candidates were 'auditioned' from a long list of applications from women with, mostly, no experience of broadcasting, journalism, or performance.[29] The programme's current producer, Rex Moorfoot, was interviewed by the *Evening News* under the headline '*Panorama* has job for a woman':

> We are looking for a woman commentator, but so far have failed to find one. We are conscious of women's appeal in the programme, and we are sometimes criticised—for example last Monday we didn't have a single woman's face in the programme.[30]

The first mention of a female interviewer in the Audience Research reports is for the 23 February 1959 programme, which had had items on regional accents, Cyprus, women as priests, influenza, and a competition club: 'Nan Winton . . . impressed some viewers as a good interviewer with a very pleasant manner and several viewers said they would like to see more of her'[31] but, as Lindley notes, by June 1960 she had been snapped up by News—'nice work if you can get it'—writes Lindley, continuing,

> Most men don't get offered this studio-based job until they've seen some service and look a little travel-worn. Television managers—and, it seems, the public—like their women newscasters with the bloom of youth and innocence still on them. Who can blame women for seizing an offer to stop reporting the world and start reading other people's reports about it instead?[32]

Despite this retrospective comment the paucity of women newscasters in this period, as we have seen, hardly bears him out.

Integrity, showmanship, and, above all, 'intelligent exploration of the medium', albeit in almost exclusively masculinist hands, were the principles which guided *Panorama*'s rapid development into what was (and still is) probably one of the BBC's most prestigious programmes—certainly its longest running one.[33] It is of course no

---

28 Lindley (2003: 263).

29 WAC T32/1399/1, 1958.

30 Lindley (2003: 264).

31 WAC VR/59/110, 12 Mar. 1959.

32 Lindley (2003: 265).

33 Though Lindley notes with regret in his conclusion that 'the author's pride in *Panorama* is tempered by doubts as to whether it is, any longer, right at the heart of the BBC', ibid. 387.

accident that the 'new' *Panorama* went on air as a forty-five-minute weekly programme just one week before the start of ITV transmissions, in September 1955, and the subsequent and healthy competition with A-R's *This Week* no doubt fuelled the 'intelligent exploration' of television's potential in both the public service and the commercial sector. Viewer responses to *Panorama*'s new format were, on the whole, positive: 'although we certainly got around more the intimate character of the last series was entirely lost', but, more typically, 'highly successful TV and much better than the other set-up', 'I liked getting around more, the other was inclined to be studio-bound'.[34] The international crises of the mid-1950s must also have stimulated audience appetite for this new form of journalism. Peacock recalled nostalgically that 'Panorama's finest hour will always be the Autumn of 1956. It was during those dark weeks of the Hungarian revolution and the Suez invasion that Panorama grew up'.[35] But, international events notwithstanding, Goldie kept a close eye on *Panorama*'s development, as her November 1956 memo indicates: 'I am confirming that . . . by next Monday it would be advisable to make Panorama once more a mixed programme and not confine it entirely to politics and international affairs. We agreed that to continue the crisis atmosphere for a third programme might alienate the audience.'[36] Her assessment of the audience is confirmed in an Audience Research report on the 11 June programme broadcast live from the Middle East: 'Panorama should abide by its magazine format and not attempt to emulate documentary', though the viewer cited acknowledged that devoting the programme to one subject was 'expedient in the present instance'.[37] Interestingly, here the respondent assumes the documentary form to preclude its presentation in magazine format—hence a current affairs programme with a single item is understood to be 'emulating' documentary. The programme had comprised Woodrow Wyatt reporting from Kuwait and Bahrein and a Dimbleby-led filmed piece about tankers and oil refineries. By 1956 *Panorama* had, clearly, settled into a format of mixed items always including, though never limited to, present current affairs. For at least one viewer this format had become tediously predictable as an Audience Research report for the 13 October 1958 programme, which included items on Brazil, the Isle of Man government, the Wolfenden Reports on homosexuality and prostitution, the closure of Croydon airport, and the US lunar probe projects, indicates: 'Somewhat uninspired, especially in regard to interviews: man-on-the-spot,

34 WAC VR/55/465, 11 Oct. 1955.

35 Peacock (1966: 96).

36 WAC T32/1191/3, 13 Nov. 1956.

37 WAC VR/56/308, 2 July 1956.

woman-on-the-spot, pro, anti, uneducated accent, posh accent. Usually in that order. Take a look at yourselves and have a Panorama programme on Panorama.'[38]

In general, however, Audience Research reports for Panorama's first five years deliver a lively sense of the audience's real and thoughtful appreciation of the programme and its contribution to the development of televisual form. There is a growing sophistication over this five-year period in viewers' responses to the form of different items, for example to interview manner and techniques, to whether questions raised were satisfactorily answered. There is evident pleasure in Panorama's explication of complex issues, especially but not only those relating to foreign affairs, and an acknowledgement of the vitality of this immediate moving image material in allowing some understanding of events in unfamiliar places. There is also great pleasure in reports from foreign locations *not* troubled by political events, such as for example those from Bermuda, Norway, Brazil: here television's power to 'see' faraway places coincided with the developing appetite, in the later 1950s, for foreign travel and the soon-to-be ubiquitous 'package' holiday.

A former editor of Panorama, Roger Bolton, writing in 1986, suggested that 'audience research studies show that the majority of the audience for the BBC's flagship current affairs programme Panorama comes from the lower reaches of the class structure', relating this observation to the imperative for programme makers to remember that 'nobody *has* to watch, and most people wish to be entertained as well as informed'.[39] Between 1955 and 1960 the BBC's own audience research figures indicate that Panorama was securing about 25 per cent of the total available audience, with a greater proportion amongst the Band 1 than Band 3 viewers,[40] and Asa Briggs corroborates this, noting that in 1958 'it was reported that one adult in four in the UK was watching Panorama'.[41] Panorama was programmed at 8.00 p.m. on Mondays against the US import series Western *Wagon Train* on ITV. A stable slot was considered key to the strategy of maintaining audience loyalty: in 1960 a run of timing changes elicited vociferous complaints from the programme team, Michael Peacock writing, 'the loyal viewers will switch on anyway. It is the floating 10% or 20% which we must catch if we are to remain a majority programme.'[42] For these loyal viewers, 'Panorama, many said, was to be relied upon to keep viewers au fait with current affairs, opinions

38 WAC CR/58/553, dated 4 Oct. 1958 probably meaning 4 Nov. 1958.

39 Bolton (1997: 261).

40 Band 1 = BBC only, Band 3 = BBC *and* ITV.

41 Briggs (1985: 302–4).

42 WAC T32/1191/7, 23 Feb. 1960.

and topics (sometimes of a very unexpected kind) that had their entertaining side as well.'[43] The routine 1–2 page reports on programmes issued by Audience Research record a consistent and over-all approval of the programmes, always carefully quoting both pro- and anti-comments and noting which are exemplary, which unusual. There was frequent criticism of items deemed by viewers to be overly political or 'heavyweight' but, equally, 'light' items were often thought to be inappropriate. Every report included either commentary on, or directly quoted viewer response to, the anchormen (most often Dimbleby who was perenially popular despite a minority of detractors who found him pompous) and there is also always a comment about the technical aspects of the programme—that is to say its lighting, sound, set—especially if these were deemed to be substandard. Apropos the 1 February 1960 programme for example, Audience Research noted that

> Robin Day was adversely criticised for appearing too like a Prosecuting Counsel. He lacked sympathy with those he interviewed, it was said, and a number of viewers disliked his overbearing attitude and tendency to interrupt . . . Ludovic Kennedy appeared to some a rather negative figure—too serious and somewhat indifferent to the subject.[44]

The programme had included items on the railway crisis, Algerian rebels, the power of theatre critics (discussed by Sam Wanamaker and Bernard Levin), and the trade in horses between France and Ireland. These Audience Research reports offer a most useful insight into the ways in which, at that time, both programme makers and viewers alike were conscious not only of the appropriateness, or otherwise, of programme content but also of the technical and cultural novelty of the new form. They reveal that viewers, just as much as makers, of television were concerned to play their part in consolidating and refining it in accordance with their view of the part television could or should play in national culture. As a travel agent's wife commented on the 2 June 1958 programme which had included items on France and Algeria, the restoration of Westminster Abbey, and fairgrounds in Britain, the programme was 'intelligent without being humourless, socially conscious without being snobbish. A proper use of television.'[45]

The programme format, as it took its definitive shape in these early years, settled into a sequence of five or six disparate items usually including at least one foreign affairs story, an item on an issue in the

43 WAC VR/57/523, 10 Oct. 1957.

44 WAC VR/60/66, 27 Feb. 1960.

45 WAC VR/58/298, 18 June 1958.

domestic political spotlight, an item of potential general concern sometimes triggered by a newsworthy event or the publication of a report, and usually though not always a lightweight or 'trivial' item clearly included in the interests of maintaining both 'balance' and entertainment value—such items, particularly when they concerned 'women's interest' as they sometimes did, came in for more than their fair share of criticism in the Audience Research reports. From time to time *Panorama* 'specials' delivered the programme from a foreign location, or focused, as with the Suez crisis, on a particular issue. The team combined a journalistic awareness of the 'scoop' story with a constant eye to the possibility of extending television's range, characteristic amongst broadcasters at this exciting time. Thus detailed and highly complex arrangements—both technically and politically complex—were made in 1961 to broadcast from Moscow a special edition on the Mayday Parade. These followed ATV's announcement that it planned a broadcast from the British Trade Exhibition in Moscow on 17 May, hence scooping ITV in being the first to broadcast live from the heart of the 'Soviet bloc'. In the event *Panorama* scooped itself by managing to divert the Mayday arrangements into a live broadcast on 13 April of Gagarin's heroic return from the first manned spaceflight, with Dimbleby's unrehearsed commentary to the live footage as it appeared.[46] Other live broadcasts from overseas covered political events such as the July 1960 Democratic Convention (Los Angeles, 1960), ceremonials such as the opening of the Vatican Council (Rome, 1962) or devastating natural catastrophes such as the Skopje earthquake (Skopje, 1963). It is all too easy, after fifty or more years of broadcasting, to forget the experimental nature of what now seem both obvious and routine elements of what we expect from television, and to underestimate the risk-taking, the intuitive leaps, the laborious negotiations that must have accompanied each innovative step. Though the programme settled fairly speedily into a familiar and predictable form there were also 'one-off' experimental departures such as the Gagarin scoop, or the 17 October 1960 special on Polaris. Between 8.00 and 8.55 p.m. in a slightly extended programme time, a CBS film, presented by Ed Murrow, about the development of the Polaris missile was broadcast and then from 9.25 to 9.45 p.m. the implications for Britain were considered in a live studio discussion. The majority of viewer responses recorded in the Audience Research report concerned reactions to the the film and its 'awe inspiring' content, rather than to the form of the programme, though

> some viewers felt the technical brilliance of the film made it an entertainment in itself inducing at times a state bordering on euphoria so that they almost forgot the deeper implications . . .

46 Miall (1966: 116).

most viewers in this sample . . . gave full marks to the idea of a live discussion timed to allow an interval for them to absorb the full meaning of what they had seen and heard.[47]

In order to exemplify this sketch of *Panorama*'s early development I want to offer some idea of the detail of a couple of the mid-1960s programmes it has been possible to view—bearing in mind that, apart from some filmed inserts, the majority of earlier programmes are no longer available. Much of the preceding outline of programme form and content may seem familiar, since it was the foundation of the British current affairs programming in which we are now all so well versed. Nevertheless I think it important to recall as far as this is possible the visual detail, tone, and sequencing of the programme since it is this which constitutes the matrix through which the current events were perceived by contemporary audiences.

■ *Panorama* **(29 June 1964)** By 1964 *Panorama* was at the height of its reputation as one of the most respected programmes on British television. Richard Dimbleby is the secure and confident master of ceremonies in this 29 June 1964 programme which comprised three distinct items, each subject to multiple forms of presentation. A proposition is exemplified through a location piece, or by means of a studio discussion offering varied points of view. The emphasis is on questions. The programme opens with Dimbleby speaking to camera, welcoming the audience: 'Good evening. *Panorama* tonight looks at some length at morals and law', continuing to advise that some parts of the programme may be unsuitable for children. The tone is urbane, familiar, assured. The first item in the programme was a studio discussion about police relations with the public, touching on corruption and its investigation. Dimbleby references some recent problems over police behaviour, suggesting the expansion of motoring as a factor contributing to the increased contact between the police and the public, and leading into the discussion with the question 'What can be done?' put to his two guests Lord Shawcross QC, former Attorney General and Arthur Evans, Secretary of the Police Federation for England and Wales. There follows a substantial discussion, adroitly steered by Dimbleby, focusing on the question whether or not the police should be their own investigators, and referring to several recently publicized cases of police misdemeanours. With the camera close-up on Dimbleby he makes the link to the next item: 'Now from law, the police, to the question of morals. *Panorama* decided to investigate what problems face young people in two countries, very different from ours, in Italy and in Sweden.'

47 WAC VR/60/613, 8 Nov. 1960.

A filmed report follows in which the *Panorama* reporter in Rome interviews various male Italians in the film industry who speak of the endemic poverty and unemployment in the south, concluding 'there are many more forces at work to tempt girls into the brazen business of patrolling the roads out of the city'. The conclusion is an interview with a 21-year-old gang leader, three years in prison already behind him, before we move, via Dimbleby in the London studio, to a second film insert, this time from a coffee bar outside Stockholm, in Sweden. The reporter's voice-over comments on images of Swedish 'rockers' in their cars, drinking, with their girls. There's an interview with a social worker on 'night patrol' and with a girl in a 'children's village'—an experimental resource for accommodating delinquent children. We are shown well-equipped State youth centres, and there's an interview about Swedish society with the Minister for Welfare. The polarization of these two 'case studies' allows the idea that British experience falls comfortably in between that of the Italians and the Swedes—a clever demonstration of *balance* in practice, perhaps—but the item's inequitable treatment of the two examples more than smacks of agenda setting. Whereas in Italy we're given an exclusively masculine assessment of a social problem experienced by young women—that is to say, prostitution as a means of livelihood—in Sweden the emphasis is on the state's efforts to anticipate and control youthful misdemeanours. Hence British stereotypes of Italian-ness and Swedish-ness are reinforced: male Italians speak about the sex trade, male and female Swedes speak about their welfare state.

Returning to the London studio Dimbleby turns briskly to the final item which, trailing the next programme, contains a lengthy compilation of five-year-old news footage edited to offer a snapshot account of recent and dramatic events in the Congo, followed by a studio discussion about the UN's handling of the conflict. Robin Day reports from the studio on the current status quo, followed by the five-year-old clip—now it's 1960 and again it's Robin Day—in which he asks of people apparently selected at random in the street, 'What are the problems facing the Congo?' A clip of the Congo Parliament in 1960 is described as a 'tragic farce', and further clips call attention to the series of crises—Lumumba's murder in 1961, UN Secretary General Dag Hammerschold's death in a plane crash, air raids in Elizabethville—which together, Robin Day suggests, pose a threat not only in the Congo itself but also to the viability of the entire UN operation. He poses the question 'What is your verdict on the UN record?' to two Englishmen, a journalist and an ex-member of the Colonial Office, who make clear their fundamental disagreement on every aspect of the issue. Here the programme closed, on a sombre and provocative note, effectively setting an agenda through which audiences might consider the matter. Finally Dimbleby announced next week's subject, the Commonwealth Conference.

■ *Panorama* **(11 January 1965)** This programme, too, had three substantial and quite different kinds of report. The programmes titles roll over an exterior shot of a city street from which we cut to Dimbleby watching the same pictures captured through an unmanned surveillance camera on the roof of a building. Only now do we learn that the item concerns the innovatory use, in Liverpool, of such cameras for crime control. As in classic storytelling the audience's curiosity is aroused by this opening narrative 'hook' and our attention secured as Dimbleby, in the Liverpool control room, interviews the Chief Constable whose idea this was, discovering the technology involved, raising the spectre of the technique's 'Orwellian significance', and asking about the films' status as evidence in court. The police chief confesses he hadn't considered the latter and gives an undertaking that the technique will never be used for anything other than crime and traffic control. He suggests, rather lamely, that the film couldn't be used in court since this would entail revealing the whereabouts of the cameras. From the 'brave new world' of state-of-the-art crime control techniques in Liverpool, via a close-up of Dimbleby making the link, we go to a by-election in Leyton, East London. Patrick Gordon-Walker, the then Labour Foreign Secretary who had recently lost his Smethwick seat in the general election, is a candidate. Both campaigns had been marked by racial conflict and the current scenes from Leyton include a racist fight which breaks up the election meeting, the Fascist leader Colin Jordan and his supporters with their 'Keep Britain White' cries and banners being much in evidence. Members of a football crowd are interviewed about their attitude to 'blacks', we get a glimpse of a special service at a local church, and the *Panorama* reporter interviews each of the three main candidates before giving a face-to-camera summary of the campaign—essentially interpreting what we have just 'seen', before returning us to Dimbleby in the studio. The juxtaposition of these two items—futuristic crime control in Liverpool and the dangerous racism likely to produce crime in Leyton—implicitly proposes questions to the audience about the direction of British society: questions not explored further when, returning to Dimbleby, the final item is headlined. This is a filmed piece about reporter Michael Barrat's visit to the Gambarene leper colony in West Africa, run on unconventional lines by the celebrated Albert Schweitzer. Barrat speaks to benefactor Marion Preminger, present for her annual visit to the colony, about Schweitzer's philosophy of reverence for life, extended she says to the management of the jungle and the farm as well as to medical and other human facilities, about his idiosyncratic refusal to use available technology such as a local generator, or jeep transport, and about his autocratic command of the colony: 'the routine of Gambarene is ordered by the bell'. 'When a sage reaches 90', she says, 'you don't question him.' In a rather dizzying cut we are returned to the Liverpool control room where Dimbleby asks the duty officer what's been going on, then the credits—separate for each item—roll. The questions suggested in the juxtaposition of the first two items aren't answered, but Schweitzer's (albeit autocratic) reverence for all life is offered, again only implicitly, as one way of evaluating the apparently intractable social problems of racism, violence, control.

Women on screen, as reporters, studio guests, or subject matter, were largely absent from the 1964 programme, except for the teenage victims of poverty, depravity, or simple peer-group pressure, who dominated the film inserts from Italy and Sweden. In the 1965 programme there is a single plain-clothes policewoman who, unlike her male colleagues, says almost nothing, there are a (very) few women at the election meeting—none of whom speak—and there is Marion Preminger in the Schweitzer item. The overwhelming impression given in both programmes is of a confident, diverse, and overwhelmingly masculine world. This can partly be accounted for by reference to the question of programme hierarchy in which *news* is dominant, and the declared intention of *Panorama*, along with other BBC current affairs programming, to compensate for what they perceived as the paucity of news in the mass press. Yet the clear intention in the sequencing of items in both programmes, not to mention in the brief to which current affairs programming worked—that is to say, the intention to reflect and explore contemporary British society—renders this masculinist bias mischievous, to say the least. But here of course is a self-serving circle: the agenda of public affairs is a male one to which *Panorama* must subscribe in order to demonstrate its seriousness.

Marriage Today   By the early 1960s questions about the social relations of men and women, their expectations of each other and their 'place' in the social order—what we might now term gender politics—were prominent on the public agenda, to be found in the print media, on radio, and not least on television. In 1962, for example, *Perspective* ran a programme on courtship, in 1963 the series *This Nation Tomorrow* had included a programme *Sex and Family Life* which generated substantial correspondence, and within six months of its establishment in February 1964 the Family Programmes Department had two six-part series on air, *Marriage Today* and *The Second Sex*, and an ongoing evening programme *Gilt and Gingerbread* in the planning stages. This was to be an 'avant-garde/feminist . . . magazine for women which men will want to watch'.[48] In 1966 a fourteen-part series *Women Women Women* (BBC2, 12 May–10 Nov. 1966) intended to 'look at women in Britain today—their lives and their attitudes'. The majority of the producers and directors of this series were men: once again the female subject is 'looked *at*', hence both distanced and objectified. *The Second Sex*, produced by Elizabeth Cowley and also for broadcast on BBC2, was, however, striking for its all-female contingent: four professional women debated the given topic, chaired by a woman— the only men being a trio accompanying the female singer, Shirley Abicair, and they were playing off-screen. Perhaps this was a rare instance of *men* being objectified. The six parts were entitled *Men as Lovers* (11 Sept. 1964); *Men as Husbands* (18 Sept. 1964); *Men as Children* (25 Sept. 1964); *Men as Fathers* (2 Oct. 1964); *Men as Superiors* (9 Oct. 1964); and *Men as Equals* (16 Oct. 1964). The studio was arranged with a bar, coffee table, fresh flowers, drinks, and cigarettes and the tone intended to be lightweight and informal: 'The women will be seen in an "after dinner" setting talking over coffee and brandy. The producer wants . . . to use attractive, interesting women who do not regularly appear on television'.[49] Sadly this intriguing programme is no longer extant, but despite its informality it did appear to propose an exploration of the masculine—or at least of the major ways in which men and women interact, that is to say of gender relations—from the point of view of the female subject. Such privileging of the female subject position was highly unusual and strikingly absent from *Marriage Today*'s positioning of women, as we shall see.

Marriage Today, broadcast on BBC2 over the same period, was a rather weightier six-part series of forty-minute programmes pro-duced by the newly formed Family Programmes Department but planned under the aegis of, and staffed by personnel from, the dis-banded Women's Programmes Unit. The programme titles were *Getting Married* (9 Sept. 1964), *A Social Institution* (16 Sept. 1964), *A Business Partnership* (23 Sept. 1964), *An Intimate Union* (30 Sept. 1964), *Breakdown* (7 Oct. 1964), and *An Excellent Mystery* (14 Oct. 1964). The first programme dealt with marriage ceremonies, the second with the institution understood in terms of community, housing, mobility, and opportunity. In the third programme the legalities of the marriage contract and its history were explored, as were questions of income and finance—housekeeping money, wages, and pension provision—and women's rights at divorce or the death

48 WAC T32/395, 30 Nov. 1964.

49 WAC T32/1572, 7 Aug. 1964.

of their husband. The presenter or, in then-current parlance, the anchorman, Alan Little, closed this programme with: 'How far do women today see marriage as a means to avoid going out to work—how far does this attitude exist, side by side with the modern ideal of "shared partnership" and "feminine equality"?'[50] The fourth programme, *An Intimate Union*, dealt with sex and birth control—particularly its recent history—and gave statistics on marriage, divorce, and family size. The closure focused on two experiences of childbirth of which the first was the Johnsons. Their wedding had featured in the first programme and their family life in the second and the father had been present at their daughter's birth, an experience both recalled with pleasure—here was a truly 'modern' couple. The second entailed a divorced woman's recounting of her experience—she had given birth alone while her husband had taken his lover to the theatre.[51] In the fifth programme the subject was divorce: history, statistics, legalities, and costs. Reasons for marriage breakdown were explored, statistics concerning both male and female adultery offered, and the consequences of breakdown for children and for women's economic situation were discussed. The programme closed with Alan Little reassuring the audience that the 'large majority stay married and mean to—still 90% of marriages last'.[52] The final programme turned to generational changes in attitudes to marriage, looking at practical questions in relation to some perceived contradictions in modern marriages and how these might be approached through education, the law, facilities for working women, sexuality, and religion. It closed with an interview, filmed in New York, with anthropologist Margaret Mead who pointed to education and the concomitant expectations it provoked which, she suggested, were nevertheless vital to the well-being of the social whole, and to longevity and mobility as the other major threats to traditional ideas of marriage. The series' overall focus seems to have been on female experience and its consequence for societal well-being conceived both in economic terms and apropos the socialization of the next generation. A more detailed account of one programme will give a clearer sense of the form and tone.

■ *Marriage Today: A Social Institution* (BBC2, 16 September 1964)

Presenter Alan Little's closing remark to the second programme 'Has sexual equality gone far enough, or too far?' conceals an elision of gender politics typical of the mid-sixties, though acknowledged implicitly in a couple of revealing comments surviving in the typed summary of a November 1963 production meeting planning the

50 WAC T32/914.

51 WAC T32/917/1.

52 WAC T32/913, 4 June 1964, p. 4.

series. This entailed discussion about the content, form, and sequencing of both the research and the construction of each programme and allows access to the general principles agreed in the planning process.

> Doreen Stephens, Ed. W.P. Tel: 'Marriage Today' would be for peak hour viewing time on Channel 2. It should be a general programme for men and women equally—not a feminist programme.
> Lorna Pegram, Producer: We should find out what the experts have to say from reading their reports, etc., and it is a good idea to record the experts first, then the ordinary people afterwards. . . .
> Doreen Stephens: After the programme has finished, it should cause an argument in every house where it has been watched.[53]

There are interesting (and familiar) assumptions here: for example, the separation between 'experts' and 'ordinary people', and the assumption that a 'feminist' programme would not be 'for men'. But what I want to draw attention to in consideration of the second programme in its broadcast form is, first, the polemical intention 'it should cause an argument in every house' and secondly the egalitarian intention 'It should be a general programme for men and women equally'. I have no quarrel with either of these intentions, both of which are utterly steeped in the ethos of the BBC Talks Department at the time and are, in any case, laudable intentions for a programme series presuming, as this one does, to offer a portrait of contemporary life in Britain—to mirror the audience to itself. But at the same time I can't help but note that this is a team *exclusively* composed of women, a recently re-formed unit with a new access to prime-time scheduling, and that they are 'swallowing whole' not only the characteristically polemical address of current affairs but also the fictional elision of difference in the gendered audience, while at the same time hoping to provoke 'an argument in every house'. This argument would presumably be between the 'ordinary people' in their familial couples— 'men and women equally'—in front of their domestic screens. What the arguments should be *about*, however, is less clear; certainly perusal of the programme in question—as well as the production notes for the others—*doesn't* suggest a focus on the politics of gender, as the title *Marriage Today* might imply, but rather on those of age and class, as well as a polemical attention to perceived social *change* and its positive or negative value. So what the programme effectively does, I think, is to adopt a masculinist voice in speaking about social mores and change, typically assuming that this is equivalent to an egalitarian address, and then locating perceived social problems in a specifically *female* experience. *Marriage Today: A Social Institution* (16 Sept. 1964), in line with the producers' intentions and with the remit of the Family Programmes Unit, represents an interesting and careful attempt to 'stand back', as it were, and to look at contemporary society through the institution of marriage as well as to look at the institution itself.

The programme opens with a woman's voice 'I was born in Liverpool' over high-angle long-shot images of children at play in Victorian terraced streets, emphasizing the housing with a pan across the terrace façade which dissolves to another long-shot of a woman and a child walking away from camera in a contemporary, low-rise detached housing estate. The same voice-over tells us, 'I don't think the estates are old enough to have fostered any community sense'. Straight away there is an opposition offered between 'the old' and 'the new' in which something has been lost, and the sense of lack is located with the young mother, the woman whose first-person voice had interpreted the filmed images to us. The title sequence follows and then an authoritative male voice-over addresses us, 'Where you live affects how you live', and in so doing suggests a link between us and the female 'I' of the opening speech, as well as confirming the visual suggestion of the importance of housing and location to the issue of marriage and society. A fairly lengthy introduction ensues over a montage of moving footage and still photographs offering a 'history' of the family and pointing out significant differences for the families of 'today'. This disquisition touches on economics, 'more recently full employment, social security and the welfare state have made for changes in family life'; on health and longevity, 'Prosperity and advancing medical knowledge mean people live longer . . . 100 years ago the average life span for a woman was 50 years, today she can expect to live until she's 74'. The emphasis here and in the accompanying still photograph of a Victorian family group on which the camera zooms in to rest on the figure of the mother, is once again on the woman. He continues, touching on family size, the decline in Church membership, on education and mobility: 'Widening of educational opportunity and the ease of transport have made society more mobile . . . people need no longer stay put in the class or area in which they were born'. This is spoken over an image of a group of young men in a street, cut to cars, a traffic jam, and cut again to a close-up of a helmeted couple on a motor bike as the voice-over summarizes, suggesting that youth today have 'a greater freedom than any previous generation'.

Up to this point the emphasis has been on changes largely suggested to be positive but nevertheless the images of *then* juxtaposed with those of *now* suggest a homogeneity of the past which recalls the sense of loss signalled in the opening images. This is, to say the least, a spurious homogeneity. But now the tone of voice and of image shifts as the discourse focuses, as it were, on the special qualities of the present. Over a rather menacing medium close-up of a forest of television aerials against the sky the voice continues, 'But in place of the rigidities of the old social order new gods have arisen . . . of every 3 households, 2 have TV sets . . . the mass media may be imposing a new and massive uniformity on the whole nation.' The consequences of this uniformity, however, seem to be primarily experienced by women since an image of a breakfasting couple—she looks at him, he reads the newspaper—dissolves to a close-up of the woman's face as the voice continues, 'With fewer children and more labour-saving devices women are freer from household drudgery but more subject to boredom and loneliness' over a long-shot of an empty street in a suburban housing estate.

Now the programme's lengthy preamble is complete and we are introduced, still by the disembodied male voice, to a couple who are first seen in their home, rather ineptly hanging a picture in their newly decorated hall (it falls off the wall) and then in the studio alternately talking to camera. She is the woman from the pre-credit sequence and continues her nostalgic reminiscence about her child-hood in inner-city, working-class Liverpool, contrasting this with her present good fortune but also noting her sense of unease with her current life: 'I can spend the whole day doing things, but I feel that I overdo things. . . . I find now that I go to the doctor a lot . . . quite unnecessarily . . . my mother or a relative would have been able to say' and 'I look around at my detached house . . . all the things . . . we didn't do a great deal for it. I do appreciate it . . . I'm very grateful'. Interspersed with her speech is that of her husband who speaks of his career, of his wife's wages supporting him through his Ph.D.—'I wasn't ashamed at all but of course we did quarrel a lot'—of living near his work which motivated their move away from Liverpool, of their neighbours on the estate who have 'come from all over', noting that the 'estates are not old enough to have fostered community spirit. People don't know where they stand'.

Finally we come to our presenter, Alan Little, now no longer a dis-embodied voice but a young, middle-class, professional man seen in medium close-up in the studio talking to camera—directly to us, the audience. 'Well there we are. One marriage in a changing society. But how far are the Johnsons typical of marriage today as a social institu-tion? Do they personify any general trends?' This signals a change in the programme's format as his rhetorical questions are picked up by a series of 'experts' also in the studio. These are all men: a research psychiatrist (Hugh Ballard Thomas), a practising psychologist (Peter Fletcher), and a sociologist (John Highett). Though the production notes indicate that many female experts were found and listed during research for the programmes, in fact the great majority selected to appear were men. Perhaps because their brief is to fulfil the role of 'expert' they all focus mainly on the problems they perceive. Like the programme's authorial voice they tend to understand these primarily as problems in and for the woman, agreeing that the smaller family is a weaker social unit introducing dangerous differences to the community, and noting the 'improbability of a man and woman being all in all for each other' in the isolation produced by new mobility and smaller family units. The isolation and anonymity of the modern family in new housing estates is compounded, they agree, by the *cultural* uniformity imposed by television. Here they assume—despite Pat Johnson's account of other, more active, leisure pursuits—that families are necessarily a part of the mass television audience homogenized in its apathy, passive before quantities of 'mindless' or 'frivolous' programming. The one positive note, about a 'new reciprocity to the couple' (decorating the hall together, however incompetently) is lost as Alan Little steers the talk in the direction of part 2 of the programme which will deal with poverty and housing. The primary emphasis is now on housing rather than on the couple and we are with a vicar in the Gorbals as he shows and tells of slum housing and its effects on tenants who lose hope, he says, and self respect. The material of this filmed insert is reminiscent of Edgar Anstey's 1934 documentary *Housing Problems*, with the significant difference that there are none of the face- or voice-to-camera testimonies from inhabitants which so enlivened this film.

Whereas in the first part of the programme there's a degree of uncertainty about the borderline between *us* (the audience, the ordinary people, the citizens of the changing Britain under scrutiny) and *them* (the Johnsons, the mobile young, the isolated housewives), in the second part there is a much less equivocal division. Here the middle-class voice of the BBC speaks confidently to its middle-class audience. This is BBC2 at peak viewing time,[54] 8.40 p.m. on a Wednesday, in competition with *Z-Cars* and *Sportsview* on BBC1 and with *Ben Casey*, *The News*, and *Boyd QC* on ITV.[55] Moving on from liberal disquiet at the conditions of the poor, Alan Little introduces the next 'expert' Griselda Rowntree, the only woman in this role, who talks briefly about a recent national survey on marriage confirming that housing is indeed a central issue.[56] Thus she is invited to purvey

---

54 We should note here also that in 1964 the new BBC2, like the BBC of the earliest 1950s, was only available to audiences in London and the south-east.

55 The viewing figures as recorded by the BBC Audience Research service for 16 Sept. 1964, and expressed as a percentage of the total UHF viewing public, estimated to number 950,000 and excluding children under 8, were as follows: *Marriage Today* 3%; *Z-Cars* 34%; *Sportsview* 22%; *Ben Casey* 22%; *The News* 17%; *Boyd Q.C.* 13%. *Marriage Today* was followed by *The Danny Kaye Show* 12%. WAC T32/918.

56 The survey had comprised 3,000 interviews.

evidence, rather like a witness in a court case, and is not invited to participate in discussion—however stilted—as are the previous, male 'experts'. The Johnsons, the young couple whose wedding had been a subject of the first programme, now appear, talking to camera, as exemplars of the marriage survey's statistical information. Thus Rowntree's speech is demonstrated—this woman's discourse cannot, it seems, stand up in the way that the rather less well-substantiated assertions of the three male 'experts' apparently can.

Finally our presenter Alan Little introduces three couples seated around a table in the studio for what is promised to be a discussion about housing. He introduces them by means of still photographs of their current accommodation, demonstrating in the process their disparate positioning in terms of location, class, and income. They are a rural couple, a low-paid urban/industrial couple who live with their six children in two rooms, and a middle-class couple of whom the wife is Austrian and who have moved house and job frequently. While not intended to exemplify the whole of 'British society', they *are* offered as points of radical difference within it. The so-called discussion is a painfully stilted affair in which Little asks questions of each in turn, touching on community, on neighbours, and enquiring about differences in experience from previous generations of the respondents' own families. The whole thing lasts about four minutes. On our own with Alan Little again we watch him sum up, and then, over a montage of images rather different from those we've seen so far, he introduces the questions to be aired in the following programme. 'Is the relation between husbands and wives changing too? Are the clear-cut roles of men and women getting confused?' The images are of a man with a pram, of young men with shoulder-length hair walking in a sunny exterior and eating ice-cream cones, and, finally, of an androgynously dressed young couple: the camera pans down their leather trousers to hold on a close-up of their leather-booted feet, as he delivers the final line, 'Has sexual equality gone far enough, or too far?'

How are we to understand his question? As I have indicated, the substance of the second programme concerned broad social movements—education, welfare, health, increased mobility, greater material comforts (for some)—of which the consequences seem to be a weakening of the family unit and some psychic disturbance in the wife/mother who has been 'cut off' from the support she supposedly once enjoyed in the close-knit extended family community of the rosy past. Certainly the idea of sexual equality having gone 'far enough' implies that contemporary women are 'more equal' than their mothers and grandmothers were, and that therefore they wield more power, socially, than their female forebears. But there is no evidence in the programme of any shift in power relations: it is all about broad social changes of which women seem to be more victims than beneficiaries. If anything, the programme has implied a *dis*empowerment of contemporary women. Images of young men have accompanied information about increased opportunities, and images of not quite so young women have accompanied the ensuing problems. It's almost as though the programme is warning contemporary women of the pitfalls of 'sexual equality': certainly it denies them any agency in power relations. What is lost, perhaps, is stability, the known and the fixed—hardship and drudgery notwithstanding. In the wider context of gender power struggles of the sixties (and subsequently) what is at stake, of course, is the stability of the *masculine*. Is there, perhaps, a displacement of this anxiety at work here, a displacement onto the feminine, somehow put at risk in the women of 'today' by the prospect of a new-found equality 'gone too far'? And is this how the all-female production team understood their intention to 'address men and women equally, not to be feminist'? Here is a compelling microcosm of hegemonic struggle over gender in which representatives of the 'oppressed' group (women) are seen to be colluding with the discourse of their 'oppressors' (men).

Though the viewing figures were low, they were nevertheless substantial, and the programme received some good reviews, Monica Furlong for the *Daily Mail* in particular noting the all-female production team and insisting on a distinction between 'the experts' and the humanity of the speaking subjects.[57] Pre-production meetings had noted the intention to address women *and* men, 'not to be feminist' as Stephens had put it, as well as to 'cause an argument in every house'. It is an interesting programme revealing much about the anxieties and complacencies of the early 1960s yet, despite the apparent acknowledgement of a politics of gender and the all-female production team's embracing of a provocative stance, the dominant visual and aural tone is one of a masculine knowledge probing, sometimes attempting to empower, but always *controlling* female subjects. The production team's attempts at provocation, in other words, are thoroughly constrained by the masculinist discourse they adopt. Within the modern family the focus is on the women, whose relation to their history, their surroundings, and their daily life is frequently offered as problematic. *We* look at *them* through male eyes and so we are positioned as masculine.

Living for Kicks (A-R, March 1960)   Dan Farson, the presenter of this 45-minute investigative programme, had by 1960 made a reputation as an engaging and innovative interviewer committed to exploiting television's potential for 'examining society'. Under contract to A-R, he was in a position to

[57] *Daily Mail*, 17 Sept., 15 Oct. 1964.

propose and research subjects of his own choosing, and this 'film' about Britain's new generation of teenagers was broadcast on the cusp of the new decade, in March 1960. Hence most of the questions it poses relate to the later 1950s and it offers a compelling snapshot of British youth—and their difficult relationship with the parental generation—just before the so-called permissive 1960s got under way. Like many of his programmes it dealt with a contentious contemporary issue: Farson had a journalist's eye for the topical subject, but deployed this in the service of social, rather than political, explorations. Looked at today the programme seems remarkably tame, the interviewing soft and stilted, the responses stiff and incoherent, and the voice-over commentary raising questions and contextualizing the images and interviews often bears a pretty tangential relation to the on-screen images. Nevertheless the images themselves are telling ones, and the interviews certainly allow plenty of space to respondents: they may have been rehearsed but they certainly were not scripted. Ambient laughter in some of the coffee-bar interviews suggests the out-of-shot peer group's response to what was said, reminding the audience that the teenage interviewees were performing to each other as much as they were to Farson and his camera team. The glimpses of the contemporary British environment—the seafront at Brighton, a civic building in central Northampton, the canal at Limehouse in London—which frame the crowded coffee-bar interiors dominating the programme suggest bleak, drab, and empty urban spaces, a suggestion confirmed in Farson's closing interview with Lady Albemarle in which she characterizes contemporary Britain as 'a world which is pretty humdrum, pretty boring, and pretty much on tramlines, usually'. I want to offer a detailed account of the programme itself before returning to the question of its representations and what these might suggest about contemporary gender politics, as well as to the interesting issue of contemporary responses to the programmme. I note, also, that the entire production crew (as listed in the programme's on-screen credits) was male.

The programme opens with a high-angle medium-shot, panning slowly across teenagers dancing in a crowded and well-lit interior: the titles come up over this image and Acker Bilk playing 'Stranger on the Shore' is the non-diegetic sound. Close-ups of various individual young men and women give way to shots of couples before the titles finish and we cut to a close-up of presenter Dan Farson, a plump and earnest man in his thirties, speaking directly to camera hence to us, 'at home':

> So much has been said about teenagers recently that I must say
> I flinch at stepping on this well-trodden ground again. I'm
> certainly not going to attempt to reach any profound conclusion.

All we hope to do is observe a new type of teenager, a teenager who is making more money than was ever dreamt of in the old days, who's got a new spending power and with that power is able to enjoy himself, or fails to enjoy himself, in a completely different way.[58]

Farson's voice-over introduction continues over a montage verifying, as it were, the substance of his discourse. A January 1960 *Daily Herald* front-page headline 'The Teenage Millionaires—50s-a-week pocket money' fades to a mid-shot of a pretty teenage girl as she looks through a pile of 45s,[59] tries on shoes, looks at them in the shoe-shop mirror, all over a sound track with Lonnie Donnegan singing 'Putting on the Style' and followed by a tilt-up to show us a line of elegantly dressed young men—three-quarter jackets, shirts and ties, much-loved shoes. Hence Farson's initial focus is on the economic power of this newly important consumer group: they buy half of all record players, 44% of motorbikes and cycles, he tells us, and a quarter of all cosmetics. But though he does ask about spending power, the main thrust of his subsequent questions to the teenage interviewees concerns their attitudes to courtship, sex, and marriage and to the (assumed) difficult relations with their perplexed parents. In a rather disingenuous voice-over conclusion to his introductory remarks he prefaces the first set of interviews with 'We shall not show the mass of teens who use these advantages to the utmost. They are no problem. But there are teenagers who seem to be slightly lost in their newfound freedom, who seem to live in a world slightly apart.' This isn't about *all* teenagers, then, rather it concerns a minority 'problem' group. Yet though Farson claims these teenagers are 'lost' and, later, 'sad', there is no evidence of this in the demeanour of the healthy, happy, and clearly fun-loving coffee-bar crowd that we soon see again on screen.

Images and voice-over combine to show us that we are in Brighton: shot of surf on the shingle, pan up to the Palace Pier, track round to bleak and empty streets with one or two cars as Farson introduces the Whisky-A-Go-Go coffee-bar and teens descend its basement area steps over Farson's summary introduction of his first interviewee: 'One of the main attractions is a coffee bar called the Whiskey-A-Go-Go and known as The Club by the teenage patrons, and one of the main characters who go there is a sort of beatnik, Royston Ellis, also a teenage poet.' Royston's voice-over declaims an execrable 'poem', in the background Adam Faith sings 'What do you want if you don't want money', and after a close-up of crowded dancers we're shown the fresh-faced Royston in a lengthy shot-reverse-shot interview with

---

58 This and subsequent dialogue quotes are transcribed from the programme as broadcast.

59 There were 45 r.p.m. vinyl records usually carrying one track on each side, and retailing at about 6s. 8d. (c.33p) thus well within the teenagers' budget.

Farson. Royston says some pretty extreme things about churchgoing (the pointlessness of it to today's youth), parents (their wilful refusal to recognize teenage autonomy), and sex (routine before marriage, few girls are virgins when they marry), and Farson picks these up in later interviews with other young people, few of whom concur with Royston's summary, despite Farson's often leading questions. But nevertheless, Royston's final remark 'we're just a bunch of kids out for kicks' gives the programme its title and Farson his starting point. Here an implicit connection is made between teenagers 'slightly lost in their newfound freedom' and the pursuit of pleasure in 'living for kicks', and Farson doggedly pursues this agenda as he tries to elicit just what their pleasure is from his not very articulate respondents. Behind his questions lies a moral point, that the pursuit of pleasure as an end in itself is likely to produce 'lost teenagers', hence there's a lack, one which society ignores at its peril and one for which the teenage subjects themselves are not to be held accountable. Though his 'conversations' with various teenagers touch on clothing styles, parental strictures, the recent cessation of National Service, he returns again and again to his preferred question of sexual practices. Over the lead in to the next section we have Farson to camera again, fading into a high-angle shot of a back street by a canal, some washing lines, some people standing by their front doors:

> I think it would be true to say that the teenage attitude to sex is rather different today. . . . Doctors say that sex before marriage can be a problem because of the guilt complex that can be aroused. However boys and girls do mature at a much earlier age than before the war. . . . One solution is the teenage marriage. But unfortunately it must be admitted that the divorce rate is much higher among those who married in their teens. . . . A blissful example is the couple who live near me at Limehouse Lock.

Farson asks his blissfully happy young neighbour—the 19-year-old Sylvia, mother of two—about the advantages and disadvantages of an early marriage. Though her husband is in shot, carrying the younger child, he is not interviewed and the impression remains that it is Sylvia who carries the responsibility for oversight of the marriage: she is happy to 'dance indoors with the babies' rather than in coffee bars with her peer group, she is glad that she will grow up with her children, but she would like to go out to work since her husband's wages are low and she could get 'things for the 'ouse'.

After the commercial break we return to the sound of rock and roll music and the exterior of a Tooting pub, The Castle, with its sign referencing the supposed tedium of watching television in the domestic environment: 'leave that gargoyle goggle box and get happy here'. There's a cut to the interior and a pan across two tables, the first largely men, the next women, and finally past the clean-cut rock band to mixed couples dancing. These teenagers seem slightly older than the previous group, but then this is a pub, these are licensed premises. In the sequence of the images is the very strong visual suggestion that this pub is a fruitful location in which to find a partner. Once again Farson interviews several teenagers, including the young male singer, focusing where possible on the signs of difference (the 'problem' announced in his opening words)—behaviour, relations with parents, dress styles—and on the question of whether or not teenagers are happy, given the great new freedoms they enjoy. Moving on to the fourth and final location we cut from a medium-shot of couples dancing in the crowded London pub to a tilt down the façade of a civic building, and a pan round yet more bleak and empty streets. Farson's voice-over resumes: 'A reasonable charge against teenagers is that they are too easily bored. This is why I went to Northampton, to find out what sort of entertainment teenagers can find in a town like this. I learnt that the one place where the rowdier element could go is a coffee bar started by the church.' In Northampton, it seems, there's a 'rowdy element' of twenty–thirty youths who have been banned from the town's only other teenage leisure facilities because of their disrupt-ive and (mildly) violent behaviour. The church coffee bar has been started in order to 'save' these youngsters by offering them, three nights a week, a place to meet, dance, and mix with their peers. As Farson tells us, nearly 400 teenagers regularly pack into the 'bleak rooms . . . pathetically anxious to have a good time' but they also spill outside, causing disruption and distress to local residents: they break windows (when Farson pressed the neighbours for details we learned that it was two), tear down drainpipes, make noise all evening, keep-ing local children awake (till the club closes at 10.15 p.m.). Here Farson focuses on local adults, probing their claims of violence and disruption for details of the offending behaviour, and suggesting mildly, in the process, that the complaints are unhelpfully exaggerated. He speaks to a man who runs the venue from which the 'rowdies' have been banned, and who declares the church experiment worthy but nevertheless a failure, and to two neighbours, a woman and a man, both of whom have made complaints about the church's club. Farson's is the voice of reason, and after this rather depressing ex-ample of representative adults he returns to his interviews with the teenagers themselves, pursuing this time the question of their pleas-ure, enquiring about their career ambitions, their holiday plans, their leisure pursuits. All their answers do suggest very limited imag-inations, but none of them seem sad, lost, or unhappy despite his steer to the audience to view them in these terms. Over Adam Faith singing 'Poor me', the image fades into a close-up of Lady Albemarle with whom Farson now discusses 'the film' and its implications for the future of British society.

Though, according to Farson's opening remarks, we have been looking at a minority of Britain's generally well-adjusted teenage population, these now seem to stand for the whole age group as Albemarle agrees about their typicality and wonders, with Farson, about the adult audience's likely response to the film's content: 'Well I was rather wondering how the audience was reacting to this particular programme. Whether they're feeling at the moment surprised, shocked and rather hostile to young people. I think that it's a very easy reaction that people have nowadays. I don't think it's a very constructive reaction'. She dismisses objections to teenage dress styles—'I think they're rather romantic, rather colourful, rather unconventional'— and broadens the discussion to reference the recent Crowther Report on secondary education, and the current population explosion in the age group: 'we've seen these young people but we've got to remember that by 1964 there's going to be a million more, the bulge is coming out of the schools, national service is ending'. She is a confident, self-assured woman speaking for herself and demonstrating a thoughtful and informed concern with the long-term implications of current concerns with teenage mores for the future health of British society, and refreshingly she locates problems in society itself rather than in the 'problem' teenage group. In what seems an almost mischievous counter to this reasonableness—or maybe just the broadcaster's endemic search for 'balance'—Farson includes a second 'coda' to the film in the form of an interview with the mother of one of his teenage respondents. She had written to Farson about her 'lazy good-for-nothing son' and consented to a filmed interview. In his gentle probing of her disquiet Farson elicits that the boy is the eldest, that she has younger children with a second husband, that her son 'hasn't worked for five weeks', and that she depends on his income to help support her large family. The contrast between these two women couldn't be greater: their class position, the understanding or lack of it, their articulacy. What is really interesting is that both of these 'post-film' interviews draw attention to the nature of television itself in their acknowledgement of the temporal gap between the process of making the film and the studio-based responses to it, despite the fact that for the 'audience at home' both must be consumed within the same time frame. So the reactions of the domestic audience to the film's content are anticipated, moderated, prefigured, almost, in these codas which are followed by Farson's voice-over closing summary as we see a montage of earlier club and bar scenes of dancing teenagers:

> 80% of all children leave school at 15 and one cannot deny that many of them go into boring and repetitive jobs and live in dull homes, but I'm sure that most of these troubles between parents and children are in fact timeless, have always existed, but are now out in the open. . . .

In the slice of the teenage world that I saw I was left with one disquieting thought. There seemed to be an element of sadness there, a wistful hankering after better things. All the new opportunities and all the new wealth have not necessarily brought contentment.

Despite Farson's attention to changing sexual mores, the programme has suggested a consideration of class and generation rather than of gender. At first glance the relative appearance of male and female youth seems pretty equal—many of the images are of dancing, crowds, couples. However, on closer examination I find that of Farson's teenage interviewees nine were girls, sixteen were boys, excluding the several couples to whom he also spoke. These interviewees are the ones offered the opportunity to speak, as it were, for their generation and once again there's a predominance of men, though it's doubtful that Farson was aware of this, or that it would have mattered to him if he was. His sample adult respondents included two men and one woman (in Northampton) and the two women delivering their 'post-filming' assessments whose differing class backgrounds made such a striking contrast in the closing codas. By far the strongest impression left by the film, its framing voice-over commentary, and its codas is one of class-based anxiety and real incomprehension about the medium-term social consequences of the economic power of this new group—affluent teenagers—for whom, as yet, there was no social provision outside a few coffee bars and youth clubs and the homes where, it seemed, none of them wanted to spend much time. As one teenage girl said

> GIRL: They don't approve of the boys I go out with, think I should stay in more.
>
> FARSON: And do what, at home?
>
> GIRL: Nothing—just row with them and watch television, I suppose.

There is absolutely no mention of race, clearly not yet conceived as an issue with relevance to the 'teenage problem' despite the recent 1959 Notting Hill riots: children of the most recent and largest wave of black immigrants who came to Britain during the 1950s would not yet have come through the education system whereas, as Lady Albemarle had observed, the post-war bulge—the baby boomers— was just about to leave school, thereby increasing the numbers of this problematic group. The question of nationality, of national identity, on the other hand is implicit throughout, since the anxiety felt by the adult generation, Farson's curiosity about the realities of 'living for kicks' are about what Britain will shortly become, what Britishness is, and how and in what ways it was changing. There's an elision between such questions and the apparently shocking moral standards of the generation under scrutiny in which longer standing anxieties about British decline and British cultural autonomy, it seems, are coming to the fore. Though Lady Albemarle noted, reasonably, that this generation should not be held accountable for the problems they inherited and therefore live with, nevertheless the hysterical response provoked by the programme recalls the perennial 'moral panics' whipped up by a sensationalist press. In this case the 'panic' was soon to be commandeered (in respect of television's contribution to the supposed national decline in moral standards) by Mary Whitehouse and her co-campaigners. Headlines such as 'Teenage Mob in Farson Coffee Bar Battle' (*Daily Mail*) and 'Sexpresso Kids In TV Probe' (*Daily Sketch*) alerted authorities in Brighton, the police raided the coffee bar looking for necking couples, and local councillors declared themselves appalled at the representation of 'Brighton's teenagers'. 'the programme . . . was pornographic and designed to show up beastliness and the worst in people who had not the slightest idea where their words would go, by a very skillful interviewer'.[60]

Here again, I think, is a problem with the perception of veracity and, more seriously, about *who* may speak. Counciller Thomsett, quoted above, displaced his own anxiety by suggesting that a 'skillful interviewer' had somehow creatively deployed the words of his unknowing respondents in order to further the ends of his perverse representation of Brighton's youth. What is even more interesting is how the controversy settled into the question of whether, and to what degree, the programme had been 'staged'. Here again the audience responded to difficult content with an interrogation displaced onto production practices: not *what* was shown and told but rather *how* it reached 'our screens' became the issue. Farson was accused of deploying actors (teenage respondents having been paid the mandatory 1-guinea fee for their participation) thus 'faking' the documentary element of the programme, and A-R felt sufficiently compromised by these (according to Farson) totally unfounded claims to be obliged to refuse offers from all over the world for sales of the programme.[61]

All my examples—*The Wednesday Magazine, Panorama, Marriage Today, Living for Kicks*—propose more or less explicitly to disseminate informative, sometimes entertaining, sometimes provocative assessments of contemporary British society and the changes it—hence also by definition the television audience—was currently facing. Here is an early example of what John Ellis later referred to

---

60 Quoted in Farson (1975: 66).

61 Ibid. 63–7.

as 'witnessing' and 'working through' social problems by means of their representation on broadcast television.[62] All the programmes, too, propose questions to their audiences to which they do not offer answers, though the characteristic 'steer' of the presenter does suggest the parameters within which answers may be sought, hence there's agenda-setting by omission, as it were. Most striking for my own exploration of the gender politics of the period, though, is the strikingly *in*equitable representation of women on screen, in any capacity, and the paucity of women in production, the BBC Women's Programmes Unit and subsequently the Family Programmes Department notwithstanding. Like the ubiquitous use of the male pronoun to include women—and thereby simultaneously in a sleight of hand to render them invisible—the overwhelming impression from the various programmes is of a masculine world. Opportunities are *for* men, problems are *in* women. Men speak for us, interview world leaders, interrogate politicians, describe the world to us. Women, if they speak, must have their discourse verified, but more usually they are uncontentiously offered in what was clearly understood, in the 1950s and 1960s, to be an appropriately disempowered subject position. In the few exceptions to this—Lady Albemarle in *Living for Kicks*, for example—her position of authority is validated by her class rather than her gender.

62 Ellis (2000).

4

Drama for the Mass Audience

Drama and Cultural Value   The developing understanding that there was a reciprocal relation between the content of broadcast television and national culture and identity was not, of course, confined to current affairs broadcasting. If anything, the broad field of drama was considered to be even more crucial in the equation, and within this field the most pressing question concerned the cultural 'value' of broadcast drama. It has become a trope of television scholarship to make an easy distinction between 'quality' and 'popular' drama where 'quality' references not only high production values, celebrated and accomplished writers and performers, but also an at least implicit acknowledgement of the canon against which theatrical drama was measured. Yet though it may be simple to distinguish between, say, Shakespeare on television and an imported sitcom such as *I Love Lucy* or *The Burns and Allen Show*, value judgements about their aesthetics, their fitness for purpose, or their use-value to audiences are not so clear. One of the more fascinating aspects of this fluid period of television history is, precisely, the various and gradual ways in which audiences, producers, and critics came to assess the relative merits of different forms of drama programming. One year on from the introduction of ITV, the *Daily Mirror* television critic Clifford Davis, in a review of Granada's *Play of the Week*, exhorted his readers to watch John Osborne's *Look Back in Anger*:

> Sydney Bernstein, Granada TV Chief, steps in where the BBC fears to tread with his presentation of John Osborne's intense, bitter play—Look Back in Anger . . . When an extract from the production was offered to the BBC last month they were prepared to screen only twenty minutes from the Royal Court Theatre. 'The rest of it wasn't suitable for family audiences' they said. Bold Mr Bernstein, however, has no such qualms. 'There has been no censorship', he tells me. This means the 'meat' of the play—strong language, face slappings and original, controversial theme— remains intact. . . . You may not like Look Back in Anger. It is brittle and brutal. You may be shocked—but that is what

playwright Osborne intends. But its arrival on the screen tonight is an important event in the history of TV drama. Don't miss it.[1]

In 1956 the self-conscious competition between the BBC and the ITV companies was at its height: it was a competition in which, initially, the BBC's output was assumed to be 'highbrow' in relation to the altogether more populist appeal of the companies, at that time still struggling to generate revenue and as yet financially insecure. The *Daily Mirror* was a tabloid paper addressing the same mass audience which the ITV companies needed to secure. Davis's review references both the BBC which 'fears to tread' mindful of its 'family audiences' and the ITV company, Granada, which delivered the play in its entirety—'[t]here has been no censorship'—thus implicitly trusting its audiences to make up their own minds, something the paternalist BBC was too timid too risk. Davis notes that Osborne 'intends' to shock and suggests, too, that the arrival on the television screen of this piece of contemporary writing, signalled as 'high culture' through its Royal Court provenance, is an 'important event in the history of television drama', one not to be missed. In this way Davis both forewarns and flatters his readers by assuming their critical engagement with controversial drama. The BBC's then Head of Drama, Michael Barry, later admitted that his assessment of what was appropriate to the domestic audience was 'out-dated':

> The first cannon [*sic*] in selecting what shall be produced is an assessment of professional competence in writing and performance. Parallel with this is the awareness of the home audience and the fact that there are extremes of thought and action, accepted in the theatre, that may not be acceptable in the family circle. This is both a moot and a changing factor. For example, I will admit to believing that the whole of the play 'Look Back In Anger' was unsuitable for home viewing. In the event it was transmitted by a commercial programme company and accepted by the viewers. I had no doubt of its professional competence nor of its significance in the modern theatre, but my assessment of the shock that its language and morality might cause to a television audience was out-dated.[2]

On the whole the attempt to interest the mass audience in 'high' culture is more familiar than its obverse, a defence of 'low' culture, though *I Love Lucy* was singled out more than once as being the epitome of 'true television'—a rather two-edged remark in the defensive mood of the mid-1950s. By the mid-1960s, programmes such as

1 *Daily Mirror*, 28 Nov. 1956, p. 16.

2 WAC T16/62/2, 21 Dec. 1957.

Z-Cars, The Avengers, and single plays such as *Cathy Come Home* were being discussed and evaluated as much for their inherent *televisuality* and the contemporary relevance of their content as for their conformity or otherwise to any theatrical canon. Just as in the criticism of the time so, too, in subsequent scholarship far more attention has been paid to 'quality' drama, hence my focus in this chapter and the next on popular drama and the various ways in which this was developed in the experimental and expansionist context of this formative decade.

Drama at the BBC

By the autumn of 1955 the BBC had over ten years' experience in drama production and, according to Jason Jacobs's excellent study, had streamlined their production practices and their organizational base. He writes:

> The changes in drama planning, organisation and production completed during this time [1947–50]—the script library, a more standardised drama schedule, new studios and equipment, telerecording—were to come to fruition and full use during the early 1950s. It was this period which saw the consolidation of a drama standard, and the routinisation of work practices, which would only face restructuring again when the competition arrived in the form of ITV in 1955.[3]

The BBC Drama Department were able to look back on their achievements and to consider what further changes might be necessary in order to meet the threat of competition from ITV for 'their' audience. Various summary papers document this process of taking stock, a major anxiety being the perceived need to recruit and train writers to fill the apparently ever-expanding need for programme content. Amongst many issues was the question of where the line should be drawn between drama and light entertainment. Much of the material perceived as 'popular', addressed to the new mass audience able to choose between two channels, was considered the purview of Light Entertainment, yet the Drama Department was also concerned with exploring new dramatic forms appropriate both to the medium and to its audiences, which they wished to build. Cecil McGivern, Controller of Programmes, wrote in 1953 to the Heads of Television Drama and of Light Entertainment as follows:

> an occasional but regular farce . . . would be a very useful programme ingredient. At present the ingredient is almost completely missing.

3 Jacobs (2000: 108).

a) should Drama or LE be responsible for it?
b) and should it be in a theatre or in a studio?
I have my own views.
a) Drama—but Drama doesn't condescend to notice it.
b) In a theatre.
May I have your views, please.[4]

McGivern also had his eye on generic developments, writing again in March about thrillers, which 'are legitimate television fare in regulated quantities' and 'are *very* popular . . . and at present they are sporadic and too few'.[5] A couple of years later the new Controller of Programmes, Kenneth Adam, complained in detail about what he saw as the inappropriate introduction of 'incidents of violence and terror' to *The Grove Family* and assuming, interestingly, that the 'error' was a consequence of slack administration:

> a rather bad mistake was made by suddenly introducing into the last episode of The Grove Family incidents of violence and terror which in my view are quite foreign to the romantic atmosphere of a soap opera . . .
>
> I have asked for a description of the administrative set-up behind The Groves . . . all this strikes me as very hand-to-mouth compared with the careful consultations which took place over the policy of The Archers in my day when the storyline was discussed and accepted by Chief Assistant Light Programmes, Head of Midland Regional Programmes, and by Godfrey Basely as well as the producer concerned. Something of this sort, I am sure, ought to take place in the case of any soap opera where you engage the attention of listeners regularly, though it need not be so elaborate in the case of a weekly serial.[6]

These examples suggest both impatience with and uncertainty about the proper management of what was gradually being recognized as the major element in BBC Drama output—that is to say generically specific and widely accessible drama.

Though the question of new writing and new writers continued to exercise managers until well into the 1960s, it was recognized, too, that the scale of popular drama production offered opportunities for writers to 'cut their teeth' as it were, by contributing to established series. This attention to management structures and the consequent checks and balances that ought to ensure appropriate content indicates an acute awareness in the upper echelons of BBC management

4 WAC T16/62/1, 16 Feb. 1953.

5 WAC T16/62/1, 2 Mar. 1953.

6 WAC T16/137/3.

of the importance of getting popular drama output right in order to secure audiences. More interesting, however, is the detailed attention accorded by both producers and audiences to the visual and technical detail of broadcast drama: here is the search for the televisual which characterizes the period, and consideration of its implications for the development of specifically televisual dramatic forms.

Developing the Televisual

Part of television's appeal to its early audiences was in its instantaneity, and while this was of more consequence in the context of current affairs, talk programmes, and the revered Outside Broadcasts, it also figured in the live transmission of one-off dramas. In the early 1950s, as we have seen, television plays were broadcast live from the studio, there was no post-production, and repeat broadcasts entailed repeat performances. Of greater concern, however, to writers and producers than the increasingly onerous necessity for a single live performance was the search for what we might now term 'televisual specificity'; that is to say, for subjects, forms, and performance styles particular to the new medium. Instructions to writers, critical response, and audience feedback all make reference, in their differing ways, to this aspect of production strategy. A 1960 memo from the BBC's central Script Department suggested to potential writers for television that 'two of the medium's happiest assets are the camera's mobility and its inquisitiveness' and cautioned further that, 'although you may have an audience of many millions, it is not (as in the theatre or cinema) a mass audience. It is largely composed of individuals sitting in their own homes'.[7] The combination of a mobile 'inquisitive' camera and the domestic context for viewing the (very) small screen tended to privilege the medium-shot and particularly the close-up which, on the nine-to-fourteen inch screens typical at the time, meant that the face seen on screen was roughly the same size as those of the domestic viewers themselves. This, combined with their close proximity to the screen, heightened the suggestion that actors were *present* with the audience for whom they performed.

It's worth recalling Raymond Williams's useful concept of television's *flow*[8] here, and to bear in mind that though it was in the interests of producers, schedulers, and audiences to respect generic differentiation between and within programming areas, it was also the case that audiences tended, on the whole, to watch television per se rather than specific programmes. Here the direct address, in close-up, of the news presenter, the light entertainment host, or the

---

7 WAC T16/62/3, 1 Apr. 1960.

8 Williams (1990 (1st pub. 1974)).

current affairs interviewee intentionally bound the viewer into a supposedly intimate relation with the on-screen face. The habit of viewing thus engendered was also brought to bear in viewing drama and deployed, often quite consciously, in binding the viewer into the fiction offered. A particularly clear example is the case of *Dixon of Dock Green* where the preamble to the weekly show had Jack Warner, in costume as PC Dixon, standing outside the Dock Green police station talking directly to the viewer, often about the broader implications of the previous episode. The scene then cut to PC Dixon inside the police station, and the fictional story commenced—though now the characters did not look directly at the camera nor address viewers overtly. But it is true to say that viewers' engagement with the fictional Dixon was achieved through this clever deployment of cross-generic techniques, through the 'borrowing' of news/current affairs performance styles in the service of establishing the diegesis.[9] There were pitfalls, though, and injudicious or excessive use of the close-up could work against the desired viewer engagement, as Peter Black complained in a 1956 *Daily Mail* review:

> David Boisseau's production [Act of Madness, adapted from John Wiles's stage play] miscalculated the difference between the effect of words spoken into a theatre auditorium and into a TV screen. The former can afford a shout; the latter needs an intimate talk, or a production that suggests it. . . . Unfortunately Mr B kept his cast in close-up; the combination of big faces and unnatural dialogue was fatal. As every viewer knows, a TV close-up is valuable only when it shows the character's thoughts[10]

This aspect of the performance style appropriate to television had been quickly recognized by actors themselves as a 1939 interview with Sybil Thorndyke indicates:

> It's like the kind of acting you do in your own sitting room when you're working on a part, and that's always the nicest kind. You think and breathe things and they come over[11]

Thorndyke's comments refer to her experience in performing 'quality' drama in the earliest years, but they are nevertheless influential in producing the received wisdom about what was 'appropriate' in the 1950s exploration of the new medium's potential.

At the other end of the spectrum from the intimate, thinking, and breathing close-up is the distanced spectacle. Though the spectacular was certainly appreciated and had its place in television's output—for

---

9 The fictional world proposed through the narrative.

10 *Daily Mail*, 8 Nov. 1956, p. 11.

11 Goldie, cited in Jacobs (2000: 118).

example in the theatrical *Sunday Night at the London Palladium* and similarly lavish light entertainment productions, or in the Outside Broadcast event, of which the most famous was the 1953 Coronation—it was often regarded with suspicion in drama. James Thomas, reviewing the BBC's *Clive of India* for the *News Chronicle*, for example, wrote that 'to cram the crowded canvas of Clive of India onto the TV screen in 100 minutes turned out to be beyond the ingenuity even of the BBC's resourceful master of the dramatic, Rudolph Cartier'.[12] Cartier had been responsible, amongst other productions, for the celebrated 1953 six-part series *Quatermass* in which he did manage successfully to deploy the spectacular, but in a very careful juxtaposition with the intimate so that viewers were enabled always to read the one in relation to the other. The writer Nigel Kneale had explicitly wished to use the *Quatermass* series to explore television's dramatic potential and the innovative use of the small screen that he and Cartier developed electrified audiences and paved the way for later experiment, such as their 1954 production of Orwell's *Nineteen Eighty-Four*. The characteristic model, however, remained the small-scale domestic drama, and it is this which most certainly dominated the home-produced popular product, even in those series, like *Dixon* or ITV's *Emergency Ward 10*, not primarily located in a domestic setting. The small scale of the screen, the relative intimacy of the viewing context, and the proposed contiguity between performer and spectator all encouraged character-based drama. For example Bernard Levin, reviewing Ted Willis's *The Young and the Guilty*, noted appreciatively that 'the total effect is of the kind for which television was invented: one which gives the main weight to character rather than situation'.[13]

With the benefit of hindsight it is interesting to note that this perceived requirement for character-based, domestic, and small-scale drama was accommodated within the 'popular' end of the spectrum while those responsible for 'quality' output became increasingly confident to innovate in both form and content. What is also discernible in the memos, reviews, and viewer reports from the period is a continuing attempt to *measure* television drama in relation to the older forms on which it drew; that is to say, radio, live theatre, and the cinema. The acknowledgement of television's debt to, and difference from, these media forms a constant refrain in the discursive climate of the period. Direct address to camera, unthinkable in classical narrative cinema because it destroys the basic illusion necessary to the fiction's construction, becomes a familiar device of televisual performance. Television in the mid-1950s also allowed the continuous

12 *News Chronicle*, 31 Dec. 1956, p. 3.

13 *Manchester Guardian*, 8 Dec. 1956, p. 5.

performance which actors enjoy in live theatre but were denied in cinema's different production regime, as Sybil Thorndyke had noted:

> Television is going to give us an entirely new kind of acting. Different from stage acting because the nearness of the camera makes it more intimate. But even more different from film acting because the acting is continuous and the emotional pattern of the character is decided by the actor as he acts and not by the director on the floor or by the cutter in the cutting room.[14]

Intimate, nuanced, and, in live performances, *continuous* performance of character—such as that outlined by Thorndyke—becomes the hallmark of successful television drama.

Radio, particularly in its light entertainment and comedy genres, offered a rich source for popular television output in Britain as in the USA, and not only formats but also performers made the transition. Jack Warner was still performing in Radio's *Meet the Huggetts* when he signed his contract for *Dixon of Dock Green*; *Life with the Lyons* moved wholesale from radio to television, appearing for a substantial part of the 1950s in both media; the imported *Burns and Allen Show* had begun on radio as had many other US programmes.[15] A *News Chronicle* review of the situation comedy *Whack-O* complimented both scriptwriters and performer for their successful transition:

> Into the banality of TV comedy, Messrs. Muir and Norden have at last thrust the reluctant bulk of Jimmy Edwards . . .
> Edwards' noisy, angry style has been distilled by Muir and Norden into the best situation comedy on any channel at the moment. The veteran radio script team has resisted the temptation to join the current swim of semi-surrealist Goon humour. They have settled down brilliantly to the job of translating the racy gag-for-gag style of 'Take it from Here' into visual terms[16]

Familiarity, domesticity, character-driven and intimate plots: all these are of course hallmarks of the situation comedy genre which came to dominate the schedules of the later 1950s and early 1960s. Typically these would entail a very limited number of sets and the spatial relation of viewers to performers certainly referenced, if it did not entirely duplicate, the familiar theatrical proscenium arch. The quasi-theatrical setting for many of the popular early sitcoms— particularly the US imports such as *I Love Lucy* and *The Burns and Allen Show*—offered undemanding though nonetheless pleasurable

---

14 Goldie, cited in Jacobs (2000: 118).

15 Thumim (2002).

16 *News Chronicle*, 26 Oct. 1956, p. 6.

entertainment to the new mass audience and relatively low production costs, a winning combination as Bernard Delfont noted in a *TV Times* feature: 'The theatre and television will continue to go hand in hand . . . Well I think shows like I Love Lucy are true television. We want to think up shows with a British background, not of the same kind as I Love Lucy but of the same kind of television.'[17]

Sitcoms, including the perenially popular *I Love Lucy*, figured large amongst the American product imported by both the BBC and the companies to fill the expanding transmission hours in the later 1950s. Despite a constant minority bewailing what they saw as the excessive presence of low-grade material on British screens, such programming did find ready and appreciative viewers, generally amongst the early evening 'family' audience. Westerns and gangster series also found eager audiences. In these shows, though the focus on character development across successive episodes remained central to the drama, the settings in which action occurred were by no means theatrical ones. Here television's other celebrated ability—to bring images of exotic locations into the domestic viewing space—was central to viewers' enjoyment, as many of the BBC's audience research reports testify. Despite the small screen size Westerns and gangster series offered spectacular action in equally spectacular locations, achievable in the American production context because of the greater use of film and as a consequence of the reorganization of many Hollywood studios during the 1950s to generate product for television.[18] Westerns, of course, remained and still remain a specifically American genre but the crime and gangster series for which, as McGivern had noted early in the 1950s, there was always a ready audience, could be produced at home. The celebrated series *Z-Cars* made ample use of location filming where *Dixon of Dock Green* had depended more heavily on studio-based performance. It is interesting to speculate that, as the 1950s gave way to the 1960s, and developing technologies permitted new production strategies in the UK, *location* began to assume greater significance and the implicit 'proscenium arch' became less evident as the organizing principle for the *mise-en-scène* in the majority of popular drama series. The emergence of television versions of radio's soap operas where the action unfolds in a combination of studio sets and limited locations—that is to say, the 'studio' is expanded to include, as in *Coronation Street*, not just a series of interior spaces but also the linking exterior spaces which suggest a *locale* rather than a *stage*—is a specifically televisual development. It's worth noting, too, that in radio soaps there was never any need to limit action to interior spaces and that characters

17 *TV Times*, 13 Apr. 1956, p. 4.

18 Anderson (1994).

could move freely within the implied *locale*—as in the case of the exceptionally long-running rural soap *The Archers*.

In considering the emergence of new dramatic forms specific to television the question of genre, unsurprisingly, assumes great significance. Within the broad field of popular drama and comedy series it was relatively uncontentious: producers and viewers quickly arriving at a consensus whereby broad differentiations such as comedy, Western, gangster, crime/police were functional descriptors of programme content and address. But in other fields, such as 'quality' drama and documentary, the question of genre was both more problematic and more fluid as conflicting assessments of particular programmes indicated. Within the scheduled slots for 'quality' drama, for instance, there was a constant struggle over the appropriate proportions of new writing, adaptations from the classics, costume-based historical drama, and so on. Schedulers wanted to be able to offer a sufficiently predictable experience to attract viewers while producers wanted the opportunity to explore new form and content. Reviewers felt free to make comparisons right across the range of television's output, on occasion considering the effectiveness of dramatic production in relation to the power of news and current affairs and vice versa, as this 1954 *New Statesman* review indicates: 'if only we had the capacity to give the NATO deliberations in Paris the kind of actuality with which the BBC producers endowed their play last Sunday!'[19] The play in question was the 12 December 1954 Kneale/Cartier production of Orwell's *Nineteen Eighty-Four* and the broadsheet critics were fulsome in their praise. *The Times*, for example, recognized the production as a seminal moment not just for television drama but for television as a whole: 'If anything had been needed to underline the tremendous possibilities of television the reactions of the last few days have provided it.'[20] However, as Jacobs notes in his detailed study of the production,[21] the viewers were not so happy—in fact the majority of letters to the BBC regarding the production were hostile. He suggests,

> If the Coronation proved that television had access to a mass national audience, *Nineteen Eighty-Four* demonstrated that television could also frighten and perhaps harm that audience . . .
> Cartier reports that he received death threats, and the BBC had to hire bodyguards to protect him. Perhaps this indicates that the shift from less 'cosy' drama to that which pulled no punches in its representation of intense distress and discomfort,

19 *New Statesman*, 18 Dec. 1954.

20 *The Times*, 16 Dec. 1954.

21 Jacobs (2000: 139–55).

had ramifications beyond the internal debate about technical etiquette: the audience could no longer trust the intimate screen.[22]

A little over ten years later the Peter Watkins film *The War Game* was considered by the BBC who had commissioned it to be so disturbing that they refused transmission altogether.[23] In these two examples lies the conundrum facing broadcasters; that is to say, innnovations in both form and content had to carry the audience with them, or, in other words, the implicit 'contract' between producers and viewers which is at the heart of generic classifications must be respected.

The generic 'seepage' between drama and documentary was equally troublesome as the very mixed responses to a 1956 document- ary about prostitution, *Without Love*, indicated. In this case, inter- estingly, reviewers were divided as to whether drama *or* documentary were the appropriate genres within which to tackle such 'difficult' subject matter. L. Marsland Garner, writing in the *Daily Telegraph*, clearly found the deployment of actors in a 'fictional reconstruction', albeit one made in the service of documentary exploration, to reduce the impact of the documentary:

> As a lover of the informative documentary, I was sorry to see, in this particular programme, some confirmation of my belief that drama is steadily ousting fact.[24]

However, James Thomas in the *News Chronicle* appeared to think that drama was a more appropriate generic vehicle for 'putting over hard, unpleasant facts':

> this documentary, for what it was worth, was created with care and conviction and cast with a touch of brilliance.
> But just what *was* it worth? Was it even a documentary?
> It was a play, well done. A documentary would have marched more fearlessly towards the truth. It is becoming clear that the documentary play should now be reserved only for non-controversial subjects. It has neither the range nor the striking power for putting over hard, unpleasant facts[25]

This tension about genre informed much of the commissioning environment throughout the 1950s during which time, as we have seen, the so-called mass audience was being built in a competitive context. Jacobs, writing about the early years of the BBC's quality drama output, suggests in conclusion that 'after 1955 television

---

22 Ibid. 155.

23 It found an audience at private or 'club' cinema screenings, e.g. at the NFT, but was not broadcast until 1985.

24 *Daily Telegraph*, 17 Dec. 1956, p. 8.

25 *News Chronicle*, 21 Dec. 1956, p. 6.

drama was to develop its styles and interests not towards film modes, but instead towards politics, documentary and current affairs . . . In this way the visualization of 'getting close' was part of a public look, of a looking at the world rather than the stage.'[26] Though this cross-generic impetus is most evident in quality drama and in the organization of news and current affairs which, in their turn, 'borrowed' many performance modes from both drama and light entertainment—as, for example, did the current affairs magazine programme *Tonight* and, later, the short-lived and contentious satirical programme *That Was The Week That Was*—it is also to be found in the rather slower evolution of popular drama in the period.

Fitness for Screen and Audience

The Reithian imperative to 'inform and educate' while also 'entertaining' the audience was the guiding principle behind the BBC's operations up to, and after, 1955. A large part of the anxiety expressed both within and outside the BBC regarding the commercial channel's output turned, essentially, on the assumption that a profit-driven system could not—by definition—be trusted to subscribe to this view of television's function. The regulatory functions of the IBA contained an implicit endorsement of Reithian principles and the 1962 Pilkington Report's condemnation of Independent Television rested largely on their assertion that ITV had failed sufficiently to accommodate the key categories of information and education with their output of entertainment. But just what did these regulatory bodies— the IBA and the BBC's Governors—expect from the new mass medium? Scratching the surface of contemporary discourse reveals a powerful mix of paternalism—that is to say, that one group 'knows what is best' for another group—with adherence to the canons of high art against which, at that time, the artefacts of popular culture must by definition be found wanting. Another way of putting this would be to say that a form of cultural snobbery dictated that the majority of popular television programming, since it was not 'art', was inherently damaging to its audiences and therefore could be said neither to inform nor to educate while it entertained. A further dimension to this cultural anxiety was the imbrication of American values with the British perception of popular culture, which in turn tied in with post-war resentment of increasing American global power and influence. Given that pre-war and immediately post-war audiences for the BBC's single channel television operation were the largely middle-class viewers who could afford the currently high cost of receivers and lived within reach of a transmitter, this emphasis on

26 Jacobs (2000: 160).

dominant standards of high culture is unsurprising. Given also the class-based nature of British society at that time—the famous meritocratic ideal of the 1950s notwithstanding—it is no more surprising that disquiet about the cultural 'value' of post-1955 broadcasting should often be couched in terms which deplored the lack of educative and/or informative material, while in fact what is really being expressed is a class-based resentment about the expansion of the audience to include the mass population—including, therefore, the 'lower' classes—whose (different) interests were henceforward also to be served by the broadcasting systems. Thinly veiled disapproval of different (gendered) interests also surfaces, even in the writings of female critics such as Mary Crozier in the *Manchester Guardian*, reviewing Elaine Morgan's play 'You're a Long Time Dead': 'this playwright's work is always worth watching, though often it is about women's magazine level . . . Her tendency is to make the drama rather too strong and sweet'.[27] A similar cultural snobbery informed some responses to the very proximity of high art with the world of commerce:

> 'they' on the other channel were doing, of all things, 'The Aspern Papers' . . . what chiefly excited my imagination was trying to think of the appalled grasping for words which the Master would have executed to try to express his amazement at the climactic advertisements! If there is one place in the world where you do not expect to meet exhortations about gums and carburettors it is Henry James' Venice!'[28]

Here 'exhortations', 'gums', and 'carburettors' are synonymous with the messy, profit-driven world of the mass audience while 'Henry James' and 'Venice' stand for the values of high art: it is the juxtaposition of the two which this reviewer found inappropriate, not to say contradictory. Such anxiety and disquiet manifested itself much more strongly with reference to drama and light entertainment output than it did with responses to news and current affairs, where, as we have seen, different aspects of television's possibilities were acknowledged.

In line with the idea that television should inform and educate, hence implicitly should seek to raise the cultural awareness and standards of its audience, those engaged with production felt some responsibility for stimulating contemporary art and culture. This sense of responsibility manifested itself both in the search for new, specifically televisual form, as in the celebrated collaborations of Kneale and Cartier, and in the broader and continuing search for

27 *Manchester Guardian*, 18 July 1960, p. 5.

28 *The Listener*, 3 Nov. 1955, p. 761.

'new writing'. In the memos circulating between practitioners and managers at the BBC and no doubt also in the companies—certainly at Granada—there is a constant tension between the practitioners' desire to experiment, to break new ground, and the managers' desire to ensure satisfied audiences, achieve high ratings, and keep the budgets balanced. Jacobs suggests that this had been the case since the early 1950s: 'The appetite for a television drama that would exploit its visual mobility and transcend the drawing room was evident in the BBC in the early 1950s, but it was to meet with critical and managerial resistance.'[29] Much of this resistance was centred on discussion of the single play which, in the later 1950s and early 1960s was clearly recognized as the locus of cultural value—potentially if not always actually. Philip Mackie of Granada's Drama Department wrote to Sidney Bernstein on this point in 1962:

> the 60-minute play has established itself as a form admirably suited to TV.
>
>   . . . play-slots on British TV have established themselves as just about the only openings for original creative writing. (Series are hack-work, good or bad as the case may be . . .)
>
>   TV must always experiment, or it will move in ever-decreasing circles till it disappears into its own rut. A series can't experiment: the investment is too large. A play can: the investment is small . . .
>
>   The BBC's drama laurels have faded, and we've rather forgotten Armchair Theatre now . . .
>
>   . . . time we had a revolution, don't you think?[30]

Mackie's point about the relative investment in series or single plays, however, did not stand the test of time any more than did his assumption that series must inevitably be 'hack-work'. One of the reasons for the gradual disappearance, from the late 1960s onwards, of the routine and regular appearance of the single play was the difficulty in attracting and maintaining audiences for a scheduling slot that lacked the narrative continuity characteristic of series drama. The idea that audiences must be 'built' was well recognized and the exceptional difficulty of doing this for the single play acknowledged, as MacMurraugh-Kavanagh demonstrates in her provocative study of the BBC's *Wednesday Play* slot.[31] Sidney Newman's reorganization of the BBC's Drama Department, following his arrival there in 1963, gave equal weight to the series, serial, and the single play. The minutes of what seems to have been a particularly acrimonious meeting of the BBC's Drama Department in 1964, attempting to plan the next year's

---

29 Jacobs (2000: 125).

30 Granada Archive Box 1017, 26 Mar. 1962.

31 MacMurraugh-Kavanagh (1997a).

scheduled output, recognized that the necessary address to the whole demographic was being better achieved in series/serials than in the single play: 'there were not enough programmes with a) young people's appeal, b) enough appeal to women. Only serials covered this point.'[32]

The encouragement of new writers and new writing was one reference point by which producers of television drama measured their worth, and the other was television's relation to live theatre. This had been troublesome during most of the 1950s as the regular presence of (quality) drama on television was thought to present a threat to the live theatre's ability to attract audiences—though the contrary argument that television *engendered* an appetite for drama which would stimulate theatre attendance was also frequently made. An Arts Council report on the relation between the two assumed television's responsibility to ensure the latter: 'if and when these problems are resolved, the massed forces of television might well be persuaded to recognise their obligations to the living theatre and to accept some responsibility for its survival'.[33] Jacobs, ignoring television's possible usurpal of live theatre, suggests rather optimistically that 'the new dominant aesthetic for television drama, which continued into the 1960s, was that it offered an authentic national theatre, for and about working class concerns, majority concerns—a far cry from the bourgeois drawing room, the intimate "cosy" sets'.[34] Though he refers here to the later 1950s 'quality' drama output, it remains a moot point whether 'majority concerns' were really addressed in quality drama or whether, as seems highly likely, the appetite for intimacy, for cosy sets and drawing rooms was satisfied in the staple forms of popular drama: in sitcoms, comedy shows, and, later, in the ubiquitous soaps. The drawing rooms may no longer always have been bourgeois ones but the sets were just as cosy. The point that emerges from the juxtaposition of these two references to television and live theatre is that both assume such a relation does, and should, inform critical responses to television's drama output. The Arts Council expects television to 'recognise its obligation' to live drama and Jacobs, eschewing altogether the question of 'the live', claims that by the 1960s television offered an 'authentic national theatre'. The notion of 'majority concerns' doesn't in itself acknowledge the various forms through which such concerns might be addressed. Clifford Davis's *Daily Mirror* review of Granada's production of Osborne's *Look Back in Anger* notwithstanding, the difference between the production of 'classic' writing and the production of new, often 'difficult' writing

32 WAC T16/62/3, 17 July 1964.

33 WAC T16/62/2.

34 Jacobs (2000: 137).

is elided in such a formulation. The fact that a play concerns itself with the 'working class' doesn't *of itself* guarantee a working-class audience. In contrast, many of those actually writing or directing for television were interested in finding forms that, precisely, did *not* depend for their value on association with live theatre and could, indeed, attract a mass audience.

Running alongside these concerns about stimulating cultural production by finding and nurturing new writers, and with developing genuinely televisual forms which did not depend on a theatrical provenance for their value, was a concern with generic balance. The dominant strategy deployed by both the BBC and the companies in order to attract, build, and maintain audiences was the regular weekly 'slot' in which a 'television play' could be reliably anticipated. These included, for example, *Play of the Week* (prod. A-R, Granada; transmitted on ITV, 1956–61) and *Television Playhouse* (prod. A-R, Anglia, and Granada; transmitted on ITV, 1956–61), *Sunday Night Theatre* (BBC, 1955–9), a series of 'prestigious plays' with largely theatrical and/or literary provenance, *The Sunday Play* (BBC, 1963) and *Sunday Night Play* (BBC, 1960–3) offering 'new writing especially for television', *Festival* (BBC, 1963–4) 'dramatic plays to entertain the intelligent viewer', and *First Night* (BBC, 1963–4) 'written expressly for television with the emphasis on action and conflict'. *Armchair Theatre* (ABC, 1956–69), according to Vahimagi, 'represented ITV's golden age of writing and production' and *The Wednesday Play* (BBC, 1964–70) 'became a byword for challenging, left-of-centre drama'.[35] In designing and planning these slots managers were also acutely aware of the need for 'balance'—a term which, above all others, seems to characterize the managerial approach to all television genres as well as to the mix of content within them. In the field of drama, though, unlike its usage in current affairs, the term indicates *generic* as well as *political* balance. Whereas in cinema generic categorization is a relatively straightforward affair achieved in the consensus of interests operating between producers, exhibitors, and audiences to differentiate product, in television it is a rather more slippery term. Within the field of popular drama generic terms such as sitcom, crime, Western, and so on function more or less effectively but, almost by definition, the field of 'quality' drama was—and perhaps still is—more troublesome.

The various television drama departments attempted to vary the diet, as it were, by offering a mix of classic plays, literary adaptations, and new writing and further to distinguish between these by the use of such descriptors as costume, realist, period, contemporary, social,

---

and so on. There was an assumption that different sectors of the audience would display their allegiance to some but not all of these, and thus that the holy grail of 'balance' was to be achieved by judicious alternation in the interests of satisfying all sectors of the potential audience. But this worked against the principle of building audience loyalty to a particular scheduling slot by offering relatively predictable material within it. The BBC's David Whitaker, in a 1962 paper surveying the previous eighteen months' output in the *Sunday Night Play* slot argued that 'There is a strong case for running a series of plays of a similar nature (sophisticated comedy, detective fiction etcetera) but for a Sunday Evening a general mixture eventually takes precedent.'[36]

An early 1960s Granada paper lists one-act plays from 'classic' writers such as O'Casey, Galsworthy, Shaw, and Pirandello in an evident search for appropriate titles, concluding with a note that 'The One Act Theatre seems to have grown up very recently and while appreciating that you don't want to go too modern, I would anticipate that there is a far richer source of material from—say—Ionesco onwards.'[37] The paper also noted that 'the few longer one-act plays are difficult and abstract' and that 'many of the better plays have already been done', suggesting that the impetus towards new writing was at least in part driven by the dearth of existing plays short enough to 'work' on television, where the generally preferred length was sixty minutes, and endorsing an implicit desire for novelty in the relentless march of the weekly slot. A 1960 paper from A-R's Head of Drama, Peter Willes, addressed to 'script-writers and/or their agents' laid out in some detail A-R's requirements in terms of both quantity and content:

> A-R is looking for 26 60-minute and 18 90-minute scripts each year; however, since there is practically no source for 60-minute scripts other than the original television script, whereas a certain proportion of 90-minute scripts will always be adapted stage plays and novels, in reality there is at least *twice* the demand for 60's than there is for 90's . . .
>
> *We want:*
> More variety of settings. More scripts which concentrate on people's working lives as opposed to their home lives. One living-room or kitchen looks very like another . . . the script which does not take place in the living-room, the office and the pub but in the shop, the factory or the fair-ground, has an immediate pull over its rivals.

36 WAC T16/62/3, July 1962.

37 Granada Archive Box 0830, file: Mrs Head.

More variety of plots. . . . there must be, surely, any number of domestic and workaday conflicts and small dramas which sex neither causes nor solves,—and we would like a change of diet, please.

More action and stronger stories. . . . too many scripts would make practically the same impact if they were not seen at all but only heard. By action, I do not mean just fights and running about, I mean scripts which 'move' and tell a story visually—not merely in words.

We do not want:

Routine thrillers, farcical comedies or fantasies. The number of thriller serials and series, both live and on film, make us very choosey indeed about thrillers for our normal drama programmes, despite the fact that they are eternally popular. Similarly, the technical difficulties of broad or farcical comedy, and the un-popularity of fantasy, makes these types of entertainment less likely to be accepted than romance, sophisticated comedy, or straight drama.[38]

These exemplary papers illustrate the kind of attention what we would now call 'commissioning editors' were giving to soliciting the kind of writing they felt appropriate to their respective 'quality' drama slots, and indicate also their wish to differentiate their output from what they saw as the more predictable and mundane output of serials, series, and popular drama generally. While they were focused on this tricky balance between the predictable (which secured audiences) and the novel (the hallmark of orginality, and thus, potentially of 'art') they also emphasized the importance of the *visual* component of televisual drama: writers must conceive their stories through images just as much as through words, while also conforming to requirements of length and interval, writing parts appropriate to 'star' performers, and acknowledging the technical implications for production of their stories. But above all the question of *suitability* for the television screen and for the domestic audience exercised critics, managers, and producers. Typically reviews of television drama in the broadsheet and tabloid press returned again and again to this issue, indicating a consensual curiosity about just how the new medium might best be exploited. Granada's 1956 *Play of the Week* production *Shooting Star* about professional football elicited conflicting responses, implicitly referencing this question of suitability. Peter Black, for The *Daily Mail* wrote:

Granada TV last night brought off the kind of success that all television badly needs and rarely achieves—the play that succeeds

---

38 WAC T16/62/3, 28 Oct. 1960.

on more than one level, as an entertainment and as a tart
social comment. . . . this play showed what can be found
when dramatists examine the native British scene for what it is
worth[39]

Bernard Levin, on the other hand, saw it differently in his *Manchester
Guardian* review:

in intention it was worthy enough; but the viewer's road back to
the BBC is paved with worthy intentions . . . it was dull.
    It was that grim thing a play with a social conscience but on a
trivial theme . . . To be good television a play does not have to
be a masterpiece. Sixpennyworth of good writing and a dash of
conviction will work wonders.[40]

When Levin did find what he recognized as good writing he was
fulsome in his praise, though not without an almost obligatory dig at
Independent Television per se, and, as Black in the *Daily Mail* did
with respect to *Shooting Star*, he applauded the contemporary subject
matter of Ted Willis's *The Young and the Guilty* which, he wrote, was

first rate television . . . which enhanced, instead of (like so much
independent television) degrading the human dignity of his
characters. Integrity and box office: these two have been strange
bedfellows indeed on independent television . . . Mr Willis'
dramatic restraint, in fact, is truly remarkable: so much so that
I am sure he will be accused, in some quarters, of being dull . . .
there is nothing dull about real life, properly observed, and it is
real life that Mr Willis is portraying[41]

The irony evident, with hindsight, in much of the contemporary
discussion about drama production is that, though producers and
critics alike were at pains to differentiate between the prestigious
goals of the single play and the apparently 'trivial' achievements of
popular drama, their demands for appropriate material for television
received in the domestic context were in fact being met in much of the
broadcast output of popular series, serials, and, latterly, soaps; that is
to say, again, character-based drama in a variety of domestic and
work-based settings with plots taken from the 'small dramas' of
everyday life. An occasional critic touched, tangentially, on this
insight; for example, Peter Black's *Daily Mail* review of a production
of Ibsen's *Pillars of Society*: 'the best television drama is that which
poses problems of decision in a small, recognisable society; and what

39 *Daily Mail*, 1 Nov. 1956, p. 9.
40 *Manchester Guardian*, 3 Nov. 1956, p. 5.
41 *Manchester Guardian*, 8 Dec. 1956, p. 5.

is the Berwick family but the Grove Family turned inside out with all the nastiness coming through'.[42] Black's acute observation begins to muddy the boundaries between high and low culture, as did also the increasingly significant production of serial drama in various forms—Ted Willis's *Dixon* scripts being an early example. Here was good writing, workplace, domestic, and urban location settings, and 'small dramas' of everyday life offered in a predictable format that encouraged and built audience loyalty to the extent that the series lasted over twenty years (1955–76).

The general sense to be gained from perusal of these various memos, working papers, instructions, and, not least, published reviews, is of a field in flux. Though historical hindsight suggests a clear division between popular and quality drama, at the time, it seems, this was not quite so obvious. A 1958 memo from the BBC's Head of Programme Planning, Joanna Spicer, addressed to the Head of Drama (television), suggests that at that time the planning strategy was to develop a 'bank' of subjects agreed to be suitable for production, and the detail of the memo indicates that the full generic range was to be included and that both 'quality' and 'popular' scripts were to be sought.

> We agreed that the method of drama planning which we want to achieve is to have a 'bank' of subjects agreed for production, covering both Drama Department and the Regions . . .
>   Subjects are wanted in all categories, that is to say,
> Major 'special' projects
> 'World Theatre' plays
> Adaptations and specially written productions in all lengths . . .
> Theatre farces (four a year)
> Revivals of former television productions
> Drama serials, adventure type and classical type
> Saturday evening serials capable of continuation over a period of six months and adapted to resources available at the week-end
> The question of 'family serials' once or twice weekly is under review.[43]

The inference to be drawn from the memo is that the border between popular and quality was not, in the initial soliciting of material, a crucial one, though there is an implicit hierarchy in this list which begins with 'Major "special" projects' and ends with ' "family serials" once or twice weekly'. From the tone of contemporary memos, critiques, and reviews one can deduce a contemporary judgement which is rarely overt but rather implicit in the terminology deployed,

---

42 *Daily Mail*, 26 Nov. 1956, p. 6.

43 WAC T16/62/2, 26 Aug. 1958.

as for example in Levin's asides about independent television and the presumption that, as he put it, 'integrity and box-office are strange bedfellows'. There is also a thinly veiled misogyny in reviews which, suspecting a particular appeal to a female audience, use this as evidence of the low cultural worth of the programme in question. A *Daily Telegraph* review headlined 'Matinee Mama is outmoded', for example, mischievously elides the distinction between the subject and the audience of the play in question:

> Times change, and we change with them. Felicity Douglas' 'The Patchwork Quilt', an ATV production . . . is the sort of piece that caused a muted rattling among the matinee tea trays a couple of decades ago, but it wears a rather outmoded air in this day and age. Here we had what used to be called a woman's play . . . one of those self-centred, unthinking, all-embracing Mamas who love nothing better than a family reunion.[44]

Even Peter Black, the *Daily Mail* television reviewer, had no qualms in invoking the feminine (interestingly also the elderly feminine) as an uncontentious indicator of the low-grade in his otherwise positive piece about the final episode of the BBC's *A Matter of Degree*: 'the whole thing was a refreshing lift for the BBC's provincial new play department which seems lately to have specialised in the sort of thing written in poker work by old ladies who keep gift shops in Chumleigh St Chads'.[45] There are different interests at work, of course, for critics and producers. While critics validated, or denigrated, the increasing volume of material broadcast to the expanding audience, producers struggled to keep pace with the necessity not only to secure and produce sufficient material but also to take account of developing technologies and increasing costs. These latter imperatives must be taken into account when considering the generic evolution of dramatic forms in this volatile and expansive period of television history.

The Industrial Imperative and the Search for Content

The demand for increased volume of production and the rise in costs of all aspects of production—scripts, actors, sets, and costumes all incurred freelance fees and material expenses—required, in both the BBC and the companies, a view of production as a quasi-industrial process. Forward planning, streamlining, cost-cutting: all these imperatives entered the managerial discourse of the later 1950s alongside the continual search for new content. A 1957 paper from Michael Barry, BBC Head of Drama, to the Controller of Programmes gives an

44 *Daily Telegraph*, 20 July 1960, p. 13.
45 *Daily Mail*, 21 June 1960, p. 14.

interesting overview of the problems facing drama production and the increasing scale of the operation over which he presided. Similar concerns were evident in the commercial companies, Granada, for example. Barry's paper, like many in the immediately post-1955 period, is littered with defensive and denigratory remarks about 'the competitor' but focuses on the pragmatics of drama planning with particular emphasis on costs and benefits. He begins by asserting the centrality of drama production to the whole BBC operation:

> The tradition of the Sunday night play . . . is as old as public-service television and a review of audience figures shows how strongly drama has maintained a leading position among programmes and is able to hold and build audiences.

He suggests that the effective deployment of budget would be best achieved by splitting the production operation into three parts—the play, the actors, and the presentation—thus effectively moving towards an industrial conception of the processes. He continues:

> In all three we face an increased expense, on the one hand arising from competition and on the other caused by the increased cost of everything used from wood and nails upwards . . .
> . . . the price of a full length play from a desired author has risen from eight to twenty-eight percent of the play's production budget.
> . . . the division between economy and austerity is narrower than commonly thought and a glance at the competitor's screen will reveal standards unacceptable to modern programmes. On his side, I know that our plays are monitored to log the swaying wall or jammed door, which the audience is equally quick to fault

Invoking the impressive statistic of 'nearly two thousand plays produced' (presumably since the 1936 commencement of broadcasting) he points also to the BBC's work in bringing on young writers and young actors, evaluating their relative costs and noting how frequently the investment in training, as it were, brings benefits to competitors—not only in television—whose better rates of pay tempt writers and actors away from the BBC:

> We have a fine record for starting off new or comparatively unknown actors, but it may not be realised how avidly the casting directors of film and theatrical managements use our screen.

Finally he acknowledges the crucial contribution of the staff producer and, implicitly, the necessity to ensure that sufficiently high calibre individuals are attracted to the role:

The capacity of their minds and imaginations, their ability to use television as a story teller, their sense of style and appreciation of economy truly applied to the problems of production will make or mar all that we see on our screen. Much has been said and rightly said of our duty to the outside contributor. Equally the value of the programme producer should be assessed as being of paramount importance to the television operation.[46]

The search for content and the development of new forms and genres which characterizes the decade 1955–65 must, as this 1957 paper demonstrates, be understood in the context of an increasingly large-scale operation which, for economy's sake, had to be conceived overall while maintaining the necessary autonomy of the creative personnel whose collaboration ensured the product. This development, along with new technologies, had important consequences for generic development within the general field of drama.

The practice of telerecording performances, allowing transmission-ready material to be 'in the can' as it were, or in order to facilitate repeat broadcasts, began during the 1950s, though it was not yet routine by the mid-1960s, many productions—particularly single plays—still being broadcast live. At the same time the use of film for inserts into live performance was widely and increasingly deployed. In both cases the costs—of videotape and of film—were substantial and seem initially to have been seen as an inappropriate drain on the drama budget. At issue too, particularly in the case of video recordings of continuous live performance for transmission, was the question of payments to actors and the tricky negotiations with the actors' union, Equity, which continued throughout the period. Initially Equity permitted only the 'telerecording' of a *second* live performance in order to guarantee their members' fees for two performances. Subsequently they agreed to repeat broadcasts being the telerecording of the initial, live, performance but stipulated not less than a month and no more than a year between the first and repeat transmissions.[47] Negotiations were not finally concluded until the early 1960s when the 'New Equity Agreement' outlined regulations pertaining to rehearsal, recording, permissible hours, and rates of payment.[48] Film was initially used for inserts into live performance but, increasingly, the economies consequent on producing the whole programme on film as well as the concomitant scheduling advantages became clear and in series and serials this practice became the norm. Such production methods were often indicated in the published

46 WAC T16/62/2, 1 Aug. 1957.

47 Jacobs (2000: 115).

48 WAC T32/1789/1, 17 Jan '63 New Equity Agreement (applying to all contracts after 28 Jan '63); and 24 Jan '63 Programme Contracts Notice no. 227.

schedules with the byline 'a television film' in order, presumably, to distinguish the programme from films made for the cinema which were also broadcast on television, despite the attempts on the part of the distribution branch of the film industry to minimize such transmissions which they perceived as a direct threat in the context of the then rapidly declining cinema audiences. Perhaps the reluctance of some drama producers to embrace the practice of taping as routine might be explained by reference to these two avowedly popular forms—serial television drama and cinema film—which both depended on filming/taping and *against* which television's 'quality' drama output was aligned with the continuous live performance of theatrical drama. Philip Mackie at Granada, in a memo concerned with the organization of drama production, grudgingly acknowledged that taping was a possible solution to the problems he faced: 'The fact that technicians would have to come in for about three hours on a Sunday is unfortunate, but many necessities are unfortunate . . . The only possible alternative we can see is taping our plays on a previous mid-week day. We don't much like the idea of taping plays.'[49] The acceptance and understanding of ways in which new technologies such as videotape recording, or telerecording, could positively enable the development of televisual drama was gradual and, interestingly, realized initially in serial drama. Jacobs notes that as late as 1954 some serial drama was still being produced live but that by 1955 'the use of telerecordings and serial production allowed a new flexibility by which the BBC could respond to the attack of ITV drama output'.[50]

The other important advantage to filmed, rather than live, production, well known in the USA where many Hollywood film studios had 'retooled' for television production was that not only were repeats easy to schedule but also programmes on film could be made available to the export market.[51] Writing about 1950s television drama in the USA, Paterson notes

> there was a certain inevitability about the changes. Series were easier to schedule and allowed the networks to amortise fixed costs over a longer period . . .
>
> The filmed drama series . . . had a number of advantages . . . regular characters and situations with a returning audience, schedule anchorage, efficient production, easy sale of advertising. . . . [they] dominated ratings in the USA from the early 1960s, and were sold across the world to equal success with international audiences: *Cheyenne, Bonanza, Dragnet, The Untouchables, Star Trek*—derivative often from film action genres.[52]

49 Granada Archive Box 1017, 23 Jan. 1959.

50 Jacobs (2000: 115).

51 Anderson (1994).

52 Paterson (1998: 58, 60).

Many such series found their way onto British screens, allowing both the BBC and the companies to fill the increasing broadcasting hours with material guaranteed to attract sizeable audiences. Inevitably these provided generic models to both audiences and producers. The increased volume of product required from 1955 onwards necessitated a quasi-industrial approach to production, as well as the importing of ready-made programmes from the USA. The streamlining, cost-cutting, and other organizational efficiencies characteristic of industrial production methods naturally privileged the evolution of forms, such as series and serial drama and light entertainment shows, which could be delivered by such methods.

A 1956 BBC Programme Planning memo noted a 10% increase in transmission hours over the preceding year, and indicated roughly where the increase had been, in terms of genres. While 'Talks, Demonstrations and Documentary Programmes' had increased by 220 hours, and 'Light Entertainment, including Musical Comedy' by eighty-nine hours, 'Drama' had increased by a mere six hours. It seems likely that the disparity in these figures can be accounted for by differing production costs and that much of the increase in programming in this period would have been achieved by bought-in, that is to say imported, material, as the memo's conclusion suggests: 'As part of the 10% increase in hours and of the increase in LE material, there has been an increase in weekly 25 minute entertainment film series placings.'[53] The 'entertainment film series', in the BBC parlance evident in both internal memos and in *Radio Times* billings, is frequently a euphemism for imported, American, material. When the Pilkington Committee's Report was published in 1962 the issues of home-produced versus imported material and of obtaining sufficient product to fill the schedules were still very much alive. Apropos their recommendation that the proposed third channel should go to the BBC the Chairman of ITA, Kenneth Adam, was reported as saying, rather waspishly, that 'overproduction [is] much the most serious threat to television. The sources of supply are bound to dry up and the result will be to fill in with any kind of cheap rubbish.'[54] It has always been the case that the US product has enjoyed more global exposure than that of any other national television, partly as a consequence of its huge home market and consequent scale of production and partly following in the wake of Hollywood cinema's global reach. The lesson that material planned and executed on film or tape could have a potentially lucrative life after its first transmission was not lost on British producers. The BBC explored the possibility in the later 1950s of exporting *Dixon* to the USA and to Australia (both attempts were

53 WAC T16/243/4, 25 May 1956.

54 *Daily Mail*, 14 Sept. 1962, p. 6.

unsuccessful) and Philip Mackie at Granada reminded his programme committee, 'Let's plan these . . . series with careful consideration of their potential for overseas sales.'[55]

In the broad field of drama the series and serial forms were discovered to be effective means of engaging audiences through their promise of predictable, regular provision of well-liked genres and characters. The early 1960s saw the start of several series celebrated at the time, as well as subsequently, for both their writerly and production quality and their widespread popular appeal to audiences. Writers of 'quality' drama such as Troy Kennedy Martin, for example, began to produce material not only for single play slots but also for the police series *Z-Cars*, while many on the production team of *The Avengers* came from distinguished careers in cinema. Sydney Newman, best remembered for his innovatory and sometimes radical approach to the single play both at the BBC and, earlier, for ABC, was also responsible for establishing the long-running science fiction series *Dr Who*. These and many other series made relatively sophisticated use of newly established televisual conventions which had developed during the experimental and competitive latter half of the 1950s.

'Discovery' of Popular Genres

While the economics as well as the development and deployment of new technologies within what was recognized by all concerned to be a rapidly expanding industry had an undoubted effect on the generic and stylistic evolution of television drama, the fundamental impetus informing this evolution was to find forms that engaged and satisfied audiences. There's a sense in press reviews, industry memos, and the BBC's invaluable audience research reports, routinely circulated to programme planners and producers, of *discovery*—of an ongoing search for forms that would enable the nurturing and dissemination of 'good writing', the deployment of performance styles appropriate to the small domestic screen, and the provision of storytelling that would offer both pleasure and use-value to audiences. The dominance, in drama output overall, of series and serials and, latterly, soaps acknowledged production and scheduling efficiencies but also recognized that audiences positively welcomed the *familiar* in terms of characters with whom they could become engaged and who would predictably return, week after week, to the screen. But the familiar meant more than this: it also referred to the representation of well-known settings for the dramas—the contemporary, the domestic environment, the local scene. While many imported (American)

55 Granada Archive Box 1017, 1965.

series certainly provided the pleasure of familiar characters, home-produced material offered the additional pleasure of plots and *mises-en-scène* recognizable by audiences as contiguous, if not identical, to the world they themselves inhabited. Two police officers wrote of the first *Dixon* programme in July 1955 that 'The attention to detail was very good and much appreciated. This was a busman's holiday for me but I enjoyed it. The performance, the setting and the action were true to life'. Though some viewers found it, certainly if judged as a crime series, too tame, humdrum, and with a central character 'too good to be true', the majority grasped what the series *did* offer and 'whole-heartedly enjoyed this "simple, human" story of "homely" people—the sort of characters they could believe in, whose behaviour and con-versation was refreshingly "natural"... it was suitable viewing for the whole family'.[56] Three years later the series was well established and routinely eliciting responses emphasizing the pleasures of familiarity, not to mention the sense of loss accompanying the series' upcoming break in transmissions: 'This is a real family favourite and we will certainly miss meeting Dixon and all our other police friends on a Saturday. Essentially simple, the stories "rang true" and always had a homely, natural touch. The regular team, especially "Dixon", were so good they were like real people to us'.[57]

The recognition that 'simple' and 'homely' stories were, indeed, an aspect of drama provision which audiences were coming to value and seek informed programme planning strategies and marks a divergence between 'popular' and 'quality' drama provision in the latter part of the 1950s. Where quality drama was often conceived as *challenging* its audiences in the best traditions of 'high' culture, pop-ular drama took on the job of *reassuring* audiences with a predictable diet which, effectively, represented them back to themselves. The mid-1950s series *The Grove Family* attracted similar comments from its audiences—over 90% of whom claimed to be regular viewers, never missing an episode—to those elicited by *Dixon*:

> Many viewers... said they were 'apt to forget the Groves *are* acting, they are so natural...'[58]

> The Grove family... continues to keep a firm hold on its audience... some viewers confessed to a special liking for Bob Groves—'a typical family man', or Mrs Groves—'so sweet-tempered yet speaks her mind'. Granma Fagg, however, is obviously regarded as the leading character of

56 WAC VR/55/334, 27 July 1955.

57 WAC VR/58/168, 17 Apr. 1958.

58 WAC VR/55/51, 9 Feb. 1955.

the serial—'which would not be the same without her foibles and her sharp tongue'.[59]

Clearly both the Dixon entourage and the Grove family members were *recognized*: whether because they mirrored the audience to themselves, or because they offered a consensual ideal of the period with their emphasis on 'family values' which, in the latter part of the 1950s, were perceived as coming under threat from various social forces such as the new category 'delinquent youth' or the influx of immigrants from the soon-to-be-ex-colonies, is less clear. Certainly the anxieties manifest in the 'social problem' films of British cinema in the later fifties, or in the work of the 'angry young men' of British writing are strikingly absent from these well-loved domestic dramas.

In line with the ethos of Public Service Broadcasting many of these familial dramas bore traces of social engineering, in the sense that the public bodies to which they referred, or within which the fictions were based, were frequently consulted for 'advice' which, for writers and producers, was no doubt intended to secure the verisimilitude of the representation. Ted Willis, the originator and primary writer of *Dixon*, for example, wrote to producer Douglas Moodie enquiring whether the BBC already had a 'top-level' arrangement of this kind: 'Incidentally, I feel that a copy of each script should go to the police, for routine checking. If you would let me have copies . . . I will see to this. Or is there a top-level arrangement at the BBC for doing this?'[60] For the public bodies themselves, the unprecedentedly huge audiences offered an irresistible opportunity to 'inform' the public. The *Grove Family* files at the BBC Written Archives, for example, contain a letter from the Ministry of Pensions asking that the programme make reference to imminent changes in retirement pensions[61] and the *Dixon* files have several such letters. One from the Royal Marines publicity officer thanks producer Douglas Moodie for displaying their posters on the *Dixon* set and notes the increased level of civilian enquiries following transmission of the programme[62] while another, from the Controller of Police Canteens, asked that a subsequent storyline might focus on the police canteen.[63] The routine address to camera which opened each episode of *Dixon*, typically commenting on the events of the previous episode, frequently had a strong public information content. A 1958 episode featured the story of a destitute widow with three young children whose husband had been killed in a

59 WAC VR/55/125, 29 Mar. 1955.

60 WAC T12/75/1, 16 May 1955.

61 WAC T12/137/4, 18 Feb. 1955.

62 WAC T12/75/6, 12 Mar. 1959.

63 WAC T12/75/6, 7 Dec. 1959.

cycling accident, and Dixon's address to camera in the subsequent episode put the story straight, as it were: 'Since 1946 anyone finding themselves in such an unfortunate position would, thanks to an agreement between the major motor insurance companies, receive reasonable compensation.'[64] The practice of excessively overt 'public service' information in these to-camera speeches caused disquiet, in some quarters. A memo from Kenneth Adam while he was BBC Controller of Programmes noted that 'DG [Director General] thinks we are in danger of overdoing the Dixon image—he disapproves of the length of the 'message' at the end of each episode, and of his appearance in religious programmes (Did you know of this? Did you see it?) I shall probably raise this at Planning Committee tomorrow.'[65] And audiences, too, sometimes took exception to the more obvious and heavy-handed deployment of 'propaganda' as responses to the 21 March 1956 episode of *The Grove Family* entitled *Prevention and Cure*, which dealt with the issue of home security, indicated:

> The idea of a policeman coming to tell Mr Groves how to safeguard his house was '. . . a clever blend of entertainment with instruction' . . . and viewers appreciated the advice but 'there were . . . some . . . who obviously resented their favourite serial being used in this way. 'Entertainment should *be* entertainment, not just a lot of propaganda' and viewers found the detailed description of safety devices, etc, very boring . . . and too much like a documentary[66]

A rather less didactic approach, though one equally informed by the Public Service brief to inform and educate while entertaining audiences, was taken by the producers of ATV's serial *Emergency Ward 10*. The Director General of the ITA, Robert Fraser, was engaged in correspondence on the question whether the Spastics Society, a registered charity, had received unfair 'plugs' in some episodes and received the reply

> it is our intention, if possible, throughout the series to introduce various different matters of a similar nature . . . so that the programme in the course of its existence helps in doing a generally good public relations job in educating the public . . . in regard to the facilities available for treatment of various different types of unusual illness[67]

64 WAC T12/75/5, undated memo 1958.

65 WAC T12/75/6, 20 Dec. 1960.

66 WAC VR/56/154, 13 Apr. 1956.

67 ITC Library file 5081/2/6, 2 Dec. 1957.

There's a fine line to be drawn, here, between a paternalist assumption that popular entertainment can and should be exploited in the interests of the public good and the perennially thorny question of mass television broadcasting being hijacked in the interests of hegemonic control. Where, precisely, the examples cited here would lie is perhaps a matter for individual thought: what *is* of interest is to note that not only producers but also audiences were, at least some of the time, alert to this aspect of broadcasting's social power. Many series, of course, eschewed such directly informational content but it seems to me that the representations offered in such fictions, *precisely* because they seemed to their audiences to be 'simple', 'homely', 'natural' also participated in this power by validating, or questioning, various forms of social and gendered behaviour. To offer reassurance to viewers, as I suggest many of these programmes did, is also to engage in hegemonic struggle on the side of the status quo. As popular television drama became more sophisticated through the course of the 1960s it allowed more radical positions to be explored. The well-liked emphasis on characters developed over time, delivering the pleasures of the familiar to their audiences, was retained, while at the same time plots and locations implied a critique of the status quo. Peter Black's glowing *Daily Mail* review of a 1962 *Z-Cars* episode suggests something of this:

> If there is a better television series anywhere in the world I'd like to see it . . . John Hopkins' script expanded this [storyline given in previous paragraph] into another close and angry look at one of the uglier bits of urban life. The blocks of flats in which people live as indifferent to each other as though they all belonged to some new species of bee.
>
> It is this core of reality that keeps the series in good heart. The cast and director never need to start from a cold centre.[68]

As television 'came of age', as it were, by the mid-1960s the difference in typical content of popular and quality drama became less clear. Many single plays (the very appellation 'single play', interestingly, carries the connotation 'quality') took their subject matter from the supposed daily experience of the mass audience, as did *Cathy Come Home*, while series such as *Z-Cars* and *The Avengers* occupied a kind of centre ground where televisual form was explored and the audience challenged—as had happened earlier with the pioneering series *Quatermass*. Questions of realism and of verisimilitude are at issue here but these do not, of themselves, allow a distinction between the various forms of drama output despite their usefulness

---

68 *Daily Mail*, 18 Oct. 1962, p. 22.

in the analysis of individual programmes. What must be acknowledged in an overview of television drama during this formative period is the significance of the ubiquitous and often undervalued popular forms in forming audience habits and expectations—in laying the ground, as it were, for the explosion of new television forms (not only in drama) characteristic of the mid-1960s. The question arises, too, as to the extent to which the provision of what, by many, was regarded uncontentiously as culturally low-grade material— 'trivial' was a recurring epithet at the time—was *compensated* by the concomitant paternalist 'mission' of providing socially constructive information within the format popular drama, thus arguably retaining the moral, if not the cultural, high ground.

| Contemporary Anxieties | The discursive climate surrounding reception of television programming in the later 1950s is strongly marked by two major anxieties. |

The discursive climate surrounding reception of television programming in the later 1950s is strongly marked by two major anxieties. One was the possibly negative 'effects' of television viewing on its audiences—particularly excessive viewing by children and youth— and the other concerned the extent and quality of imported American programming. We should remember that the dominant paradigm in such audience research as existed at that time was the behaviourist model in which audiences—generally conceived as 'mass' groupings despite the small-scale domestic context of viewing—were considered to be passive recipients of 'messages' which they were thought to accept uncritically. It's worth noting, too, that those writing anxiously in such terms to the BBC or the ITA or in the print media were never talking about their own viewing practices but always evincing doubts about the abilities of 'others' to be discerning. Submissions to the Pilkington Committee contained much material of this kind and indeed, in its Report the committee appears to have been convinced by the argument that broadcasting—particularly by ITV—was doing a positive disservice to the cultural life of the nation. Complaints about the effects of too much unsupervised viewing on children were common and generally centred on the issue of depictions of violence, 'unsuitable' language and, latterly, on excessive depictions of sexual activity. Mary Whitehouse's NVLA campaign to increase controls on broadcast content arose out of this but many earlier studies had already sought to explore the relations between children and television, often in the context of education.[69] Hilde Himmelweit in her 1958 study *Television and the Child* had refuted the notion of viewer passivity before the screen but suggested that there was a distinction to be drawn between discriminate and

---

69 See Oswell (1999) for more detail of these.

addictive viewing. Those directly concerned with broadcast production were alert to these debates and quick to defend themselves: the Director General of the ITA, Robert Fraser, had received a letter from the Women's Group on Public Welfare deploring the 'horror' and 'brutality' in transmissions during the 6.00–9.00 p.m. period, and particularly the number of Westerns, citing recent violent tragedies as evidence of television's deleterious effect on children. His three-page reply robustly refuted the charge, claiming the recent Nuffield Report in support, and listing many children's programmes of which the ITA was 'proud' and none of which was acknowledged in the letter of complaint. He concluded: 'those of us who work in television do not feel we are any less concerned with moral values and the good of society than are those who pass these resolutions. We are also citizens and parents, you know'.[70]

Underlying such exchanges is a widespread coming-to-terms with the fundamental shifts that the habit of television viewing was, inevitably, introducing into everyday life in Britain. Much was made of supposed domestic routines in designing the broadcast schedules and, whereas in the days before the mass television audience had been established different groupings formed audiences for different types of cultural experience, in possibly blissful ignorance of the predilections of others, now everyone had access to everything. The disquiet this caused was expressed by some in terms of the supposedly negative social consequences of some forms of broadcast content, such as depictions of violence, by others as the downgrading of cultural standards—a sentiment familiar today in the ubiquitous phrase 'dumbing down'. Both forms of objection, it seems to me, depend on the displacement onto television per se of far broader social and cultural anxieties which, though they may have *surfaced* 'on' television, were not necessarily *caused by* television. It is apropos the adjacent fields of popular drama and light entertainment that such disquiet was most vociferous, and nowhere more so than in the vilification of imported American series which, though highly popular with many, brought out a class/culture-based snobbery in others. Peter Black in the *Daily Mail*, for example, lashed out at 'A-R or Granada or anyone else who buys stuff like this':

> I get the feeling that American scriptwriters will eventually
> become as extinct as the Dodo. All that is necessary is for the
> formulae to be fed into a computer with instructions to perm any
> eight constituents. Press the button marked 'domestic bliss', 'law',
> 'medicine', 'wild west', or what you will and out pops the required
> set of storylines. A-R or Granada or anyone else who buys stuff

70 ITC Library, ITA paper 21 (61), 24 Jan. 1961.

like this must recognise it for what it is—paltry, cheap, serving only to appease the round the clock appetite of American television.[71]

Such sentiments were echoed in BBC viewer reports, for it was not only the ITV companies that saw fit to 'buy stuff like this', but they were almost always in the minority. *The Burns and Allen Show*, regularly transmitted by the BBC from 1955 until at least 1960, attracted an enthusiastic following. The first transmission took place, significantly, on 16 September 1955—one week before the commencement of ITV broadcasts. According to the Viewer Report, 'a minority "found the film crazy" and "could not understand American speech"... the vast majority said "situations were delightfully ridiculous", "dialogue sparkled with wit" and they had laughed almost continuously'.[72] Six months later the series had secured a loyal following, though dissent was now expressed not in the bemused terms 'crazy', 'could not understand American speech', but in far stronger anti-American terms: 'Only one or two viewers actively disliked... entire series "too silly for words", "typical of the third rate Yankee films we have to put up with".... Majority enthusiastic fans "these excellent comedy films are a 'must' every Friday for all my family"... "one programme we never miss"'.[73] Within a few years the anti-American feeling seems to have been established, the Viewer Report noting a minority but routine critique of anything American which seems to inform not only the adverse but also the positive comments on this 1960 episode:

> There were... the inevitable few who automatically reject anything of American origin—for them this was 'the usual moronic American rubbish'—but, on the other hand, one or two remarked that, although they did not usually enjoy American comedy, the Burns and Allen Show was at least 'bearable' in that the humour was rather more subtle than was usual in American comedy.[74]

British viewers, as this and reports on other US imports suggest, appreciated 'subtlety', and an appeal to the intelligence which they found lacking in such programmes. An exasperated tone is evident in the Viewer Report on a 1957 episode of *I Married Joan* which had been transmitted by the BBC since September 1955: ' "Its appeal has definitely waned", far too many of these "juvenile" American film

71 *Daily Mail*, 21 Sept. 1962, p. 3

72 WAC VR/55/458, 3 Oct. 1955.

73 WAC VR/56/75, 2 Mar. 1956.

74 WAC VR/60/581, 25 Oct. 1960.

series . . . and they would prefer something, preferably British, which required at least a modicum of intelligence to enjoy'[75]

The call for more programming 'of British origin' which appears frequently in these BBC reports evidences, perhaps, an increasingly widespread impatience with imported material—yet such programmes did attract and hold substantial audiences, becoming, eventually, much-loved exemplars of early television. *The Phil Silvers Show* also known as *Sergeant Bilko* elicited the following comments:

> There were . . . many . . . who would prefer a comedy series of British origin . . . The type of humour was such that the whole family could, and did, look forward to 'this weekly tonic of good fun'[76]

> 'Not another moronic American film series? Like the rest, it is immature and superficial—certainly unfit for adult viewing'.[77]

> 'As usual the story was corny and obvious but who cares when the twists and turns are so outrageously funny. Admittedly Bilko's adventures are silly, but they're such great fun and I always thoroughly enjoy them'.[78]

Those who objected to American popular series did so in terms of their intellectual level, their lack of (British) subtlety, or their superficiality, while their regular viewers seemed to have appreciated their wit, zest, and performance style—their 'great fun'. In the discursive climate of the time it is the former group whose views are circulated: it is rare to find positive commentaries in the press and all too often the assumption of immaturity or worse 'another moronic American series' pervades television reviewers' columns, feeding, one might surmise, the displacement of anxiety about cultural change onto the routine material of popular broadcasting.

75 WAC VR/57/243, 22 May 1957.

76 WAC VR/57/277, 4 June 1957.

77 WAC VR/57/219, 9 May 1957.

78 WAC VR/58/312, 7 July 1958.

5

Popular Drama: *The Grove Family, Life with the Lyons, Dixon of Dock Green*

Quality Drama and Popular Drama

In the mid-1950s the commercial imperative to fill broadcasting hours, attract audiences, and secure advertising revenue, together with the BBC's uneasy assumption that they must compete on the same ground as commercial television, as it were, produced a polarity between 'serious' or 'quality' drama (expensive to produce) and popular drama which was either cheaper to produce or a low-cost import. As the audience expanded consequent on the spread of the transmitter, networks broadcasters also learned from experience *how* to secure audiences and *what* generated audience loyalty—to channel, genre, or programme. By the mid-1960s the pool of television writers had also enlarged, thanks to the conscious efforts of the BBC's Drama Department in 'bringing on' new writers as well as to the increased opportunities offered by the existence, after 1955, of a variety of commissioning sources. The BBC's *Quatermass*, of which there were three six-part series (1953, 1955, 1958–9) was an early example of self-consciously innovative material addressed to the mass audience which initially provoked mixed but nevertheless engaged responses:

> Quite a number confessed that they had been unable to follow the initial stages of the story but most seemed quite confident that the plot would emerge more clearly as the serial progressed . . .
>
> Exciting, gripping and novel. The air of expectancy is always with you. Can't wait for next Saturday.
>
> An absurd story and too terrifying for older people and children. It should not be televised at this time on a Saturday night.[1]

> Viewers were, in the main, delighted with Quartermass II and considered it a most remarkable, fascinating and ingenious serial with suspense well kept up from part to part . . . some others

---

1 WAC VR/55/129, 9 Nov. 1955.

found it altogether too far-fetched, while others found it too eerily suggestive of 'things to come'.[2]

Within a few years equally 'far-fetched' narrative premises such as those informing the science fiction series *A for Andromeda* and *Dr Who*, or the thriller *The Avengers* were easily assimilated by audiences now conversant with a far broader range of dramatic conventions. And just as the narrative conventions and production methods deployed in fantasy series such as these were welcomed by audiences so, too, on the other hand, was a far greater degree of realism in the service of soaps like *Coronation Street*, or crime series such as *Z-Cars*. Techniques of location shooting drawn from many sources including television documentary, news and current affairs, and the 'new wave' of British cinema—not to mention the example of many US imports—were deployed in the service of drama series that aimed, through their depictions of the everyday world experienced by audiences, to offer polemical interpretations of everyday life. Though it is true that *Coronation Street*, with its focus on the local and the domestic (and possibly also because of its overt address to the female audience), was rarely cited in these terms, at the time *Z-Cars* was quickly recognized to be both radical and innovative, as an exasperated 1963 memo from the BBC's Kenneth Adam deploring the previous Sunday's BBC programme indicates: 'We were plunged back into all the slow plodding methods of the early 1950s with ridiculously contrived "location" scenes, whereas on the other channel . . . brilliantly acted with totally authentic location shooting of the Z-Cars type.'[3] Whereas the fifties BBC serial *Quatermass* had both intrigued and alarmed viewers with its formal novelty and far-fetched content, by the mid-1960s similarly innovative material was enthusiatically welcomed: the polarity between 'quality' and 'popular' drama had diminished or, perhaps more precisely, the space between had been occupied by material that evidenced a growing sophistication amongst producers, writers, *and* audiences.

This chapter takes a closer look at some examples of staple popular drama from the mid-1950s; that is, the popular drama which drew large audiences, attracted little, if any, critical attention, yet could be understood as central to engendering the habit of viewing which, later, enabled the understanding and appreciation of more complex narratives. In delivering an account of an episode from each of three more or less continuous series, I hope to suggest something of the typically popular (well-liked) characters and situations which, together, constituted the 'reassuring' model of contemporary life in Britain. Such drama was regarded in its time as trivial, ephemeral,

---

2 WAC VR/55/586, 15 Dec. 1955.

3 WAC T16/62/3, 22 Jan. 1963.

and of no cultural significance, yet I would argue that precisely because of this it offers the historian a valuable snapshot of contemporary assumptions concerning social relations in the home, in the workplace, or among other small-scale social groupings. Most of all, it delivers a sense of the accepted norms in gender relations at the time, thus potentially shedding useful light on questions central to this study; that is to say, on the representations of women and the discursive constructions of 'the feminine' through which patriarchal hegemony was challenged or reinforced.

These three programmes could all be conceived as belonging to the sitcom genre, since they deployed a routine and thus familiar set of characters and broadly familiar locations, and in each a storyline was played out during the episode to be resolved in the narrative closure which generally delivered a return to the status quo.[4] Of the three, only *Life with the Lyons* was regarded as a sitcom at the time, *The Grove Family* being referred to as a soap opera and *Dixon of Dock Green* as a police series—it was a workplace drama centred equally on the fictional Dock Green Police Station and the domestic life of its central protagonist PC Dixon. It is true that neither *The Grove Family* nor *Dixon* had overt pretensions to comedy, yet both attended closely to the small dramas of contemporary life on which, typically, the comedy in sitcom depends, and both routinely deployed moments of comedy predicated on audiences' familiarity with central characters. *Life with the Lyons* revolved around the fictional domesticity of the real Lyons family, and had enjoyed substantial success as a radio sitcom before its transfer to television, initially on BBC (1955–6) and subsequently on A-R where it ran from 1957 to 1960. *The Grove Family*, running for a little over two years (1954–7), represented an early BBC attempt to produce home-based domestic drama for the early evening family audience. *Dixon* was by far the most successful, running for over twenty years and securing a substantial and dedicated audience. Writer Ted Willis and actor Jack Warner had pitched the original idea in response to the BBC's call for more crime-based drama, the original title *The Blue Lamp* betraying its origins in the Basil Dearden film of that name in which Warner was the central protagonist. All these shows were produced in the BBC's Light Entertainment Department. Once established, both *The Grove Family* and *Dixon* employed a variety of scriptwriters and both also had close links with radio drama: Jack Warner continued to appear in Radio's *Meet the Huggetts* for some time after *Dixon* came on the air, while *The Grove Family* was frequently compared to Radio's *The Archers* with which, apparently, it shared an audience. The Lyons were

---

4 Though in both *The Grove Family* and *Dixon* storylines occasionally ran over two to three episodes.

an American family resident in the UK, and the format of their show owed much to US precedents; that is to say, it inferred a proscenium-arch performance space, it deployed a studio audience whose laughter punctuated the show (to the irritation of some viewers), and it depended heavily on the star personae of the central parental couple. *The Grove Family*, by contrast, aimed for naturalism to the extent that its producer, John Warrington, complained bitterly when actors' and authors' names were credited against his wishes:

> Somehow, somewhere, our 'preview' billing has been altered. It is now quite misleading. The Grove Family is not a serial, but a series. From the beginning H.L.E.Tel. has had, quite rightly, the idea to play down actors' names and authors' names and merely display the characters so that viewers would not think in terms of actors and written scripts but of a real genuine family. This idea was first-rate. Now we have a billing describing the family that Michael Pertwee *has created*, putting us right back to the ordinary domestic drama[5]

As we have seen (Chapter 4) both *The Grove Family* and *Dixon* were celebrated by their audiences precisely for their convincing portrayals of everyday life in suburbs of contemporary London. Though Warrington's complaint may indicate an excessively naïve understanding of the complexities of audience response to such drama, nevertheless his instinct that audiences wanted a convincing representation of the known and familiar was sound, as Audience Research reports testified.

> Viewers tended to regard the entire cast as a family unit, and a completely convincing one at that . . .
> There seemed to be a fairly strong feeling that the episodes so far in this series have been altogether too gloomy . . . 'We are so sorry that this new series has started off with so much trouble for The Groves and hope things will get brighter soon' . . .
> 'I always enjoy The Groves. A very true picture of family life with its ups and downs and its funny how you come to regard them as real people'.[6]

The Grove Family: 'Prevention and Cure' (BBC, 21 March 1956)

This drama was set in the 'Groves' suburban home, following the family's domestic life in which successive local incidents formed the basis for each episode's plot. The family comprised Mr and Mrs Groves (Mum and Dad), their four children of whom two, Pat and

5 WAC T12/137/1, 2 Apr. 1954.

6 WAC VR/56/572, 21 Nov. 1956 with reference to the episode 'No Peace for Dad' (31 Oct. 1956).

Jack, were young adults and two, Daphne and Lennie, were children, and their aged grandmother (Gran). Other minor characters were neighbours, Mr Groves's secretary (he is a small builder), and occasional characters specific to particular episodes. An April 1954 memo lists early episodes in production:

> 3 . . . 'Deadly Poison'—the boy finds a doctor's bag missing from a stolen car.
> 4 . . . 'A Hundred Not Out'—Grandma's hundredth birthday.
> 5 . . . 'The Ears Have It'—all about ear-piercing.
> 6 . . . 'Clean Sweep'—the family buy a new carpet, everyone spills something on it and a salesman sells them a vacuum cleaner.
> 7 . . . 'Royal Welcome'—a Princess visits the district and calls on the family for tea.
> 8 . . . 'A Dangerous Plaything'—the boy makes a catapult and creates havoc. Everything in sight gets broken.[7]

This March 1956 episode was written by the series' creators, Roland and Michael Pertwee, but other writers were routinely used. A December 1954 memo lists eleven potential new writers who had submitted script ideas. Of these, nine were men, two women (Sheila Hodgson and Hazel Adair). Producer John Warrington's evaluative notes are positive for all the male writers—'he is a writer we should seriously consider', 'obviously has a feeling for television and the family', 'parts of the script are full of genuine promise'—whereas both women, he felt, should be partnered with another writer—'she [Hodgson] has a feminine approach and certainly the domestic side is good with a light touch. However I feel she should only be considered as a joint writer and not entirely on her own' and 'She [Adair] is at present writing one of three "Mrs Dale's Diary" and again has good domestic feeling, but the plot is thin. I feel she could be associated with another writer to our advantage'.[8]

The general direction of the family's experiences as delivered in the scripts was overseen by the producer in agreement with senior management—evidence of the close attention paid to the programme in recognition of the genre's potential. An August 1954 memo, for example, notes that

> It has been agreed with C.P.Tel. that the Groves extend their influence in the Autumn schedules. An American family are coming to live near the Groves, and therefore the differences of background and approach to life will be discussed. Also agreed with C.P.Tel. is an interchange of artistes between the French family programme to be produced by Rene Soria, and the Groves.

7 WAC T12/137/1, 20 Apr. 1954.

8 WAC T12/137/1, 10 Dec. 1954.

Therefore the Grove Family will be covering, within the next nine months, international problems, particularly French and American.[9]

In addition to this kind of broad oversight Warrington, like other drama series producers, often received overtures from various public bodies wishing for issues of concern to be highlighted in the programme: here there's a sense that popular drama could and should operate as a vehicle for public information rather along the lines of the MOI's intervention into wartime film production. For example, the Ministry of Pensions and National Insurance wrote in February 1955 as follows:

> You may have heard that retirement pensions are going up in April. As there are some $4\frac{1}{2}$ million pensioners in the country you can imagine that it is a colossal task to put these increased pensions into payment smoothly . . .
>
> It occurs to me that Gran may well be a retirement pensioner. If in your programme on 15 March Nancy Roberts could drop an artful reference to the fact that she's got to get her pension book 'seen to'—or if, indeed, any member of the family could drop a hint about Gran's potential wealth and how she's going to get it—it would serve as a timely reminder to many thousands of viewers . . .
>
> A reference such as this in so popular a programme would be of immense value to us and could do much to secure the pensioners' cooperation[10]

No doubt a similar overture from the Police resulted in the March 1956 episode 'Prevention and Cure' though, as we have seen, some were irritated by what they considered to be overt propaganda in their entertainment: 'Entertainment should *be* entertainment, and not just a lot of propaganda', was one viewer's comment on this episode.[11]

The whole episode is concerned with home security and crime prevention through a storyline involving both a policeman's visit to the Groves to advise on crime prevention and the burglary of a neighbour's home. It opens with the usual upbeat music over the titles seen on a cloudy/sunny sky. The first scene is with Dad in his workshop/office, awaiting a visit from the local Crime Prevention Officer. Lennie runs in to find his cricket pads. The Officer arrives having just visited a new neighbour whose unpleasantness he discusses with Dad—both agreeing that she is 'an old sourpuss'. The Officer tells Dad

---

9 WAC T12/137/1, 19 Aug. 1954 memo from John Warrington to Kevin Sheldon.

10 WAC T12/137/4, 18 Feb. 1955.

11 WAC VR/56/154.

> We rely entirely on good relations with the public. We do know
> something about this business and we can give you some useful
> advice[12]

and goes on to suggest various small items typically of interest to
burglars, and to itemize the detail of various window and door locks.
We learn that the Groves' house has a mortice lock. There's a brief cut
to the younger children, Lennie and Daphne, practising cricket in the
street, and the conversation continues,

OFFICER: Have you got a television set?

DAD: Certainly I have.

OFFICER: The criminal is a student of people's habits. Make sure
your windows and doors are fastened before you start
viewing

The conversation turns to dogs and their potential to alert the family
to intruders,

DAD: Trouble is our dog insists on viewing with us!

OFFICER: Yes, most of them do . . . And don't leave furs and
valuables upstairs in the bedroom. It's much better to
have them down beside you

Dad and the Officer then tour the inside of the house, encountering
Gran and the elder daughter, Pat, and the Officer advises leaving
lights on when out. We return to the children playing in the street (the
inference is that by now the Officer has left) and their ball accidentally
hits a passing stranger. Apologetically the children bring him into the
house, which he admires as they tell him about it. Back in the street a
taxi draws up at the neighbour's door. The driver carries Mrs Praed's
trunk to her door but she refuses to tip him, and he leaves it on the
doorstep. Next door Dad is painting his fence and, mistaking him for
a workman, Mrs Praed summons him to carry her trunk indoors.
Later, around their table, the Groves laugh at Dad's 'prank': he had
teased Mrs Praed by suggesting that he was an 'ex-con'. A policeman
calls on the Groves, having been alerted by Mrs Praed to the presence
of an ex-con in the vicinity, and they let him in on the joke. There's a
cut to a rather sparsely furnished pub interior where Silk, the passer-
by befriended by the children, is drinking. It is now evening and Silk,
apparently a burglar, unsuccessfully tries the locked doors and windows to the Groves' house in which they are assembled in front of the
television. We cut to the interior of Mrs Praed's, next door, who leaves
her house to fetch a prescription, watched by the burglar. Once she
has left he breaks into the house. She returns to find her entrance
barred by the chain on the inside of her door and calls Mr Grove to

---

12 This and all subsequent dialogue transcribed from programmes as broadcast.

help her. As Groves searches her house she insults him and the intruder, Silk, jumps out of a window, hurting his ankle. These scenes, in contrast to most others, are dramatically lit, the high contrast play of light and shadow making interiors difficult to read. Hearing the burglar, Silk, in the garden the innocent Grove women ask him in, and eventually the policeman arrives and catches him. The policeman commiserates with Mr Grove over his neighbour's bad behaviour. The episode concludes with the end credits and an on-screen acknowledgement of cooperation from 'London Police'.

Though performances are adequate, the script is wooden and the settings sparsely furnished—the only exception being the Groves' living room which, as the main locus of family life, presumably appears in every episode. The informational content is barely integrated to the script, and the 'moral tale' of two neighbours crudely drawn. The references to television viewing practices—the family in a darkened room together with their dog and valuables, all focused on the nine-inch screen—both attempts contiguity with, and attempts to form, viewing habits. On the basis of this one episode it is more surprising that the series was able to attract a devoted following, as was apparently the case on the evidence of the regular Viewer Reports, than that it was 'retired' before the commencement of the autumn 1957 schedule. The action in this episode is largely conducted by male protagonists with the exception of the unpleasant—and 'justly' punished—female neighbour.

Life with the Lyons (BBC, 13 July 1955) Though contemporary with *The Grove Family*, this series is far more assured and confident in both pace and performance. The fictional illusion that we are watching a 'real' family is supported by the well-known fact that this *is* indeed, a family, but counterpointed by a format which overtly introduces characters, pauses for audible studio audience responses (laughter, applause), and generally deploys rhetorical flourishes in script and delivery. The American family comprises Ben and Bebe Daniels Lyon and their children Richard, Barbara, and Bobby—the former young adults, the latter a child—and their Scottish maid, Aggie. Neighbours and friends, making occasional appearances, are English. This episode opens with a camera zoom in to the façade of a well-to-do house, the titles appearing simultaneously with a male voice over proclaiming 'Ladies and Gentlemen, Life with the Lyons' as the camera rests on a close-up of the front door, cutting to an extreme close-up of the door and its knocker as the voice-over completes its phrase, music starts, and audience applause is heard. A young man runs into frame, opens the door, and enters the house leaving us with a close-up of the interior entrance hall as the voice-over intones 'Richard Lyons' to audience applause. The camera continues its slow zoom and a young woman crosses the frame, turning to smile at the camera as she passes, the voice-over telling us 'Barbara Lyons' as the camera continues to zoom/track in to a closed door in the background. This door opens and 'Bobby Lyons' smiles at camera as he crosses and exits the frame. The track continues through the doorway, and a man advances from the depth of the frame, traversing a domestic space and stopping in mid-frame foreground as the voice-over, to applause, announces 'Ben Lyons' and a woman enters from the rear, joining Ben by a table in the foreground to 'Bebe Daniels Lyon' and further applause. The table is an ironing board, and Bebe removes a burned item which Ben then holds up: it is a shirt with a scorched iron mark. Both are projecting their voices as on stage and 'playing' to camera/presumed studio audience.

> BEN: Bebe, you've scorched my shirt.
> BEBE: (smiling) I'm sorry darling, it'll never show. (exits)
> BEN: A man can take just so much. This is my best shirt. She's always doing something like this to me. Yesterday it was my shaving brush. When I said it was stiff she said it was OK when she used it to varnish the sideboard. (laughs) I don't know what I'm so happy about. You should see what I have to go through every morning. If you don't believe me, come on and see for yourself.

Ben is clearly addressing the audience/s—'at home' and in the studio. During his last remark he gestures screen left and walks towards medium close-up screen left, carrying the shirt.

> BEN: Come on, right through this door. Here, I'll open it for you.

'You' refers to us, the viewing audience, positioned here with the camera which pans to the left as he leans to open the door, and continues to track from a slightly high angle to reveal the dining table, set for five, and Bebe who has just entered from a door in the right-hand depth of the frame. At the left a French door opens to a small yard, and in the centre a huge flower arrangement stands behind the sofa. Bebe sits at the table as a uniformed maid approaches with a pot of tea.

There follows a series of what are, effectively, one-liner gags reminiscent of vaudeville. The show's provenance on radio is hard to forget since the visual construction of humour follows, rather than leads, the narrative. The family is at breakfast, and family relations, presumed familiar to audiences, are demonstrated. The 'new-fangled' electric toaster occupies pride of place on the table and plays a central part in this opening scene. The teenage daughter wants a new dress; the younger son is preoccupied with his rabbits and tadpoles, and the elder son is dreamily romantic about a new girl on the block. Bebe

Daniels is central: when she laughs so does the studio audience. Middle-class routines form the basis for this narrative of 'everyday life': Bebe 'helps' the maid, Aggie, and teenage Barbara is asked to 'go upstairs and dust the bedrooms'. The telephone, like the toaster, has a prominent role in the next scene which is concerned with Richard's romance and the sibling badinage it occasions. The episode is re- solved by the duplicity of the new girl, Marilyn. Richard's romantic fantasies provide the pretext for the few truly visual gags. Following the breakfast scene and the subsequent telephone conversation be- tween Richard and Marilyn, he leaves the house to post a letter to her. Bebe, smiling, follows him and opens the front door. We cut to an exterior shot of the house as Richard exits (audience applause). He walks down the tree-lined street, past the pillarbox (eerie music on the soundtrack), and 'posts' his letter in the litter bin. A thread of his sweater catches on the bin and, still in a daze, he crosses the street. In medium-shot/close medium-shot we watch as he walks while his sweater unravels, and the scene ends with a fade to black from which we cut to Bebe at the kitchen table—in a set-up similar to the opening scene—where she is making pastry. Bobby runs in, telling her he's seen Richard 'in a dream' to which Bebe retorts, 'Well you shouldn't be dreaming at this time of day'. There follows a lengthy discussion of grammatical correctness as Bobby asks whether he may have lettuce to give his snails. Finally he gets the sentence right, whereupon Bebe tells him there is no lettuce. Bebe puts the pastry through the ringer to make it thin, and Barbara enters, upset because she has seen her boyfriend, Derek, with another girl. The doorbell rings and Bebe lets Derek in. He and Barbara have a row, he's been talking to Marilyn Jones. Bobby puts his face into the pastry between the arguing couple who occupy centre stage. The doorbell goes again: this time it is flowers ordered by Richard. Richard, in full evening dress, fantasizes about Marilyn's impending visit, talking earnestly to a dress on a hanger while watched by Bobby. This scene fades to black and audience applause is heard again as the next scene opens with Ben and Bebe at an ornate dinner table. Bebe's friend Florrie enters carrying flowers.

> BEN: Florrie, don't stamp your feet like that, you'll bring the
>   house down.
> FLORRIE: Well that's more than you ever did in Variety.

Another neighbour, male, drops in. Conversation reveals that Florrie has seen Marilyn in a tea shop with another boy, she had been 'laying it on with a trowel'. The adults discuss 'boys these days' and eventually Marilyn (played by Sylvia Syms) arrives in a full-length ball gown. She flatters Ben—'you must be Richard's big brother'—and the conversa- tion culminates in an altercation between Marilyn and Barbara over Derek. Finally Marilyn leaves when another boy comes to look for her—she had made two dates. The family rallies round a distressed Richard. Barbara and Bobby bicker over the tadpoles.

BEN: Well, at last everything's back to normal.

An explosion is heard off-screen, and Bebe enters, her face blackened with soot, carrying a charred chicken.

BEBE: I'm afraid the chicken's a little well done.

The scene closes with a close-up of the table and the chicken, and the credits roll.

The variety show convention of an overt address to audience with which the episode had opened is in abeyance once Ben ushered us (the audience) into the family dining room, yet it remains close to the surface. The exemplary dialogue of the first of the episode's three 'segments', given above, reveals the narrative's structuring by means of a series of 'gags'—much as in the Variety/Music Hall antecedents of this show referenced in Florrie's retort to Ben. Audience laughter, cued by Bebe's frequent laughing, and its applause cued at the opening of each of the three segments, also serve to confirm to us that this *is* performance. The few sets and the characters' entrances and exits both work to suggest that the frame equates to the theatrical proscenium arch, and also support a reading of this domestic drama as a staged production: there is no attempt, here, to invoke codes of realism. The 'set-piece' gags depend minimally on audience knowledge of the characters. In this episode men are gullible and women scheming (the Marilyn/Richard sketch) or men are long-suffering and women silly (Bebe's pointed misunderstandings and her domestic incompetencies). Here is suburban middle-class domestic life used as a vehicle for comedy based on supposedly universal experience: sibling squabbles, the demands of children, the management of domestic routines, puppy love, female friendships and rivalries. The series depends heavily on dialogue and slapstick, the former betraying its origins on radio, the latter drawing on vaudeville conventions as did many imported sitcoms such as *The Burns and Allen Show*, or *I Love Lucy*. Like Lucy, Gracie, and many others, Bebe Daniels is the undoubted star of the show but we should note that in all these cases the comedy turns, precisely, on the lovable idiocy of the central female protagonist.

Dixon of Dock Green 'Father in Law' (BBC, 1 September 1956)

Written by Ted Willis and produced by Douglas Moodie, *Dixon* was first broadcast on Saturday 9 July 1955, 8.15–8.45 p.m.—a prime slot for the family audience. Using a combination of studio performance and inserts filmed on location in various parts of London and, occasionally, abroad (as in the 15 October 1960 episode dealing with PC Dixon's weekend trip to Paris), and a stable cast of regular actors, it aimed to cater to both the taste for crime drama, and the appetite for 'small dramas of everyday life'. It was remarkably successful in achieving both these aims and securing a dedicated audience well into the 1970s. The dominant performance mode is realist, supported by good production values in sets and locations, and, as we have seen, the series cleverly deployed both the direct address to audience, in Warner/Dixon's opening and closing greetings, and the cinematic conventions whereby the fictional illusion is strengthened through the taboo on direct address to audience, or camera. The storylines interweave petty crimes dealt with by the Dock Green Police Station with domestic events from Dixon's own life. The opening episode 'PC Crawford's First Pinch', for example, has Dixon and his wife welcoming a new recruit, Andy, as a lodger in their home, and the 'Father in Law' story detailed below concerns the marriage of Dixon's daughter Mary. The programme was felt by both audiences and the police to fulfil a useful role in promoting understanding of and empathy with the police in the interests of effective public relations. Indeed, Ted Willis went to some lengths to secure the support and cooperation of the police:

> There is, indeed, a very considerable volume of police correspondence and comment reaching Jack Warner and Ted Willis about this series. This is due partly to the very lively appreciation of the programmes apparently felt by all ranks of the Force from the Commissioner downwards and partly to a shrewd move made a little time ago by Ted Willis. He advertised in the Police Gazette etc. asking for members of the force, anywhere, to submit storylines for the programme (in return for payment, of course). The response has been very great and has improved the already excellent relations between the programme and the Force.[13]

Though some viewers found the storylines tame and the policemen 'too good to be true', the majority welcomed crime stories which didn't feature, or depend on, violence and bloodshed and which were consequently felt to be appropriate for a mixed family audience's Saturday night entertainment. The episode 'Father in Law' is typical in its dual focus on a familiar domestic event (the daughter's wedding) and petty crime (pickpocket theft), in both of which the series' values of collegial affection, human kindness, and a sense of the appropriate predominate, embodied principally in the avuncular figure of Warner/Dixon. This is quintessentially 'reassuring' drama against which, a few years later, the radical social criticism of such series as *Z-Cars* would be measured.

13 WAC T12/75/4, 31 Dec. 1957, from Head of Light Entertainment Ronald Waldman.

The episode opens with titles over the exterior of the Dock Green station, panning down from its blue lamp as we read 'Jack Warner as Dixon' and hear whistling to the tune of 'Maybe its because I'm a Londoner' on the soundtrack. We cut to a close-up of Dixon speaking directly to camera—addressing and acknowledging his audience— and introducing this week's story which is to be about the wedding of his daughter, Mary, to his protégé, the young copper Andy Crawford. Then we cut in to the story itself: some men drink in the pub, at Dixon's home women discuss the details of the marriage arrangements. We cut to a shot of wedding cars arriving, a chauffeur comes to the door, a tramp also approaches; inside, Dixon and another man enjoy a short 'snifter'. We see the bridesmaids get into the car, a crowd watches, Dixon offers Billy the tramp a celebratory drink. Finally Dixon and Mary leave the house. While (we presume) the marriage is taking place, the arrangements for the hotel reception are being checked by two guests—Grace (a policewoman in civilian clothes) and Frank, a Dock Green Sergeant, also in 'mufti'. There is a sinister guest, Pam. We cut to the exterior of the church as the couple come out, confetti is thrown, and crowds watch as they walk to their car: the scene concludes with a close-up of Dixon watching the couple. There's a close-up of the church clock, a cut to close-up of glasses pulling out to reveal guests at the reception. A smartened-up Billy (the tramp) arrives with a gift, a record of Sibelius, and couples are dancing. While the bride retires to her room to change, Frank tells Dixon about the theft of Frank's wallet from his mackintosh pocket in the hotel cloakroom. In the cloakroom Grace recognizes a woman. While Dixon performs a 'music hall' turn for the guests, finishing with a song, 'Mary', there are cutaways to the sinister guest and to the female cloakroom attendant. The scene concludes, once again, on a close-up of Dixon. Next Mary and Andy appear in their going away outfits, Dixon kisses Mary: 'Hurry up, you'll miss your plane' and 'I wish your mother could have seen you'. A phone rings and is answered by Grace who has ascertained that the cloakroom attendant is a convicted shoplifter. However, Pam, the sinister guest, confesses to the theft and returns the wallet whereupon Frank decides not to press charges, saying to Dixon, 'Don't think I'd spoil your day, do you George, just for a sloppy frustrated kid?' Three men toast the couple, Grace returns to the party, and they all drink a toast to Dixon. Cut to a close-up of Dixon in the car, returning home, and talking, somewhat sadly, about Mary:

What did Billy say about her?
A white angel with a heart as warm as a parlour fire.

Then he looks directly to camera, as in the opening shot:

Going on my holidays next week.
A spot of quiet fishing on me own.
Won't be long before I see you again.
Goodnight.
(raising a glass) Good luck.

Then the credits roll over the blue lamp while male voices sing 'Maybe its because I'm a Londoner'. The audience is left with a warm sense of satisfactory closure, a bitter-sweet event shared, and a minor crime resolved by the exercise of decency and common sense. All's right with the world, and it's a world explicitly shared between George Dixon and his audiences addressed in the typical close-up which, as we have seen, proposes a contiguity between the performer (or presenter, or newsreader) and the *individual* viewer 'at home'.

Popular Drama and Fifties Britain

Dixon's world and the world of *The Grove Family* have much in common, not least the conservatism of the social conventions depicted. Though there *is* a policewoman (a working woman) and two female petty criminals (might we think of these as women active in the public sphere?) nevertheless it's a fundamentally patriarchal social model that is offered in both, and both were explicitly congratulated by viewers for the verisimilitude of their fictions. We should note, too, that both these episodes turn on plots involving transgressive women (*The Groves*'s surly neighbour, *Dixon*'s female pickpocket) and that a securely patriarchal figure (George Dixon, 'Dad' Groves) is indisputably at the heart of each series. *The Lyons*, by contrast, has a female protagonist/star 'showcased' by her husband who also occupies the subject position in the narrative in his dual role as MC and paterfamilias. Bebe's central role, like Lucy's and Gracie's, is predicated on her performance of the 'silly woman'—a juxtaposition not without paradox. Lucille Ball's demonstration of this paradox is unquestionably the paradigm, as her brilliant comic performances call on her audiences' recognition of domestic gender/power conflicts while at the same time we retain our awareness of her public success as performer, producer, and entrepreneur.[14] In the great majority of such popular fictions in the 1950s women were similarly demeaned: either they were effectively absent as in the majority of gangster and Western series (the highly popular US import Western *Bonanza*, for example, featured a domestic group entirely composed of men), or their activities were secondary to the plot construction as in *The Grove Family* and, for example, the long-running *Emergency Ward 10* where it is

14 Thumim (2002: 216–17).

primarily the experience of the male doctors that the audience is invited to share.

In the early 1960s this began to change. Though the hugely popular and innovative police series *Z-Cars* was predominantly male in cast and crew, other celebrated fictions of the period, such as *The Avengers* or *Dr Who*, did feature central female characters, albeit still secondary to the central male protagonists. Granada's *Coronation Street* (1960–) however, featured a plot construction fundamentally based on the refusal to separate the public and the private, acknowledging the reality of the home *as* the workplace for many of its characters and consequently, of course, for the audiences it aimed to attract. The ensemble playing, the various interweaving plot-lines, indeed the very construction of the set itself, all refuse a separation between the private self of the domestic environment and the public self of the workplace. In this refusal is an alluring appeal to female viewers in whose own experience the concepts of work and leisure are in constant tension. In addition the embryonic portrayals of female friendship which figure as secondary plot-lines in many 1950s sitcoms—Lucy and Ethel in *I Love Lucy*, or Bebe and Florrie in *Life with the Lyons*—are developed to the extent that the narrative focus on several female protagonists allows for the recognition of differences *between* women not only to be acknowledged but also to be explored. Such a focus begins to counter the homogenizing tendency of earlier dramas and, significantly, of terms like 'the feminine' being assumed to be an uncontentious attribute of all (acceptable) women.[15] By the later 1960s a sitcom such as *The Liver Birds* (BBC, 1969–79) could attain a substantial following for a drama based exclusively on the experiences of a disparate group of women.

Popular drama in the late 1950s, in its aim to reassure audiences by presenting the known and familiar and, in the course of this endeavour, re-presenting presumed familiar conventions and patterns of behaviour, offered a relatively regressive view of contemporary gender relations. Yet as the 1950s gave way to the 1960s, and the television enterprise attracted new writers, producers, and directors, there's a developing sense that such fictions must be alert to social *change* as well as to the dilemmas and concerns of the day. Popular television drama, like cinema's box-office hits, tended not to challenge the status quo. Yet small shifts—representations of working women, single mothers, divorce, class mobility—*do* mark television's participation by reflection, at the least, in such change. It would seem that the imperative to satisfy audiences, and hence to maximize ratings, has the necessary consequence of validating at least those changes

---

15 Thumim (1995); (2002: 218–19).

in conventions and expectations which seemed to audiences to be representative of their real-world experience. It is at this historical moment, the early 1960s, that television's always paradoxical deployment of 'the feminine' is most in evidence. Advertisers sought large audiences; the goods they displayed were largely, in this period, small consumer durables within the purview of the 'housewife', hence they sought programming which would maximize the important audience of female consumers. At the same time, however, such television criticism as existed routinely denigrated the majority of such programming on the grounds of its 'triviality' and 'mindlessness', thus denigrating, by extension, female experience. More generally, anxieties about the *habit* of television viewing centred on the emasculatory effect—the feminizing effect—this increasingly ubiquitous habit might have on British culture.

At its best popular television drama was, by the early 1960s, fulfilling the Griersonian objective of enhancing democratic experience by 'showing the people to each other', or put another way, addressing their 'cultural identity' as Richard Paterson notes in his useful summary of international television drama: 'At root television drama plays a major role in all television systems because it aspires, even without self-conscious reflection, to address the cultural identity of its audience.'[16] Despite the denigratory remarks about the impact of television as a new routine in national daily life to be found in the Pilkington Report and the contemporary discourse accruing around it, it seems clear with hindsight that the habits of viewing and patterns of production engendered during this formative phase of British television broadcasting had a profound, and not necessarily negative, effect on the individual's patterns of perception. Paterson suggests further that 'There is a remarkable parallel between the themes of successful situation comedies and the social history of modern society. In the 1960s the key British sitcoms dealt with class and social mobility (or lack of it): *Hancock*, *Steptoe and Son*, *The Likely Lads*, and *The Liver Birds*.'[17] In such an account audiences, through their allegiance to particular programmes, demonstrate the programmes' use-value: despite the epithets 'quality' or 'popular', all programming attracting large and regular audiences may be understood to have some relevance to the daily experience of viewers. John Ellis has usefully suggested the notion of 'working through' to describe what this relevance might be, noting that certain contemporary concerns—examples from this period might be the effect on the family of increased numbers of women working outside the home, or the consequences of the housing shortage—surface across a variety of television genres

16 Paterson (1998: 62).

17 Ibid. 66.

within the same time period and offer, to audiences, ways of thinking about or 'working through' them. With Ellis I would argue that serious consideration of popular drama in this formative period of television broadcasting is essential to an understanding not only of television itself and its enormous possibilities (for good and for ill) but also for understanding the slow struggles characteristic of hegemonic shifts and renewals.

6

Women, Work, and Television

By the mid-1960s television was the dominant form through which culture, information, and representations—hence definitions—of Britain's citizenry, were purveyed and consumed. Where were the challenges to patriarchal hegemony, the refutations of such challenges, and, most important of all, where did those *dis*empowered in patriarchy—by definition women—seem to be accepting the injunction, or the invitation, to collude in their disempowerment? In the preceding chapters I have endeavoured to draw attention to this aspect of the emergent television insitutions. Here I want to summarize my observations and, by placing these small and disparate interactions side by side, as it were, to be alert to the crucial importance of what, at the time, may have appeared insignificant or innocuous actions: in hindsight, I want to argue, such actions aggregate to form the 'stuff' of everyday life so deeply implicated in cultural and national identity. As Brecht famously noted, there's no such thing as neutrality in politics: those who claim silence effectively lend their support to the status quo. The Gramscian idea of collusion as a principle by which we may come to understand how disempowered groups accept their subjugation is useful in understanding the complex relation between the category women and the national institution, television, in this post-war, pre-women's movement decade. This was a decade also characterized by near-full employment, consumer confidence, and an economy which, in hindsight at least, appears to have been remarkably stable, contemporary anxieties notwithstanding. Looking back on the television institutions' formative decade, and with Gramsci's notion of the mechanics of ideological work in mind, three points arise. In general it seems that representations of women and the feminine *on* television by and large *demonstrate* collusion by women in their disempowerment. Employment practices—for example, in the ubiquitous use of the apparently neutral but nevertheless slippery term 'suitable' in evaluations of personnel—seem, in their consequences if not in their intentions, to *ensure* the collusion of women. Television criticism, unsurprisingly, appears to *assume* the collusion of women in their subjugation.

As we have seen, such television criticism as existed exhibited two characteristic features across the political spectrum. The first was a fascination with the potential of the new technology which some saw as full of promise for the 'polis' of the future while others were convinced it was the harbinger of a terminal cultural decline. The second was the assumption that, democratic precepts notwithstanding, in practice women were, rightly or wrongly, second-class citizens and that 'the feminine' in itself posed a threat to the masculine vigour which (should) mark the public sphere in a vibrant democratic state. All sorts of anxieties, as I hope to have suggested, clustered round these twin poles of technology and gender—including those arising from the end of Empire, from cultural and economic relations with the USA, and from the international politics of the cold war as well as the more parochial concerns with morals, ethics, and behavioural conventions inside Britain. On the whole I think we can say that in television criticism, written by *both* men and women, the collusion of women in masculine dominance is assumed. Representations of women on television—certainly in the examples cited—most certainly demonstrate such collusion, unchallenged until the then radical appearance of *Coronation Street*, *The Avengers*, *Till Death Us Do Part*, and other justly celebrated serial dramas. Barry Norman, writing for the *Daily Mail* in 1964, clearly but innocently evidences the widely held assumption of masculine dominance, on and off 'screen'. His readership would have been expected to include both men and women in this mass-circulation 'middlebrow' newspaper. He's routinely commenting on the previous evening's viewing which had included several repeated programmes across the three channels by then available. *The Avengers* with Honor Blackman's original Cathy Gale was on ITV, a repeated play on BBC2, and *Steptoe and Son* on BBC1, and clearly *I Love Lucy* had appeared at some point in the evening. Norman complains of the 'belching flatulence to which television is so often prey' arising, he surmises, 'from being fed largely on a diet of canned goods'. However, he concluded:

> The evening provided . . . the chance to take a nosatalgic look at Honor Blackman, alas to be seen no more in The Avengers, and to compare her with Lucille Ball. For they can be compared. What they have in common is the ability to do totally unfeminine things while remaining unmistakeably feminine. Miss Blackman can be as 'butch' as she likes; Miss Ball can, as she did last night, go to a dance on rollerskates, knock waiters over and fall into a fishpond. But while doing these things they never let you forget for a moment that they are attractive and desirable women. I cannot think of any other girl on TV, with the

possible exception of Millicent Martin, of whom one could say the same.[1]

Blackman's strenuous physicality and Ball's genius for slapstick are celebrated because of the unlikely coexistence of these 'unfeminine' skills with the actors' 'unmistakeable femininity'. And this femininity is then defined, interestingly, as evidencing the qualities of 'attractiveness and desirability': that is, they are understood *as* feminine because of their appeal to male approbation and desire. For this current *Daily Mail* reviewer, moreover, they are the only 'girl(s) on TV' of whom this can be said, 'with the possible exception of Millicent Martin', celebrated for her weekly satirical song in *That Was The Week That Was*. However, despite Norman's no doubt well-meant but nevertheless demeaning comments, by the mid-sixties it is the proto-feminist challenge to women's assumed collusion with male dominance which formed the pretext for many popular fictions—much of the sparkling dialogue of *The Avengers*, for example, turning precisely on this point.

Whereas in representations of women on screen—and in the writing that allowed such representations—there appears to be a slight, though definite progression from the routine subjection of women in the early 1950s to the (albeit uneasy) foregrounding of gender politics in the mid-1960s, there seems to have been a reverse movement in the employment of women.[2] Though in the early 1950s there was a handful of women in senior positions and 'the only thing they wouldn't let us do was read the news',[3] by the end of the 1950s senior women were increasingly rare. Another *Daily Mail* reviewer, Michael Gowers, noted with apparent pleasure but in a typically backhanded tone, the (to him) novel appearance of women in the production workforce of the mid-1960s: 'Last night's episode of Z-Cars . . . was the first to be contributed by a woman (Joan Clark). What with the almost all-women production team on "Martin Chuzzlewit" and a woman producer for "Dr Who" the Monstrous Regiment is really on the march—Bravo!'[4] Thinly disguised, I suggest, by 'almost all-women', the supposed humour of the sobriquet 'Monstrous Regiment' and the concluding cheer is recognition of a threat posed to male dominance in the field of television production, if not in society more widely.

1 *Daily Mail*, 23 Oct. 1964, p. 3.

2 There are no figures to support this intuitive sense based on perusal of various WAC papers from the period. Interestingly, enquiries to BBC Research revealed that no records of the gender balance of employees were kept at that time, hence the question of the relative proportions of men and women in the BBC's workforce between 1955 and 1965 is, effectively, unanswerable.

3 Mary Malcolm and Sylvia Peters speaking in *A Night in with the Girls*, prod. Mary Dickinson, BBC2 (15 Mar. 1997).

4 *Daily Mail*, 30 Jan. 1964, p. 14.

The language betrays unease, though one might reasonably express surprise that in 1964 such female access to production should be so unusual as to merit comment. I think this unease with the presence of the feminine is to be explained, as I have argued earlier, by the increasing masculinization of the institution as its dominance in British cultural and political life was assured.

During the 1950s, despite sporadic examples of an apparently progressive approach to gender politics, the issue as a whole is more striking for its absence—in the secure patriarchal hegemony of the period this is less surprising than its occasional presence. More pressing was the question of class: perceived conflicts of interest between various sections of the audience, male and female, and within the broadcasting institutions at all levels were far more likely to be articulated in these terms. The advent of commercial television and its competition for audiences with the BBC was popularly summarized in the terms of class conflict where the middle-class BBC was seen to be challenged by the cheeky, working-class ITV companies. That such shorthand summaries were far from the truth is beside the point: the fact is that ITV's financing required a broad audience crossing class and income barriers and that the expansion of the audience in the latter fifties in any case rendered the BBC's earlier address to its geographically more limited and middle-class audience obsolete. Those who deplored the 'dilution' of broadcasting did so in class terms, those who welcomed it frequently invoked the supposed class-lessness of the decade's meritocratic ideal. In the broad hegemonic struggles of the fifties, then, class was seen to be at issue whereas gender was not. In exploring historical concerns with the benefit of hindsight it is important to acknowledge what is actually evident: in Britain in the fifties the dominating issues were shifts in class divisions, where economic status was becoming more important than birth or education, and Britain's declining role in international politics consequent on the loss of Empire and an increasingly poor performance in international trade. But though it was not until the later sixties that gender politics assumed anything like an equivalent importance there are nevertheless moments, earlier, where the question can be discerned.

In what follows I want to focus attention on three terms—women, work, and television—since I suspect that it is in the imbrication of these terms and their invidious, though often concealed, fluidity that we may uncover some of the mechanics of hegemonic struggles and/or renewals in the period with which this book is concerned, 1955–65. The term 'women' denotes the female gender, of course, but also and at the same time connotes the guardians of family values, and the conventionally dependent group of adults who are to be protected and provided for. It also references the abstract notion of the feminine, lauded as an appropriate attribute of women as in Barry Norman's approval of Honor Blackman's and Lucille Ball's perform-ance styles, but at the same time defined as the opposite pole to the (preferred) masculine, hence negatively. This symbolic function of *Woman* was, as we have seen, rather disingenuously acknowledged in a 1957 *Panorama* memorandum dealing with cartoon puppets then being made, though in the event not used. In addition to various named (male) world leaders three 'symbolic' characters had been prepared, namely John Bull, Uncle Sam, 'and a female figure to repres-ent variously the U.N., Peace, etc.'. But, and here is the interesting problem, women were in addition also real citizens exercising social power, hence their collusion in such subordinate definitions must be secured if patriarchal dominance was to be maintained.

'Work', it seems to me, is in this context a similarly tricky concept. Apparently straightforward, denoting the various endeavours in which adult citizens engage in order to ensure their economic sur-vival, its meanings become less clear in respect of both women and television. Women's work, as the later women's movement vocifer-ously declared, is invariably *un*paid, invisible, and unaccounted. In this formulation 'women's work' refers to domestic labour support-ing the male breadwinner and his children—the workforce of the future.[5] For female subjects this poses an anomaly which became increasingly visible as quantitative evaluations of worth came to dominate a consumer-led, market-driven economy. The formula-tions 'work outside the home' and 'waged labour' became a clumsy necessity to indicate that for women, whether or not they were wage-earners, the home was not only the locus of leisure and relaxation. Broadcast television intervenes here because of the publicly available images of (women's) domestic labour as well as because of the per-ceived problem that women's domestic efforts might be comprom-ised by the new habit of viewing. As Mary Hill, announcing ITV's morning programming for women had asserted: 'the woman at home, like any other worker, is entitled to . . . a mid-morning break . . . If you are one of those who just can't sit still there are lots of jobs that can be done while viewing'[6] Elsewhere[7] I have drawn attention to the absent mother whose empty armchair is at the centre of a PG Tips tea advert-isement carried by the *TV Times*.[8] The family group is gathered in front of the television, but the mother, as a sign on her chair tells us, has 'gone to make tea': her domestic labour thus continues through the evening's period of family relaxation before the screen. Both the

---

5 Oakley (1974).

6 *TV Times*, 22 Sept.–1 Oct. 1955, p. 14.

7 Thumim (1995).

8 *TV Times*, 28 Oct. 1955.

injunction to the looked-for female audience for daytime program-ming, and the then-ubiquitous image of the family group gathered in domestic harmony before their screen make implicit reference to the contradictions, for women, contained in the conventional assump-tion of the domestic environment as a place of leisure.

The meaning of the third term, television, as this book has demon-strated, was under construction throughout the period. Whereas in the earlier 1950s the primary denotation was one of technological possibility, by the mid-1960s it referenced instead the public articula-tion of current ideas, images, and definitions of the society to which all—producers, performers, audiences—belonged. It's therefore also worth looking a little more closely at the presence of women in the broadcasting workforce as well as at the actual representations on screen—the images of women routinely purveyed—before con-sidering what consensus concerning gender politics was proposed through the television institution.

Women's Employment in Broadcasting

Through its various examinations—in news/current affairs, in drama, in light entertainment—television also *represented* society. As the audience expanded and the habit of viewing became established, television's celebrated facility for exploring the 'drama of life' (Levin), or for the investigative interview (Farson) increasingly contrib-uted, through the simple presence of its mediated images, to viewers' understanding of the society which they themselves formed. In respect of gender politics two questions arise. We can enquire first into the relative numbers of men and women seen on screen, which would contribute to audiences' sense of how society was composed, espe-cially but not only those aspects of society with which they were not personally familiar. Secondly we can ask about the numbers of women employed in television and the degree of authority they were able to exercise, particularly in contributing to what, eventually, came to be seen on the screen: always bearing in mind how those few women, like Goldie, Adams, and Doncaster, who did exercise some power, often subscribed to the prevailing masculinist assumptions about the gender specificity of certain tasks, as for example produc-ing. A 1963 memorandum entitled 'Hazards of Drama Production in the Present Schedule', for example, notes in conclusion that 'it is my personal opinion that women are not suitable as PA/Floor Managers. I have noticed during this winter that, on average, experienced men get the camera rehearsal through much faster.'[9] Characteristically, here, the 'experience' of men is understood as an attribute of their

9 WAC T16/62/3, 22 Mar. 1963, memo from Stuart Burge.

masculine gender, while for women their lack of experience (having been, as we have seen, denied the opportunity to gain the necessary experience) is offered as a reason not to deploy them in (here) drama production. It is impossible to give definitive answers to these questions about the proportions of men and women on screen and in the workforce: much programming was ephemeral and has not survived; records were patchily kept and often 'gender blind'; the sheer volume of programming—over fifty hours per week on two channels over a ten-year period—precludes any exhaustive account. Nevertheless it is instructive to consider the figures that are available as 'snapshots' as it were, likely to be representative of the situation overall. In BBC Talks, as we have seen, there was a preponderance of male over female personnel and the same pattern was true in A-R's *This Week* and probably of current affairs production in most of the other commercial providers, and I have indicated how current affairs provision seems to have become progressively masculinized through the decade. What is perhaps more surprising is the similar picture that emerges from drama production, in the BBC at least (noting the division of labour whereby much 'popular' drama was provided through Light Entertainment and 'quality' drama through the Drama Department). This was recognized apropos writers in the concluding remark to a 1964 memo of a BBC Drama Department meeting, the Head of Serials noting that 'young writers were frightened of women'.[10] The remark betrays the assumption that 'young writers' were male, as well as acknowledging the paucity of a woman's point of view in the majority of currently commissioned work.

Even though, by 1964, several women had achieved sufficient seniority and/or trust in their abilities to produce and direct mainstream programmes like *Z-Cars* and *Dr Who*, they could still be referred to in the *Daily Mail* review cited above as the 'Monstrous Regiment . . . on the march'. A 1960 BBC paper about the costs of actors from the Head of Drama, Michael Barry, gives a list from Bookings of fees recently paid to named performers: there are 59 women and 101 men: almost a 2 : 1 ratio of men : women.[11] A 1956 Granada list of their television personnel in London has 29 women and 34 men, though there is no indication of their jobs and it would probably be safe to assume that many of the 29 women listed were in secretarial or support roles.[12] Later lists, such as the 1959 Programme and Production staff,[13] the 1960 Freelance Personnel,[14] and the

10 WAC T16/62/3, 17 July 1964.

11 WAC T/16/62/3, 14 Mar. 1960.

12 Granada Archive Box 1466, 1956.

13 Granada Archive Box 0978, 1959.

14 Granada Archive Box 1466, 8 Aug. 1960.

1960–1 Numbers on Staff,[15] give no indication of gender. A particularly tantalizing Granada list from 4 January 1961 lists personnel at 31 December 1960 by 'executive' and 'personal staff' showing which personal staff worked to which executive staff and their locations in London or Manchester.[16] All the personal staff are female, being given the titles Mrs or Miss with their surnames, whereas the executives are recorded by surname only, therefore in a gender blind form. Given the other Granada lists we might surmise that the majority of these were male. This is a supposition borne out in the 2003 publication *Granada Television: The First Generation* in which short reminiscences from key staff working at Granada through its early years are collected to provide a fascinating taste of that environment: of the 89 contributors only 11 are women.[17] The consistent gender inequality evident in these 'snapshots' tallies with my observation elsewhere[18] that in films popular at the British box office during the same period there was a preponderance of men over women amongst *all* performers seen on screen, and it is almost certainly the case that a similar male dominance prevailed amongst cinema production, distribution, and exhibition personnel.

Now this is an admittedly sketchy view of the various presences of men and women and of female participation in the construction of such public representations. Nevertheless the resonance between these 'snapshots' for television and for cinema in the same period points to the systemic marginalization of women—in terms both of numbers and of power—and most certainly with respect to any comparisons that might be made with quantitative demographics from the period. In considering the representations of women and the feminine visually purveyed in the public sphere it is important to recall that during the same period female employment outside the home climbed steadily and consistently, hence we might speculate that there was a growing gap between representations of gender balance in the public sphere of work and its actual construction. This is in marked contrast to the successful efforts made during the wartime period of the early forties—in practice, in representation, and in discourse—to position women alongside their male compatriots in the public spheres of work and democratic duty.

A publication in the relatively recent 1993 BBC Charter Review series, *Reinventing the Organisation*, has an essay which explicitly addresses the question of women's employment within the BBC, noting its 'growing awareness' (this was written in 1993) that as a public

15 Granada Archive Box 1447.

16 Granada Archive Box 1466, 4 Jan. 1961.

17 Finch (2003).

18 Thumim (1992: 71–2).

service body its workforce ought to accommodate the demographic variety of its constituency.

> Women have always worked at the BBC, but never in the same numbers as men. It is only in the last 10 years that a conscious effort has been made by management to increase their presence. Pressure for change came from a complex web of factors: from women in the trade unions in the 70s and 80s, from legislation such as the Sex Discrimination Act (1975) and the Equal Pay Act (amended 1983), and from a growing awareness on the part of BBC management that as a public service body, it had to represent the women, ethnic minorities and disabled people in its audience.[19]

'Represent' here means include in the (broadcasting) workforce, but the awareness in question is also, of course, germane to the issue of who and what gets represented on screen—and self-evidently, as this book has attempted to argue, the two are closely related.

Representations of Women on Screen

If we turn from this brief consideration of broadcasting's female workforce to the representations of women available on the domestic screen, an even less progressive picture emerges. Despite the efforts of a few enlightened producers and the insights of a few viewers and critics, the dominant image of women on television in the fifties is an unrelievedly retrograde one. Though there certainly were plenty of women to be seen on the screen in variety performance, popular comedy, and drama and in the afternoon magazine programmes specifically addressed to a female audience, women were notably absent from the prestigious genres of news and current affairs on which, particularly after 1956, television's claim to be a serious contributor to democratic debate was based. In its aim to appeal to the whole audience, and to provide as broadly as possible the education, information, and entertainment required by the terms of both the BBC Charter and the ITA Guidelines, broadcast television tended to reflect, rather than to intervene in, the conventions of gender definition informing society. Outside the ghettos of women's and children's programmes women appeared as entertainers—invariably and clearly subject to a male host or compère—or as 'light relief' included as visual or aural balance in discussion programmes, quiz shows, or current affairs magazines. Thus they were primarily utilized as decorative and hence demeaned as frivolous. The one place where this schema breaks down, however, is in the arena of popular drama

---

19 Murrel (1993: 48).

which, as the decade progressed, occupied an increasingly important place in the schedules. Here not only was a simple female presence more likely to be offered, but her appearance was typically in scenarios in which the routines of domestic life were the subject of a drama or comedy foregrounding female experience. As the series, serials, and sitcoms of the later fifties—both home-produced dramas and those imported from the USA—established their hold on the audience, so too did their implicit and, sometimes, explicit definitions of the feminine enter the cultural arena, offering detailed and small-scale pictures of domestic life which countered the reactionary melodramas of the cinema circuits. Not that these images or performances were necessarily progressive in their definitions of the feminine, but their nightly presence did nevertheless assert a female experience, acting as a counter to the masculinist dominance of most of television's output. It might be argued that here is just another reinforcement of the conventional 'spheres of interest' but it is worth considering the impact of representations which reference viewers' experience as directly as many of these dramas did. The following exchange of dialogue between the central female characters in *The Grove Family* certainly supports the gendered status quo, Mum's willingness to subjugate herself being a classic example of the collusion that, as I have argued, ensures the maintenance of patriarchal hegemony. The episode concerned the Grove Family's recent acquisition of a motor car, and the closing utterance is given to this mid-1950s ideal wife and mother:

GRAN: I suppose you realise what this will let you in for?

MUM: Yes Gran

GRAN: Cooking at the roadside under difficult conditions.

MUM: (blandly) It wouldn't surprise me if they were appalling conditions.

GRAN: And realising all that, you didn't put your foot down?

MUM: No Gran

GRAN: Which can only mean one thing—that you're a slave to your family and a fool, Gladys.

MUM: Yes, I shouldn't wonder, but funnily enough, I've never wanted to be anything else.[20]

Yet viewers had the opportunity to welcome Gran's subversive point of view, or to make up their own minds as to the wisdom—or indeed the verisimilitude—of Mum's happy acceptance of domestic slavery.

Though a glance through Vahimagi's programme notes for the 1960s[21] confirms that, in the majority of programmes, men continued

---

20 WAC T12/137/5, TV Light Entertainment, The Grove Family, File 1, 1954, episode 144 'A Complete Idiot'.

21 Vahimagi (1994).

to dominate both on- and off-screen, there is nevertheless an increased presence of women. Names such as those of writers Nell Dunn and Carla Lane, producers Verity Lambert and Hazel Adair, presenter Joan Bakewell, for example, became well known during the 1960s, suggesting that there was at last a shift in the gender balance of the broadcasting workforce. But these are few compared to the very many celebrated men whose reputations were established in this productive period. More significant for television's contribution to broader social change were the popular dramas featuring female experience, or foregrounding it, which achieved large audiences and became, for short or longer periods, 'household names'. While Alf Garnett is remembered as the dominant central character in *Till Death Us Do Part*, it is also true that most of the plot and dialogue in this hugely popular sitcom turns on his carefully scripted regressive views countered sometimes by his son-in-law, the 'scouse git' played by Anthony Booth, and sometimes by his long-suffering wife 'her indoors' (Dandy Nichols) and daughter (Una Stubbs). Much of the pleasure in watching this celebrated sitcom at the time came from the frisson of hearing Garnett's reactionary views ridiculed and opposed, and from the consequent sense that some things were, indeed, in the process of change. Similarly the earlier *The Avengers*, in its foregrounding of lead character Steed's (Patrick McNee) female partner Cathy Gale (played first by Honor Blackman, then by Diana Rigg), validated the developing view that women could and/or should be the equals of men. Other new series went still further, with premises that specifically highlighted women's experience and casts featuring a substantial female presence, even sometimes one dominated by female actors. *The Rag Trade* (BBC, 1961–3) with Miriam Karlin as shop steward in a garment factory, and both *Compact* (BBC, 1962–5) and *Crossroads* (ATV, 1964–88), dealing respectively with working life in the offices of a women's magazine and in a Midlands hotel, explored both professional and personal relationships from an explicitly female subject position. Like *Coronation Steet*, such dramas made sustained and uncontentious play with the fact that many women did indeed enjoy, or suffer, both domestic *and* workplace experience and, like the rag-trade workers led by Miriam Karlin, expected to be treated as adult citizens on a par with their male counterparts. In the mid-1960s, just as the so-called women's liberation movement began to take hold of popular consciousness, several popular drama series focused even more overtly on the experience of autonomous women—though it has to be said that, like the 1990s US sitcom *Sex and the City*, this experience invariably revolved around the characters' dealings with men. Sheila Hancock played the lead in *The Bed-Sit Girl* (BBC, 1965–6) which dealt with her secretary character's 'steady stream of doomed love affairs and office failures'[22] and her nevertheless undimmed fantasies of glamour and romance. *Miss Adventure* (ABC TV, 1964) was, essentially, a vehicle for the popular comedian Hattie Jacques in which she played a 'confidential investigator for a private-eye agency who gets herself embroiled in various deeds and disasters'.[23] At the end of the 1960s *The Liver Birds* (BBC, 1969–79) achieved far greater popularity with its stories of two Liverpudlians Beryl (Polly James) and Dawn (Pauline Collins) sharing a bedsitter: like other series this was originally conceived for a one-off *Comedy Playhouse* (14 Apr. 1969) by writers Carla Lane, Myra Taylor, and Lew Schwartz. But though the concept of women's liberation and the newly accepted rhetoric of women's equality certainly informed both plot and character development, these radical ideas were just as likely to be the butt of humour as were Garnett's absurdly reactionary views in *Till Death Us Do Part*.

In the simultaneous presence of such dramas we can perhaps discern the process articulated by Ellis, that of 'working through' issues of contemporary concern—in this case the personal and social consequences of empowered women taking their place on the public stage. And though it is true that many plot devices, not to mention narrative closures, suggested the unsatisfactory nature of women's unfulfilled ambition (invariably couched in terms of heterosexual partnerships), nevertheless the attention to female subjectivity, however falsely understood or presented, was undoubtedly influential. The generation of feminist scholars emerging in the 1970s and having been educated during the 1960s, for example, was provoked by these ubiquitous tales of female experience to develop an informed and speculative critical response to the materials of popular culture, as Charlotte Brunsdon's *The Feminist, The Housewife, and the Soap Opera* demonstrates.[24] Whereas the documentaries and magazine programmes produced by the Family Programmes Department— such as *Marriage Today* and *Gilt and Gingerbread*—had attempted to assert female subjectivity in the public sphere, it seems that popular dramas, no doubt partly because of the much larger audiences consequent on mainstream, prime-time scheduling, were more successful. Much of the Family Programmes output in the mid-1960s, including *Marriage Today* and *Gilt and Gingerbread*, aired on BBC2 which, we should remember, was launched on 21 April 1964 but was initially received only in the London area, and in homes wealthy enough to acquire new receivers compatible with 625-line transmissions. The audience for BBC2 in the 1960s, therefore, bore some similarity to the

22 Vahimagi, 135.

23 Ibid. 130.

24 Brunsdon (2000).

limited audience for BBC television in the early 1950s—that is to say, it did not match the national demographics but was a minority defined by geographical area (the Home Counties) and economic level.

Discourse In the latter part of the fifties the need to attract and secure a regular audience for broadcast television implied a careful attention to the requirements of the female audience. It is clear that this was a project fraught with difficulties since, though division of the population by gender may have made sense for simple and quantitative demographic statistics, such a division could not easily produce the qualitative information required by broadcasters in assessing the likely interests of their audience. To do this they were obliged to fall back on a combination of experience in other media (radio, the press) and their own assumptions. Since the majority of managerial and executive posts were held by men it is not surprising to find that male assumptions about female interests predominated in programme planning, nor that resources devoted to this section of the audience were relatively small. What is, perhaps, surprising is the extent to which this constraint was acknowledged despite the prevailing masculinist discourse. Throughout the fifties small items can be found in the ubiquitous magazine programmes, and to a lesser but still noticeable extent in documentary subjects, which attempt to place on the agenda of public debate questions concerning gender relations— particularly as these touched on the access to social power.[25] The BBC documentary series *Special Enquiry* for example, produced explorations about unmarried mothers (*Woman Alone*, 9.00–10.00 p.m., 5 Jan. 1956) and prostitution (*Without Love*, 9.15–10.15 p.m., 13 Dec. 1956) both of which received substantial attention in press reviews. These included passionate responses both for and against the programmes (see Chapter 2, above). The controversy generated, especially by the programme on prostitution, indicates that here television was operating progressively in giving air-space to a previously taboo subject on which strong opinions were held, hence contributing positively to public sphere debate. On *Woman Alone* Audience Research reported:

> Most viewers welcomed a programme which 'spotlighted a rarely mentioned subject' in so dignified and sympathetic a way. The

25 Of fifty-eight 'documentary and special' programmes on a 'selected list of Granada TV programmes' broadcast between 1956 and 1964, five took gender-related issues as their subject: *Homosexuality and the Law*; *The Pill (contraception)*; *The Trouble with Men*; *The Trouble with Women*; *Unmarried Mothers*. Sadly there is no indication of transmission dates. Granada Archive Box 1384.

programme was undoubtedly illuminating—to the few, even startling—but nearly all found it convincing and 'true to life'. It presented the problem in a 'reasonable and mature' manner. . . . The BBC, said viewers, should be congratulated on having the courage to tackle so delicate a subject in such a bold and imaginative way. The programme provided insight into an age-old problem and could, they felt, do nothing but good.

'As a trained nurse I have met all these people in real life' wrote the wife of a chartered accountant[26]

and about *Without Love*:

The great majority were deeply (and favourably) impressed by 'Without Love' in all its aspects. In the general view, the programme was vivid, convincing and thought-provoking to a degree, with personalities and situations well-integrated, and it was thought that those concerned with its preparation deserved the highest praise for 'spotlighting' a tragic and disturbing social problem without fear or favour, even to the point of 'showing up the hopeless and farcical laws we have for controlling this age-old evil'. The BBC, viewers went on to say, was to be congratulated for taking the courageous step of tackling so ugly a subject in such a frank and effective way. . . .

'This type of programme is difficult to analyse. We can hardly classify it as an entertainment, but we admit that it certainly was a valuable piece of moral education, especially to the adolescent, and as such we give it full marks'. Wife of a Boot and Shoe Manufacturer.[27]

Though the BBC's Audience Research recorded a largely positive response to this consciously and deliberately controversial programme, the substantial press coverage it generated was less generous. The fact that the BBC recognized the riskiness of the programme's content is acknowledged in the unusual device of following the broadcast with a post-programme discussion between, interestingly, a group of four eminent women. This decision to broadcast a debate on a documentary about prostitution, but to field an exclusively female team, suggests some sympathy on the part of BBC management with the *News Chronicle* reviewer's furious repudiation of the suggestion that prostitution concerned men as well as women:

'Only the BBC could do this sort of thing' said that worthy BBC executive, Mary Adams . . . she was right . . . and only the BBC could have screwed up enough courage to launch the subject of

26 WAC VR/56/11.

27 WAC VR/56/655.

prostitution and then faltered enough to view vice through
spectacles faintly tinted with rose . . .

The following discussion was not too constructive, either. Only
Miss Marghanita Lasky seemed able to speak the word 'prostitute'
without a genteel momentary hesitation.

For such a quartette of experts, the argument was alarmingly
naïve, based both dangerously and fallaciously on the belief that
prostitutes only exist because there is a distinct society of men
who patronise them[28]

For James Thomas, at least, Mary Adams may have been 'worthy' but
she was also wrong-headed in that she (or the BBC for whom she
spoke) failed to follow through their brave exploration of 'vice' except
through rose-tinted spectacles. This is 1956 and Adams, of course,
was claiming the moral high ground for the BBC's willingness to
broach contentious subject matter in contrast to the crowd-pleasing
antics of 'the competitor' (ITV). Thomas further denigrates women
by his deployment of the feminine form 'quartette' and by his recognition of 'genteel hestitation' and his accusation of naivety in the
broadcast discussion. What, I wonder, was it that was so 'dangerous'
about the supposedly fallacious belief? To today's reader it seems
extraordinary that the proposition that prostitution implicates men
could be contentious. Yet for precisely this reason this review, and
others like it, allows valuable insight into contemporary assumptions
and to the very great distance between consensual views of women
and the feminine prevailing in the 1950s and those informing social
debate after the 1960s. Hence, we might speculate, such programming and the passionate and varied responses elicited *contributed* to
developments in gender politics: though Mary Adams could not have
recognized the BBC's intervention in such terms, nevertheless here is
an instance of the emergent televisual institution setting, rather than
following, the national agenda.

If television's 'brief' was to 'examine the condition of society', what
model did its masculinist bias offer to women viewers? It is perhaps
paradoxical that, in the decade so widely celebrated for its emergent
women's movement, this apparently retrograde feature is to be
observed. Yet it seems to me that as the various strands of a politically
conscious feminism (which we should acknowledge to be survivors
from the inter-war 1920s and 1930s as well as from the better remembered radicalism of the Second World War) emerged through the
decade 1955–65 they met, not surprisingly, with an increasingly rigid
and vociferous opposition. It's a truism, after all, that if women are
to have more power in the public sphere then men must have less.
One way of understanding the exciting turbulence of the 1960s is for

28 James Thomas, *News Chronicle*, 21 Dec. 1956, p. 6.

its polarization of interest groups amongst which the opposition between men and women in terms of their access to power and visibility was certainly considered, consciously, in such terms. The political turbulence of the 1960s coincided with television's own increased confidence and its achievement of undisputed centrality on both the political and cultural stages.

As the furore caused by the documentary *Without Love* suggests, the language used in programme announcements, in the viewer responses collected by BBC Audience Research, and in the routine press reviews of broadcast material, all indicates a pretty solid consensus supporting the status quo in which women were still regarded as secondary citizens. Viewers' responses to the 'magazine programme to interest the family' *Home* (8.15–8.45 p.m., 17 Jan. 1955) produced by Women's Programmes (this was one of the Women's Programmes Unit's rare appearances in the prime-time evening schedules) were not positive, and the criticism was expressed with reference to 'the feminine':

> 'What's New' was considered a rather doubtful miscellany, reasonably good from the feminine point of view, but with nothing arresting in the way of novelties. . . .
>
> There was not much to choose between reactions to Roma Fairley and Kenneth Wolstenholme, as comperes. Both were considered to have made quite a good attempt to present their material, but Kenneth Wolstenholme struck many viewers as rather 'out of his element', and Roma Fairley, despite a good deal of natural charm, also gave the impression that she, too, was not yet sure of her ground.[29]

Whereas Wolstenholme was 'out of his element', Fairley was perceived as 'not yet sure of her ground': this is a subtle difference, but typical of the terms in which criticisms of presenters' style was offered. Where the male presenter has been misplaced (by producers), the female is responsible for her own shortcomings—her charm is 'natural' but she is 'not sure'. Occasionally viewers commented explicitly on instances of gender politics noted within programmes, as the response to a *Look and Choose* 'enquiry into dry and steam heat-controlled electric irons' (3.00–3.45 p.m., 26 Sept. 1955) indicated:

> The only point mentioned by more than one viewer was that the men experts were inclined to dismiss the housewives' criticisms as worthless. According to a Clerk 'the men's attitude was "That's what we make, and if you don't like it you can go without" '.[30]

29 WAC VR/55/30.

30 WAC VR/55/480.

Here the 'men experts' assumption of spheres of interest was recognized as inappropriate since it was the housewives who were to use the new irons discussed in the programme. More generally, however, such assumptions were offered as uncontroversial, as the following typical report on a *Panorama* magazine (8.00–8.45 p.m., 14 Nov. 1955) showed:

> There was . . . widespread agreement . . . that the programme had been unusually well-balanced, with 'a nice variety of things to see and hear' (Tool Maker). A Ministry of Supply Inspector enlarged upon this point in his comment: 'it catered for the womenfolk (fashions in Russia and the interview with Hartnell), and the men had their innings too, with the discussion comparing British and American transatlantic flight plans.'[31]

In line with hegemonic theory this consensus about gendered spheres of interest necessarily entailed the aquiescence of women with their allotted subject position. By the end of the fifties a note of irony could sometimes be discerned in viewers' reactions, for example this report on another edition of *Panorama* (8.35–9.20 p.m., 7 Dec. 1959):

> Here too, Robin Day, the interviewer, collected much credit for his cogent . . . questions when attempting to get at the meaning of 'wild-cat' strikes. In several opinions he was outstanding for the clarity of his reasoning when arguing points with his contacts (a Housewife remarking, 'even I, as a mere woman, could follow what was said').[32]

Whether or not the 'Housewife's' remark was intended ironically, it is nevertheless true that contradicting this acquiescence over appropriate and gendered spheres of interest were various broad social movements which, as the decade progressed, were more and more likely to find their place in televisual debates and representations. The post-war Education Act, for example, had promised equality of opportunity for boys and girls; from the early fifties there was debate about reform of the divorce laws which necessarily drew attention to current inequities; expanding consumer and service industries provided full employment and the proportion of married women performing waged work outside the home rose steadily; it was generally assumed that young women would take paid employment on completing their education. All these broad changes took place against the background of the fairly recent upheavals of the Second World War in which women from all walks of life had competently and publicly contributed to the national effort both within and outside the domestic arena.

31 WAC VR/55/566.
32 WAC VR/59/706.

While it is true that the later forties were characterized by substantial attempts to compensate for wartime disruptions by re-placing women 'in the home', and that the fifties is popularly regarded as a regressive decade for women, it is also true that some of women's more positive experiences of citizenship had not been—could not be—forgotten. It is worth recalling, in this context, that whereas popular cinematic representations of women in the fifties were invariably regressive, women's magazines, lightweight and trivial though they may have appeared in their tone and contents, did nevertheless more closely address the real experience of their contemporary readership, routinely carrying features which acknowledged women's presence in the public world of the workplace.[33] Television, however, was in a tricky position. Like popular cinema it addressed a mass audience, unlike women's magazines it was obliged to cater for the whole national audience in all its demographic variation—the specific programming for women (which barely survived into the sixties) notwithstanding. It is important to remember that during the fifties the simple fact of television's presence and the technological marvels this entailed was a significant element in the viewers' pleasure in watching programmes: BBC Audience Research reports on individual programmes always included responses to their technics, as well as to their content. But despite the managerial privileging of a masculine point of view, and despite the female audience's collusion in contemporary gender inequalities, the heterogeneous development of broadcasting through the fifties did allow progressive attitudes to gender or, at the least, a speculative approach to contemporary gender-related problems, to find a voice.

Conclusion

As I suggested in Chapter 1 the two major programme areas—factual, and popular drama—in the emergent televisual landscape seem particularly important not only for the establishment of the television institution itself but also in the context of its place in, and contribution to, the rapidly changing society of the time. In addition the magazine form, deployed across several programme types from light entertainment to current affairs, both acknowledged and developed habits of fragmented attention in viewers. Popular drama, in its increasing attention to female experience as central to its premises and plot devices, and despite its supposed ephemerality was, as I have argued, highly significant in reflecting and/or setting the agenda for change in the field of gender politics. The television institution though, was, and is, above all heterogeneous in forms, contents,

---

33 Thumim (1992: 191–6).

and audiences. As the magazine form attempted to secure audiences through deployment of variety in content and address, and as popular drama increasingly allowed the foregrounding of (some) female experience, the current affairs operation became ever more masculinist, allying itself with news at the very centre of the television institution. The BBC's *Panorama*, A-R's *This Week*, and, later, Granada's *World in Action* were all (justly) celebrated for their robust journalism, their searching documentary enquiries, their intrepid teams of reporters and cameramen, and their well-loved and trusted (male) presenters of which *Panorama*'s Richard Dimbleby is probably the best remembered. Though women were not totally absent from on-screen items, they were far more likely to occupy the position of object than that of subject, and though the respective production teams *did* include women (always in a clear minority) this neither implied nor encouraged a feminine, nor indeed a feminist, sensibility informing production decisions. Hence with respect to gender politics the (arguably) progressive interventions in the field of popular drama were more than compensated by the masculinism of news and current affairs. Since the news/current affairs operation quickly established its primacy in the television insitution at the heart of the democratic state it's worth looking back over its ten-year gestation: how and why, we may ask, did current affairs come to occupy its prestigious and influential position? Why, given the founding presence of women such as Goldie at the BBC or Doncaster at A-R, did the genre persist in presenting such an unrelievedly masculine view of the contemporary world?

For the BBC newsmen of the mid-fifties, not only was the female an increasingly discomfiting figure but so, too, was the visual image in itself suspect, as we have seen, since it might detract from the gravitas of the newsroom's spoken truths. Not surprisingly, the prospect of an authoritative female voice in vision, pre-war questionnaire findings notwithstanding, was doubly disturbing. It was Independent Television News which, no doubt as part of the competitive innovations by which ITV hoped to entice audiences away from the BBC, had in 1955 first introduced a woman reading the news. However, this innovation was a highly compromised one since Barbara Mandel was only invited to read the lunchtime bulletin to the (presumed) predominantly female daytime audience and did this against a painted set depicting a domestic kitchen.[34] The BBC did not follow suit until 1960 when, for a short time, Nan Winton read the 9.00 p.m. news on Sunday evening. She recalls that

> I didn't realise what a revolutionary thing it was . . . I didn't have any trouble from the press or from the public, it was the editorial

---

34 *A Night in with the Girls*, prod. Mary Dickinson, BBC2 (15 Mar. 1997).

staff who were a bit dodgy, men in their middle years who'd come from Fleet St . . . they certainly were a bit ambivalent about me. They were very, very serious about the News. It was a very serious business.[35]

Here again is that ubiquitous term 'serious' which, in production memoranda, in press and audience responses, and in parliamentary discourse is used to denote the value to which broadcast television must aspire if it was to attain the Reithian objectives enshrined in the BBC Charter and also in the ITA guidelines. Nan Winton's reminiscence, in the parlance of the time, makes explicit the synonymity of the 'serious' with the masculine. Stuart Hood, at that time a senior member of the BBC's directorate, also remembered the resistance encountered by this short-lived innovation:

> I thought it would be rather nice to have a woman newsreader on television. Now this was greeted with alarm and dismay and resistance by my editors. The thought that a woman could be the conveyor of truth and authority on the television screen was something they just couldn't imagine, couldn't accept.[36]

The failure of imagination to which Hood refers is detectable not only in the editorial resistance of the supposedly permissive 1960s, but much earlier, as I have suggested, in the very structure of the developing institution. Though, as Mary Malcolm and Sylvia Peters had recalled, there *were* many senior women in the earliest days of the BBC and 'the only thing they wouldn't let us do was read the news', questions of veracity, control, and the possession of 'appropriate' qualities were always central to those sections in which output was most closely aligned with the news and, latterly, current affairs operations. Leonard Miall, Head of Talks from 1954 to 1962, suggested that the Outside Broadcasts Department, for example, required special (implicitly masculine) qualities from its personnel: 'A lot of them had been fighter pilots in the RAF before joining the television service and in some ways you needed the same kind of qualities for a good director of a live television programme.'[37] Though Hood's 1960 intervention was certainly a radical one, by 1964 even he had apparently internalized the broadcasters' pervasive suspicion of female power as somehow inappropriate, or worse, threatening. Doreen Stephens, by then Head of the Family Programmes Department, was arranging regional visits in connection with children's programmes and asked him, 'Although Birmingham is not on this agenda, I could

35 Ibid.

36 Ibid.

37 Ibid.

have good reason to visit it for the 'Marriage Today' series. Would you like me to coincide such a visit, so that I could happen to be in Birmingham and, while there, attend this Women's Protest meeting to get the feel of it for you?' Hood's reply was curt and unequivocal: 'I do not think that you ought to attend the Women's Protest meeting in Birmingham. There has been a good deal of correspondence in the local press, not all of it on the side of the protesters.'[38] With hindsight this seems like a clear case of agenda-setting by omission—the very fact of the local correspondence seeming to point to an issue of concern to citizens (also constituting the television audience) and therefore one precisely relevant in fulfilling television's brief to 'examine the condition of society', as BBC producers in the early 1950s had seen it.

In the development from *The Grove Family* or *Life with the Lyons* in the mid-fifties to *Coronation Street* in the early sixties there is a clear refinement of the scope of family drama which rests on the complexity of its central characters and the quality of its writing and production values. In their way these popular dramas did as much as—if not more than—the more celebrated 'quality' output of *Armchair Theatre* or *The Wednesday Play* to contribute to the establishment of what Raymond Williams has referred to in his 1974 inaugural lecture at the University of Cambridge as 'Drama in a Dramatised Society'.[39] To take one example from the mid-1960s: the BBC's *Comedy Playhouse* (1961–4) which, like *Armchair Theatre* (ABC TV, 1956–69; Thames TV, 1970–4) comprised a generally un-related series of single plays, gave rise to some of the more celebrated series drama of the time. Johnny Speight's *Till Death Do Us Part* (BBC1, 1966–8; 1972; 1974–5) began life as a single play as did also Alan Simpson and Ray Galton's *Steptoe and Son* (BBC 1962–5; 1970; 1972; 1974) which had originated in the *Comedy Playhouse* single play *The Offer* (5 Jan. 1962). Concerns originally explored in a 'qual-ity drama' thus gave rise to influential and long-running series which exemplify Williams's analysis of what he perceived to be a qualitative change in the relation of drama to society. Williams's seminal lecture presents a provocative and engaging meditation on the place of drama in twentieth-century Western society. His principal observa-tion is that whereas historically dramatic productions of all kinds were relatively rare events, a special occasion for their audiences, the development of both dramatic writing and the new technologies of film and television have, during the course of the twentieth century, given rise to a qualitatively different experience of drama.

---

38 WAC T32/395, 13 and 20 Feb. 1964.

39 On 29 Oct. 1974.

The consumption of dramatized fictions has become, he suggests, a routine part of everyday experience for the majority. He writes:

> But what is really new—so new I think that it is difficult to see its significance—is that it is not just a matter of audiences for particular plays. It is that drama, in quite new ways, is built into the rhythms of everyday life. On television alone it is normal for viewers—the substantial majority of the population—to see anything up to three hours of drama, of course drama of several different kinds, a day. And not just one day; almost every day. This is part of what I mean by a dramatised society.[40]

The great majority of the dramas to which Williams refers concerned, as we have seen, familial relations, the routines of the home and the workplace, the experience of everyday life: just the same everyday life that, for Williams, is irrevocably altered by new habits consequent upon new technologies. And within these everyday routines—which viewers/audiences naturally understand and measure with reference to their own experience, as we have seen in the quotes from the BBC's Audience Research respondents—are, of course, those concerned with gendered behaviours and conventions. Hence questions of hegemony, collusion or contestation, and change arise from consideration of the dramas offered nightly on the nation's domestic screens—and not just the fictional dramas but also the habit of narrative and modes of speech which had begun to inform other genres of programming. Williams had something to say about this, too:

> Again I heard, as if for the first time, what was still, by habit, called dramatic speech, even dialogue; heard it in Chekhov and noticed a now habitual strangeness: that the voices were no longer speaking to or at each other; were speaking with each other perhaps, with themselves in the presence of others. But there was a new composition, in which a group was speaking, yet a strange negative group; no individual ever quite finishing what he had begun to say, but intersecting, being intersected by the words of others, casual and distracted, words in their turn unfinished: a weaving of voices in which, though still negatively, the group was speaking and yet no single person was ever finally articulate. It is by now so normal a process, in writing dramatic speech, that it can be heard, any night, in a television serial, and this is not just imitation. It is a way of speaking and listening, a specific rhythm of a particular consciousness; in the form of an unfinished, transient, anxious relationship, which is there on the stage or in the text but which is also, pervasively, a structure of feeling in a

---

40 Williams (1989: 4).

precise contemporary world, in a period of history which has that familiar and complex transience.[41]

For Williams in his prescient essay and his thoughtful television reviewing (sadly outside the scope of this book since it appeared in *The Listener* between 1968 and 1972) it is not only the daily habit of consuming dramatic fictions—dramatized stories—which marks change in the routines of everyday life but also the very quality of speech itself is affected. He hears 'a weaving of voices in which ... no single person was ever finally articulate' and though he refers specifically to the dramatic speech purveyed through televised drama I think there's more to it. Williams's recognition of such fundamental change in our modes of perception and communication seems to me to point directly to the altered subject positions which we now occupy as a consequence of our habitual consumption of all kinds of stories. John Ellis proposes that, in our routine exposure to the stories purveyed through news and current affairs programming we are in the position of 'witness': we see but cannot (usually) act on what we see. He develops this observation into the proposition that, as a consequence of this experience of 'witnessing' we use—I understand him to refer to both producers and consumers in that 'we'—other generic forms to 'work through' the material witnessed. Hence both Williams, in his 1974 recognition of new 'structures of feeling', and Ellis, in his more recent formulations of 'witnessing' and 'working through', seem to me to be concerned with the fundamental centrality of broadcast television in the formation not only of national and cultural identity, but also of subjective experience itself. How crucial, then, that this powerful medium does truly engage with the full range of social subjects, and how vital a tool it now is, and has been, in hegemonic struggle. Though in the early twenty-first century questions of gender may seem to be of less importance than those of ethnicity, racial and religious difference, we should recall that, in the 1950s, class seemed to be a more central concern concealing contestation and change in the field of gender. For the planners and managers working in, and at the same time inventing, the institution, television's brief was to examine and present society to itself: fifty years later that examination must in itself be conceived as a part of the thing to be examined. As the editor of Williams's collected television criticism, Alan O'Connor, notes in his introduction:

> The analysis of television collected in this book is part of a project, now cut short by Willams' death, to continually show such intolerable conflicts and contradictions as they are mediated, in ways not at first obvious, through the complexity of televised

41 Williams (1989: 12).

cultural forms. It is important that this kind of cultural analysis continue.[42]

Television's central role in forming 'structures of feeling' (Williams) or 'working through' (Ellis) the issues and events witnessed on the nation's domestic screens is thus acknowledged. These observations from two scholarly critics are confirmed in the rather more pragmatic 1993 BBC Charter Review (quoted earlier), particularly in its evident concern with the still unbalanced gender proportions of the workforce.

By the mid-sixties, though the upper management levels in both the BBC and ITV were almost exclusively male preserves, broadcast television as we have seen certainly purveyed a substantial quantity of programming in all genres and at all cultural levels which acknowledged women's movement towards democratic equality and, conversely, the inequities to which they were currently subject. This is not to suggest television as an unequivocally progressive force, but rather to acknowledge its role in bringing to the forefront of public consciousness those issues associated with 'women's liberation' and with the feminist interventions of the later 1960s. Even when, as was often the case, broadcast material mocked or demeaned women's aspirations, it still allowed a mass, national focus on them. Thus it could be argued that, the current affairs operation notwithstanding, television contributed more substantially than any other cultural form to changes in expectations of, and attitudes to, women's place in British society—slow, hesitant, and precarious though these changes were.

With the advantage of hindsight, as in all writings of history, it becomes possible to perceive the unfolding of past events in periods: the post-war period of social reconstruction; the 'primitive' phase of early, pre-First World War cinema; and in the case of this study the formative period of plural channel broadcasting to a mass, national UK audience. Ellis, taking the longer view of television history, suggests that this falls into three distinct periods. He summarizes these as eras of scarcity (until the late seventies/early eighties), availability (from then until the late nineties), and plenty: the last, he suggests, may still be a promise rather than a fact for audiences, and he therefore also characterizes the current period as one of uncertainty. While these terms offer a useful context within which to consider television's structures and outputs, I would suggest that within the period defined by Ellis as one of scarcity there are further subtleties to be noted: these are significant because of the way they contributed to setting television's agenda, as it were, for the period of availability as well as for the present period of plenty and/or uncertainty.

---

42 O'Connor (1989: p. xvii).

In 1936–9 and 1946–55 there was in the UK a one-channel monopoly broadcasting to a limited section of the potential audience: the mass national audience was in the process of being built, as this book has indicated. From the commencement of the ITV operation in 1955 there was a two-channel, hence plural, broadcasting environment but, though the BBC's transmitter network was nearing completion, ITV's transmitters did not reach the whole population until the early 1960s, hence the national audience for a multi-channel operation was still under construction throughout this period. Following the 1962 Pilkington Report, and the White Paper of the same year in which many of its recommendations were adopted, a third channel was allowed. BBC2 commenced operation in 1964. But within this 1955–65 period not only was the audience under construction but, as this book has attempted to demonstrate, so too were the insitutional and management structures, the genres, programme types and forms, and the scheduling practices (not to mention the assumptions informing these) which, by the end of the 1960s, came to characterize the British television operation. Ellis's conception of scarcity, in contrast to the availability he suggests as characteristic from the 1980s onwards, is, however, still a useful one since it is all too easy to forget that, until the 1980s, broadcasting hours were limited and twenty-four-hour availability of broadcast material was not yet a reality. Nevertheless it is important to remain alert to differences within this period of scarcity, and to the crucial significance, for subsequent developments in broadcasting, of this formative period, 1955–65. It is during this ten-year period that all elements of the institution—its audiences, its structures, its genres, its scheduling practices—were the subject of imaginative interventions on the part of various pioneering groups in both the BBC and the companies, amongst which Granada is particularly key because of the longevity of its own operation.

What has concerned me in exploring this period, following Williams's admonition about the centrality of broadcast television to the development of national culture and identity, to changes in the 'structure of feeling' informing our understandings and hence our social interactions, is the part television has played in hegemonic struggles over gender and power. As we have seen, the question of representations of women on screen, and of their 'representation' in the broadcasting workforce, has exercised those concerned that this unquestionably dominant national forum for the circulation of information and opinion has continued to present a biased view of the society we inhabit together. A recent example (autumn 2003) of two documentary reports will, I hope, suggest that this process of change, this excruciatingly slow move towards equality between the sexes, still has some considerable way to go. *Secret Policeman* (BBC,

21 Oct. 2003) was widely leaked before transmission as a 'shocking' exposé of insitutional racism in the Greater Manchester police force. A young male reporter, working undercover, had been accepted onto a police training programme and produced a video report of his experience, focusing particularly on instances of racism amongst his fellow trainees. Following the transmission there was considerable public response in the form of press reviews and editorials, items on current affairs programmes such as *Newsnight*, and, significantly, a spate of letters including one the next day in the *Guardian* deploring the racist behaviour of the trainees depicted, calling for their expulsion from the police training programme, and signed collectively by senior managers representing the majority of British police forces. The second programme, a *Panorama* report on the home-based care of the elderly (BBC, 16 Nov. 2003), also featured an undercover report. In this case a young female reporter, posing as an untrained care-worker and with false references and an invented career history, had attempted to get jobs with agencies supplying carers to local councils in several different towns in Britain. She had been remarkably successful with a number of agencies, and had worked, largely untrained and unsupervised, with several highly disabled, dependent, and often confused old people. Like the *Secret Policeman* reporter she used a hidden camera, interspersing her hand-held footage with to-camera 'video diary'-type inserts recording her reaction to events as they unfolded. What she revealed was a shocking picture of disrespectful treatment of the old, exploitation of low-paid carers, and a cavalier attitude on the part of both the agencies themselves and the Social Services departments who routinely called on their services. Both reports revealed serious malfunction at the heart of vital social insitutions on which we all depend for the maintenance of what we take to be a civilized society. But it was the masculine story of racist outrage in the male-dominated police force, secured by the male reporter, that achieved a wider debate on the issues it exposed, and was further validated at the April 2004 BAFTA awards as the Best Current Affairs Documentary. The *Panorama* report, transmitted in the 'graveyard slot' late on a Sunday evening, dealing with a more 'feminine' story of low pay, caring, exploitation, and with a female reporter, generated little, if any, public response: no reviews, no current affairs discussion, no letters to the *Guardian*, no celebratory awards.

There may be all sorts of other reasons for the different responses to these two rather similar contemporary examples of committed investigative journalism. However, given the provenance of the masculinist discourse outlined through this book, it seems to me that the question of hegemonic struggles over the relative value of differently gendered social issues may also be germane. The male story of bullying, smugness, hatred seems to carry more weight than the female story of exploitation, neglect, and suffering. If the enormous power of the medium, broadcast television, in all its future multi-channel, internet, and cable access forms in the era of plenty apparently just on the horizon is to be a positive social force, then surely we must engage with it discursively on whatever terrain is available to us. We must be alert to tone of voice, scheduling values, agenda setting, as alert to what is absent as to that which we are encouraged, through advance publicity and prime-time scheduling, to watch.

Bibliography

ANDERSON, CHRISTOPHER (1994), *HollywoodTV: The Studio System in the Fifties* (Austin: University of Texas Press).

ANG, IEN (1991), *Desperately Seeking the Audience* (London and New York: Routledge).

BOLTON, ROGER (1997), 'The Problems of Making Political Television' in Tim O'Sullivan and Yvonne Jewkes (eds.), *The Media Studies Reader* (London and New York: Arnold), 260–71.

BRIGGS, ASA (2000), 'The End of the Monopoly', in Edward Buscombe (ed.) *British Television: A Reader* (Oxford: Oxford University Press), 63–91 (1st pub. 1979).

—— (1985), *The BBC: The First Fifty Years* (Oxford and New York: Oxford University Press).

BRUNSDON, CHARLOTTE (2000), *The Feminist, the Housewife, and the Soap Opera* (Oxford and New York: Oxford University Press).

CALDER, ANGUS (1982), *The People's War* (London, Toronto, Sydney, and New York: Granada) (1st pub. 1969).

CORNER, JOHN (1995), *Television Form and Public Address* (London: Edward Arnold).

ELLIS, JOHN (1975), 'Art, Culture, Quality: Terms for a Cinema in the 40s and 70s', *Screen*, 16/1 (Oxford: Oxford University Press), 9–49.

—— (2000), *Seeing Things: Television in the Age of Uncertainty* (London and New York: I. B. Tauris).

FARSON, DAN (1975), *The Dan Farson Black and White Picture Show* (London: Lemon Tree Press).

FINCH, JOHN (2003) (ed.), *Granada Television: The First Generation* (Manchester and New York: Manchester University Press).

FORMAN, DENNIS (1997), *Persona Granada* (London: Andre Deutsch).

GODDARD, PETER (2003), 'The "Due Impartiality" Context: Regulating *World in Action*', paper given at the conference 'Current Affairs: An Endangered Species', Bournemouth University, Nov. 2003.

GOLDIE, GRACE WYNDHAM (1977), *Facing the Nation* (London: Bodley Head).

HEBDIGE, DICK (1988), *Hiding in the Light* (London and New York: Routledge).

HELLER, CAROLINE (1978), *Broadcasting and Accountability* (London: British Film Institute).

HIMMELWEIT, HILDE, OPPENHEIM, ABRAHAM NAFTALI, and VINCE, PAMELA, (1958), *Television and the Child: An Empirical Study into the Effects of Television on the Young Child* (Oxford: published for the Nuffield Foundation Oxford University Press).

HOOD, STUART (1980), *Stuart Hood on Television* (London: Pluto Press Ltd.).

HOPKINSON, TOM (1970) (ed.), *Picture Post 1938–50* (Harmondsworth: Penguin Books and Allen Lane).

JACOBS, JASON (2000), *The Intimate Screen: Early British Television Drama* (Oxford: Oxford University Press).

LINDLEY, RICHARD (2003), *Panorama: Fifty Years of Pride and Paranoia* (London: Politico's).

MACMURRAUGH-KAVANAGH, MADELEINE (1997*a*), 'The BBC and the Birth of "The Wednesday Play": Institutional Containment versus "Agitational Contemporaneity" ' *Historical Journal of Film, Radio, Television*, 17/3: 367–81.

—— (1997*b*), ' "Drama" into "News": Strategies of Intervention in "The Wednesdsay Play" ', *Screen*, 38/3: 247–59.

MIALL, LEONARD (1966) (ed.), *Richard Dimbleby, Broadcaster* (London: BBC).

MURRELL, RACHEL (1993), 'Taking it Personally: Women and Change in the BBC' in Geoff Mulgan and Richard Paterson (eds.), *Reinventing the Organisation* (London: British Film Institute), 47–58.

OAKLEY, ANN (1974), *Housewife* (London: Allen Lane).

O'CONNOR, ALAN (1989) (ed.), *Raymond Williams on Television* (London and New York: Routledge).

OSWELL, DAVID (1999), 'And What Might our Children Become? Future Visions, Governance and the Child Television Audience in Postwar Britain' *Screen*, 40/1: 66–78.

PATERSON, RICHARD (1998), 'Drama and Entertainment', in Anthony Smith (ed.), *Television: An International History* (Oxford and New York: Oxford University Press), 57–68.

PEACOCK, MICHAEL (1966), 'The Move to Panorama', in Miall (1966: 94–7).

PILKINGTON (1962), *The Committee on Broadcasting: The Pilkington Report*, Cmnd 1753 (London: HMSO).

SENDALL, BERNARD (1982), *Independent Television in Britain*, I. *Origin and Foundation, 1946–62* (London: Macmillan).

—— (1983), *Independent Television in Britain*, II. *Expansion and Change 1958–68* (London: Macmillan).

SHUBIK, IRENE (2000), *Play for Today: The Evolution of Television Drama* (Manchester and New York: Manchester University Press) (1st pub. 1975).

SPIGEL, LYNN (1992), *Make Room for TV: Television and the Family Ideal in Postwar America* (Chicago: Chicago University Press).

STEINER, LINDA (1998), 'Newsroom Accounts of Power at Work' in Cynthia Carter, Gill Branston, and Stuart Allan. (eds.), *News, Gender and Power* (London and New York: Routledge), 145–59.

STREETER, THOMAS and WAHL, WENDY (1994), 'Audience Theory and Feminism: Property, Gender, and the Television Audience', *Camera Obscura*, 33–4: 243–61.

THUMIM, JANET (1992), *Celluloid Sisters: Women and Popular Cinema* (Basingstoke and London: Macmillan).

—— (1995), 'A Live Commercial for Icing Sugar', *Screen*, 36/1: 48–55.

—— (1996), 'The Female Audience: Mobile Women and Married Ladies', in Christine Gledhill and Gillian Swanson (eds.), *Nationalising Femininity:*

Culture, Sexuality and British Cinema in the Second World War
(Manchester and New York: Manchester University Press), 238–56.

——— (1998), ' "Mrs Knight *must* be balanced": Methodological Problems in
Researching Early British Television', in Cynthia Carter, Gill Branston,
and Stuart Allan. (eds.), *News, Gender and Power* (London and New York:
Routledge), 91–104.

——— (2002) (ed.), *Small Screens, Big Ideas: Television in the 1950s* (London
and New York: I. B. Tauris).

TRACEY, MICHAEL (1998), 'Non-Fiction Television' in Smith (ed.),
Television: An International History (Oxford and New York: Oxford
University Press), 69–84 (1st pub. 1995).

VAHIMAGI, TISE (1994), *British Television* (Oxford: Oxford University Press).

WEGG-PROSSER, Victoria (2002), 'This Week in 1956: The Introduction of
Current Affairs on ITV', in Thumim (2002: 195–206).

WILLIAMS, RAYMOND (1989) 'Drama in a Dramatised Society', in Alan
O'Connor (ed.), *Raymond Williams on Television* (London and New York:
Routledge), 3–13 (1st pub. 1974).

——— (1990), *Television, Technology and Cultural Form* (London: Routledge)
(1st pub. 1974).

Index general

Index of broadcast programmes